Constitution-making and Human Rights in the Sudans

Sudan and South Sudan have suffered from repeated cycles of conflict and authoritarianism resulting in serious human rights and humanitarian law violations. Several efforts, such as the 2005 Comprehensive Peace Agreement and transitional justice initiatives have recognized that the failure to develop a stable political and legal order is at the heart of Sudan's governance problems. Following South Sudan's independence in 2011, parallel constitutional review processes are under way that have prompted intense debates about core issues of Sudan's identity, governance and rule of law, human rights protection and the relationship between religion and the State.

This book provides an in-depth study of Sudan's constitutional history and current debates with a view to identifying critical factors that would enable Sudan and South Sudan to overcome the apparent failure to agree on and implement a stable order conducive to sustainable peace and human rights protection. It examines relevant processes against the broader (constitutional) history of Sudan and identifies the building blocks for constitutional reforms through a detailed analysis of Sudanese law and politics. The book addresses constitutionalism and constitutional rights protection in their political, legal and institutional context in Sudan and South Sudan, and the repercussions of the relationship between state and religion for the right to freedom of religion, minority rights and women's rights.

Lutz Oette is Senior Lecturer in Law at SOAS, University of London, UK.

Mohamed Abdelsalam Babiker is Associate Professor of Public International Law, Founding Director of the Human Rights Centre and Head of the International and Comparative Law Department in the Faculty of Law at the University of Khartoum, Sudan.

Routledge Research in Constitutional Law

Series Editor: David Marrani

This series features thought-provoking and original scholarship on constitutional law and theory. Books explore key topics, themes and questions in the field with a particular emphasis on comparative studies. Where relevant, titles will engage with political and social theory, philosophy and history in order to offer a rounded analysis of constitutions and constitutional law.

Available titles in this series include:

Constitutionalism in the Global Realm
A Sociological Approach
Poul F. Kjaer

The Accountability Gap in EU Law
Marios Costa

Equal Citizenship, Civil Rights, and the Constitution
The Original Sense of the Privileges or Immunities Clause
Christopher R. Green

Democracy and the Human Rights Act
Republican Analysis of Citizen Power
Dennis Dixon

Constitutional Acceleration within the European Union and Beyond
Edited by Paul Blokker

Philosophy, Obligation and Law
Bentham's Ontology of Normativity
Piero Tarantino

Constitutional Politics and the Judiciary
Decision-making in Central and Eastern Europe
Edited by Kálmán Pócza

EU Law, Fundamental Rights and National Democracy
Eduardo Gill-Pedro

Constitution-making and Human Rights in the Sudans
Edited by Lutz Oette and Mohamed Abdelsalam Babiker

For more information about this series, please visit:
www.routledge.com/Routledge-Research-in-Constitutional-Law/book-series/CONSTLAW

Constitution-making and Human Rights in the Sudans

Edited by
Lutz Oette and
Mohamed Abdelsalam Babiker

Routledge
Taylor & Francis Group
LONDON AND NEW YORK

First published 2019 by Routledge

2 Park Square, Milton Park, Abingdon, Oxfordshire OX14 4RN
52 Vanderbilt Avenue, New York, NY 10017

Routledge is an imprint of the Taylor & Francis Group, an informa business

First issued in paperback 2020

British Library Cataloguing-in-Publication Data
A catalogue record for this book is available from the British Library

Library of Congress Cataloging-in-Publication Data
Names: Oette, Lutz, author. | Babiker, Mohamed Abdelsalam, author.
Title: Constitution-making and human rights in the Sudans/Lutz Oette, Mohamed Abdelsalam Babiker.
Description: Abingdon, Oxon [UK]; New York, NY: Routledge, 2019.
Series: Routledge research in constitutional law | Includes bibliographical references and index.
Identifiers: LCCN 2018038625 | ISBN 9781138652613 (hardback)
Subjects: LCSH: Constitutional history–Sudan. | Constitutional law–Sudan. | Constitutional law–South Sudan. | Constitutions–Sudan. | Civil rights–Sudan. | Human rights–Sudan. | Women's rights–Sudan. | Minorities–Legal status, laws, etc.–Sudan. | Minorities–Legal status, laws, etc.–South Sudan. | Sudan. Duståur. | Sudan–Politics and government.
Classification: LCC KTQ1760.O38 2019 | DDC 342.62402–dc23
LC record available at https://lccn.loc.gov/2018038625

ISBN: 978-1-138-65261-3 (hbk)
ISBN: 978-0-367-66340-7 (pbk)

Typeset in Galliard
by Deanta Global Publishing Services, Chennai, India

This book is dedicated to Dr. Amin Mekki Medani (1939–2018), an outstanding human rights lawyer and unflinching advocate for justice in Sudan and beyond, whose fortitude, humour in the face of adversity and generosity of spirit will be an inspiration for generations to come.

Contents

List of contributors ix
Preface xi

Introduction 1
LUTZ OETTE AND MOHAMED ABDELSALAM BABIKER

PART I
The challenges for peace, human rights protection and constitutionalism in the Sudans 13

1 Power, conflict and human rights in Sudan 15
LUTZ OETTE

2 In search of constitution and constitutionalism in Sudan: the quest for legitimacy and the protection of rights 41
ALI SULEIMAN FADLALLA AND MOHAMED ABDELSALAM BABIKER

3 Constitutionalism under siege: constitutional standoffs in South Sudan and their implications for the war-torn nation 63
DAVID K. DENG

PART II
Constitutional protection of human rights 89

4 Human rights protection in Sudan's constitutions: a critique of Bills of Rights 91
MOHAMED ABDELSALAM BABIKER

5 Citizenship, statelessness and human rights protection in Sudan's constitutions and post South Sudan secession challenges 118
MUNZOUL A. M. ASSAL

6 Constitutional dimensions of minority rights and the rights of peoples in the Sudans 139
NOHA IBRAHIM ABDELGABAR, MOHAMED ABDELSALAM BABIKER AND LUTZ OETTE

7 Women's rights in Sudan: constitutional recognition and lived experiences 160
EBTISAM SANHOURI ELRAYH

Appendix: Human rights provisions in the constitutions of Sudan and South Sudan and selected constitutional court cases 190

Index 213

Contributors

Noha Ibrahim Abdelgabar is a Project Manager with the UN Development Programme in Libya. She has served as a human rights expert for UN agencies, national human rights institutions, NGOs and research institutes, particularly as a Research Fellow for the Sudan Peace Project at the Max Planck Institute, Germany. Abdelgabar's doctoral thesis was on 'Constitutional Reform as a Means of Democratic Transformation in Sudan' (Hamburg University), and she has a number of publications in the field of constitutional law, law reform and human rights law.

Munzoul A. M. Assal is Professor of Social Anthropology and Director of the Peace Research Institute at the University of Khartoum. He has published widely on questions of identity, citizenship, displacement and migration in Sudan, including *Multi-dimensional Changes in the Sudan 1989–2011: Reshaping Livelihoods, Political Conflicts and Identities* (2015 co-edited with Barbara Casciarri and François Ireton), and *Past, Present and Future: Fifty Years of Anthropology in Sudan* (2015 co-edited with Musa Abdul-Jalil). Professor Assal is a member of the Board of Trustees of the Arab Council for Social Sciences.

Mohamed Abdelsalam Babiker is Associate Professor of Law, and founding Director of the Human Rights Centre, School of Law, University of Khartoum. He worked as legal advisor and human rights officer with the UN and AU peacekeeping operations in Sudan, and was appointed by the UN Secretary-General as a Humanitarian Expert with the Somalia and Eritrea Monitoring Group, Security Council resolution 2385 (2017). He is the author and co-editor of a number of works in the field, including his monograph, *Application of International Humanitarian Law and Human Rights to the Armed Conflicts of the Sudan: Complementary or Mutually Exclusive Regimes* (2007).

David K. Deng is a South Sudanese/American human rights lawyer who has spent most of the last decade conducting research and advocacy in South Sudan. His research has addressed a broad range of issues, including the challenges and opportunities of large-scale land investment, customary law and local dispute resolution mechanisms, citizens' views on peace processes, and people's experiences with, and perceptions of transitional justice. Deng is currently working on a project to support the development of victim groups with a coalition of South Sudanese civil society organizations called the Transitional Justice Working Group (TJWG).

Ebtisam Sanhouri Elrayh is Assistant Professor of Law at the Faculty of Law, University of Khartoum. Previously, she worked as a research associate in the Dutch pilot project 'Muslim Women and Development' and acted as senior legal officer for the Southern Sudan Referendum Commission. Elrayh has published a series of articles on gender and the constitution, and gender and the law in Sudan. She actively engages with women's rights in the wider constitution-making process, as well as with their rights in the private domain.

Ali Suleiman Fadlalla is a Fellow at the Faculty of Law, University of Khartoum, where he previously served as associate professor, dean and head of the department of public law. He has been a member of various Sudanese legal bodies and human rights bodies in the 1980s before working for the UN Mission for the Referendum in Western Sahara (MINURSO) from 1995 to 2003. Fadlalla has published widely on Sudanese constitutional law and history, particularly as part of the reform debates in the 1980s.

Lutz Oette is a Senior Lecturer in Law and Director of the Centre for Human Rights Law at SOAS, University of London. He has published extensively on law, human rights and justice in Sudan, particularly in the course of his work on the project for criminal law reform in Sudan (www.pclrs.com, led by REDRESS in cooperation with various partner organizations), including the edited volume *Criminal Law Reform and Transitional Justice: Human Rights Perspectives for Sudan* (2011). He is the co-author, with Ilias Bantekas, of *International Human Rights Law and Practice* (2nd edn 2016).

Preface

This book builds on and forms part of the work and engagement of a number of Sudanese and international scholars and actors on legal and institutional reforms in the two Sudans. The end of the Comprehensive Peace Agreement's interim period and South Sudan's secession/independence in 2011 prompted and necessitated a renewed debate on the constitutional framework in Sudan and South Sudan. Constitution-making processes have since featured prominently in both countries. Both editors have contributed to these processes, particularly by co-editing a study 'The Constitutional Protection of Human Rights in Sudan: Challenges and Future Perspectives' (REDRESS, Faculty of Law, University of Khartoum, Sudanese Human Rights Monitor, 2014) and co-authoring 'The Rule of Law and Human Rights in Sudan: Challenges and Prospects for Reform', as part of the Sudan Democracy First Group's project on institutional reform in Sudan in 2014.

We are privileged to be able to draw on this work, and especially the knowledge and insights of contributing authors who have brought their rich experience to bear for the benefit of this edited volume. All contributors have played their distinctive role in Sudanese constitutional discourses and processes, be it in their capacity as engaged academic scholars, or as members of United Nations missions in Sudan, civil society organizations and networks.

We would like to thank all those who have contributed to this book by expressing their support, making useful suggestions and providing critical scrutiny, particularly Abdullahi Ahmed An-Na'im, Suliman Baldo, Yash Ghai, Manar Idriss, Siraj Khan, the late Amin Mekki Medani, Abdel Salam Sidahmed and Edward Thomas. We are particularly grateful to Elmukashfie Majzoub, Teaching Assistant at the University of Khartoum, Faculty of Law, for his assistance in compiling the appendix.

We would also like to express our wholehearted thanks to Alison Kirk, Alexandra Buckley and Chloe James at Routledge for their support and patience in what has been a challenging but ultimately rewarding process.

On a personal note, we would like to remember, and pay tribute, to Abdelsalam Hassan Abdelsalam, Osman Hummaida, and Dr. Amin Mekki Medani, who passed away not long ago. They steadfastly sought to promote and defend human rights and the rule of law in Sudan, and continue to be an inspiration for those of us who live in what are testing times not only in both Sudans but also the African continent and beyond.

Introduction

Lutz Oette and Mohamed Abdelsalam Babiker

The diversity and location of Sudan at the interface of Africa and the Middle East account for its rich history and a number of fundamental challenges of religious, cultural and ethnic identities it has been grappling with. These challenges have repeatedly resulted in armed conflicts and contestations characterized by serious human rights violations. Constitution-making and constitutional human rights protection have in this context become an important measure of Sudan's ability to put in place a framework that is conducive to both peace and human rights protection. Sudan's history illustrates the magnitude of this task, and perhaps no period more so than the experiment of the Comprehensive Peace Agreement (CPA) of 2005 between the Government of Sudan and the Sudan People's Liberation Movement/Army (SPLM/A). Agreed upon to end the civil war and to usher in an era of democratic transformation, including by means of greater human rights protection, it ultimately led to the independence of South Sudan in July 2011.[1] The break-up of the country has cast the constitutional question wide open. Developments since 2011 demonstrate the significant challenges of implementing constitutionalism and constitutional human rights protection in Sudan, which continues to be multi-ethnic, culturally and religiously diverse, and its new neighbouring country, which shares much of Sudan's legacy.

This collection brings together scholars and practitioners from Sudan, South Sudan and beyond who have in various functions been closely involved in debates and initiatives on the protection of human rights and the constitution-making processes in both countries. Their contributions focus on aspects that have been at the core of constitutional debates in Sudan's history; they also have broader resonance for countries that share similar features in respect of the constitutional human rights dimension of religion, nationality and citizenship, minorities and gender. Contributors have been encouraged to engage with underlying, systemic challenges and to take a critical approach that considers the factors needed to make constitutional human rights protection effective considering colonial legacies and

1 Atta El Battahani, 'Sudan: Transition to Democracy after 2011, a Dismembered State Navigating Uncertainties', in Ibrahim Elbadawi and Samir Makdisi (eds), *Democratic Transitions in the Arab World* (CUP 2017).

political, economic and social structures in both countries. Before providing an overview of the chapters, this introduction will sketch out a brief history of constitution-making and rights protection in Sudan, situating it in the context of constitutional developments in the region.

Sudan's turbulent postcolonial history has been marked by political instability, oscillating between authoritarian regimes and short-lived democratic interludes, as well as conflict between the centre and the South, and other marginalized regions including Darfur, Blue Nile, the Nuba Mountains and east Sudan. Unsurprisingly, these factors loom large when examining the lack of effective human rights protection in Sudan's legal order, including its many short-lived constitutions.

Since gaining independence in 1956, Sudan has grappled with constitution-making. The Self-Government Statute of 1953 served as the template for several transitional or interim constitutions from 1956 until 1969. The 'Permanent Constitution' of 1973 was significantly amended shortly after its adoption and barely lasted a dozen years. While constitution-making has always been on the political agenda, signifying its importance, particularly in attempts to define, if not enshrine Sudan's Islamic or secular identity, it is hard to disagree with the assessment that Sudan is in constant 'search of a constitution'.[2] The status of Islam and secularism, and the right to self-determination, federalism, autonomy and minority rights have been at the heart of constitutional debates. Initially, these debates pitted those representing sectarian and Islamist constituencies against South Sudanese and other marginalized or oppositional secular groups.[3] While Arabization began with, if not predated, independence, the Islamization of Sudan's legal system commenced with a delay of over twenty years, during the latter part of the Nimeri years (1969–85).[4] The National Islamic Front (NIF), which came to power by means of a military coup in 1989, adopted a new constitution in 1998 (after ten years of ruling the country by revolutionary, exceptional decrees.) as part of its project of turning Sudan into an Islamic State. Yet, subsequent developments, both an internal split and power struggle within the Islamist movement between President al-Bashir and Hassan al-Turabi, NIF's spiritual leader, the CPA ending the civil war in 2005, ongoing armed conflicts in Darfur, Blue Nile and Nuba Mountains and South Sudan's secession, reopened the debate on Sudan's, and South Sudan's, constitutional framework. In 2011, a public statement made by President al-Bashir seemed to suggest that Sudan would no longer be a multi-ethnic and multi-religious State after South Sudan's

2 Ali Suleiman Fadlalla, 'Constitution-making in the Sudan: Past Experiences' (Advisory Council for Human Rights, With Support from United Nations, Constitution-making Forum: A Government of Sudan Consultation, 24–5 May 2011) 1.

3 Abdel Salam Sidahmed, *Politics and Islam in Contemporary Sudan* (Curzon Press 1997) 95–112.

4 Balghis Badri, 'A Critical Analysis of the Evolution of Constitutions in Sudan' (2014) 31 *Afh J* 3.

independence, and could therefore be turned into a fully Islamic State.[5] This political rhetoric highlights attempts to downplay Sudan's remaining – political, ethnic and religious – diversity. Seemingly designed to prepare the ground for a constitutional model that enshrines and entrenches existing power disparities at the expense of the rights of those who are opposed to the current regime or do not fit within its vision of society, these moves once again threw into stark relief the use of *Shari'a* law as a legitimating and enabling device for the exercise of power.[6] In South Sudan, meanwhile, constitutional debates have become closely intertwined with the ongoing peace process and transitional arrangements in the midst of a major political, economic and humanitarian crisis.

Sudan is uniquely situated as an African country that has a Muslim majority and close links to the Middle East. Due to political and institutional connections, it shares in the history of both regions. This applies equally to constitution-making and human rights protection. The notion of constitutionalism is widely understood to include an element of participation (of the people as constituent power) and limitation (accountability of government).[7] From a rights perspective, the objective of constitutionalism has been identified as 'uphold[ing] the rule of law, enforc[ing] effective limitations on government powers, and the protection of human rights'.[8] Africa's constitutional experience following decolonisation has been referred to as 'constitutions without constitutionalism'.[9] This assessment is valid in so far as it refers to top-down constitutional processes that had limited public participation and did not result in effective constraints on the exercise of power. However, a focus on constitutions and the absence of constitutionalism may ignore, or fail to fully appreciate, the nature and role of constitutional debates in any given context.[10] This is certainly true with regard to Sudan. Seemingly somewhat paradoxically, the challenges in constitution-making, and lack of adherence to existing constitutions, constitutionalism and the rule of law, have not lessened the intensity of constitutional debates. Following decolonisation, human rights protection in Africa's constitutions was generally weak, with constitutions typically providing – ineffective – protection of a limited number of civil and political rights only and reflecting 'liberal' models of constitutionalism that formed part of the colonial heritage. This situation changed from the 1990s onwards in the wake of democratisation processes across the continent.

5 'Sudanese president asserts North Sudan's Arabic, Islamic Identity' *Sudan Tribune* (6 February 2011), http://sudantribune.com/Sudanese-president-asserts-North, 37889, accessed 12 June 2018.

6 See on this point in broader historical perspective, Abdullahi Ahmed An-Na'im, *African Constitutionalism and the Role of Islam* (University of Pennsylvania Press 2006) 133–8.

7 Li-ann Thio, 'Constitutionalism in Illiberal Polities' in Michel Rosenfeld and András Sajó (eds), *The Oxford Handbook of Comparative Constitutional Law* (OUP 2012).

8 An-Na'im (n 6).

9 H Kwasi Prempeh, '*Marbury* in Africa: Judicial Review and the Challenge of Constitutionalism in Contemporary Africa' (2005–2006) 80 *Tul L Rev* 1239.

10 Nimer Sultany, *Law and Revolution: Legitimacy and Constitutionalism After the Arab Spring* (OUP 2017).

The South African and Kenyan constitution-making experiences stand out for their level of participation and focus on human rights.[11] The new constitutions reflect a broader understanding of human rights, including the recognition of justiciable economic, social and cultural rights, and a stronger emphasis on institutional protection and the right of individuals to litigate these rights.[12] These are important developments taking place in the context of broader, African Union (AU)-wide governance efforts to strengthen democratic structures and processes, as well as human rights protection.[13] Constitution-making as part of transitional processes, including liberal peace agreements, has complemented these initiatives.[14] The Middle East and North Africa region had remained largely unaffected by these developments. With the dramatic change of the political situation across the Arab world in 2011, the issue of constitutions and human rights took centre stage. Constitution-making was at the heart of revolutionary and transitional processes.[15] These processes had to address fundamental, structural questions underpinning human rights protection. These include the nature of the political and economic system, political powers, religion and the State, the rights of minorities and the rights of women, in addition to delineating the nature and scope of constitutional rights and mechanisms for their protection.[16] Political developments in most countries in the region have since 2011 been detrimental to democratic processes, and constitutionalism, with the notable exception of Tunisia.[17] Nonetheless, the question of constitutionalism, human rights and respect for the rule of law more broadly remains a key debate in ongoing transitions, or an issue to be resolved in any forthcoming transitions, such as in Syria.

Democratization and related constitution-making processes in sub-Saharan Africa have largely passed Sudan by over the past three decades despite its earlier democratic experiences following two successful uprisings in October 1964 and April 1985.[18] The 1989 military coup ushered a regime to power that ruled, first, on the basis of emergency decrees, and subsequently the 1998 Islamic constitution that included references to an 'Islamized' Bill of Rights, which was subject

11 Yash P Ghai and Jill Cottrell, *Kenya's Constitution: An Instrument for Change* (Katiba Institute 2011); Hugh Corder (ed.), *The Quest for Constitutionalism: South Africa since 1994* (Ashgate 2014).

12 Ibid.

13 H Kwasi Prempeh, 'Africa's "Constitutionalism Revival": False Start or New Dawn?' (2007) 5 *ICON* 469.

14 Juan E Méndez, 'Constitutionalism and Transitional Justice' in Rosenfeld (n 7).

15 Sultany (n 10).

16 Rainer Grote & Tilmann J Röder (eds), *Constitutionalism, Human Rights, and Islam after the Arab Spring* (OUP 2016).

17 Hatem M'Rad, 'The Process of Institutional Transformation in Tunisia after the Revolution, in Grote ibid; Sultany (n 10) 252–6.

18 WJ Berridge, *Civil Uprisings in Modern Sudan: The 'Khartoum Springs' of 1964 and 1985* (Bloomsbury Academic 2015); Hayder Ibrahim, Abdelsalam Nur Eldin, Mohamed Mahmoud, Abdul Wahab Himat (eds), *50 Years since the Sudanese October Revolution (1964–2014): Sudan's Early Uprising* (Sudanese Studies Center 2015, Arabic).

to *Shari'a* law and national legislation. In parallel, Sudan's legal order was significantly transformed from a common law system to a legal system increasingly influenced by *Shari'a* law. Legislation enacted since 1989 was based on a mixture of *Shari'a* law and public order considerations, emergency powers/security paradigms and immunities of law enforcement agencies. This approach resulted in discrimination and impunity that facilitated violations and enshrined lack of access to justice and accountability.[19]

The 2005 INC failed to meet expectations of strengthening human rights protection. It was the outcome of a top-down (Government of Sudan, SPLM/SPLA, external actors) liberal peace agreement that largely enshrined and entrenched existing power structures, rather than of a participatory, transparent process and broader constitutional debate.[20] Other peace agreements such as the East Sudan Peace Agreement, the Abuja Agreement, 2006 (ESPA) and the Doha Document for Peace in Darfur, 2010 (DDPD) reflected a similar mind-set and approach. The lack of democratic parliamentary oversight, an independent judiciary and effective security sector reform, a largely deferential Constitutional Court, weak national human rights institutions and the repression of civil society are key factors that contributed to the maintenance of the problematic status quo.[21]

South Sudan's secession from Sudan, and its independence, is an important foundational moment in Sudan's history, with apparent constitutional implications. For Sudan, it posed the question of the INC's status and future, and the contents of any newly adopted constitution. This question gained fresh impetus with the National Dialogue in 2014 and a number of civil society initiatives, which generated some debate on Sudan's constitutional future, and resulted in initiating debates on a new constitution-making process. As of early 2018, key constitutional questions, such as a preference for a *Shari'a*-based constitution versus 'secular', 'liberal' models, the Bill of Rights and federalism remained to be addressed, after the National Dialogue had failed to provide a suitable forum and facilitate participatory constitution-making. Instead, several piecemeal constitutional amendments made in this period (2015, 2016, 2017 amendments) strengthened the position of the President and the security apparatus. They were largely aimed at consolidating the constitutional status of some aspects of *Shari'a* law, strengthening the status of the security forces, and dismantling Sudan's weak federal and decentralized system by consolidating the President's powers of removing and appointing governors of states. These amendments were widely seen as undermining any commitment to a broader participatory and democratic process of constitutionalism.[22] In neighbouring South Sudan, the constitution-making process envisaged under the transitional constitution of 2011 was

19 See particularly on Sudan's criminal law, Lutz Oette (ed.), *Criminal Law and Transitional Justice: Human Rights Perspectives for Sudan* (Ashgate 2011).

20 Critical, Badri (n 4).

21 See in particular Babiker Chapter 4.

22 See e.g. 'Sudan's NUP rejects constitutional amendments' *Sudan Tribune* (8 January 2015), www.sudantribune.com/spip/php?article53590, accessed 12 June 2018.

aborted amidst the conflict, and renewed efforts have since become an integral part of an uncertain peace process. As in the case of Sudan, several constitutional amendments have increased the powers of the President, and ushered in a highly controversial decentralisation. As in Sudan, concerns over top-down, elite-driven processes that fail to address deep-seated structural problems loom large over any constitution-making in South Sudan.

It would be premature, and simplistic, to reduce Sudan, and South Sudan for that matter, to a stereotypical, authoritarian country in which the constitution is seen to be nothing than a piece of paper, and is used to have the trappings of a State and to provide a modicum of legitimacy. Debates surrounding the nature and content of the Constitution have been at the heart of political debates throughout much of Sudan's history, and are closely tied up with the question of Sudan's contested identity. They form part of a broader inquiry into the relationship of State and society, its multi-ethnic and multi-religious constituents, and the role of law and rights, which is particularly evident in Sudanese initiatives for legislative and institutional reforms.

In its recent history, constitutional debates came to the fore in the period leading up to independence, being dominated by the relationship between what are now Sudan and South Sudan (and Sudan and Egypt at the time), particularly the rights of Southerners. In 1953, the colonial Self-Government Statute was adopted as a transitional instrument. The Statute guaranteed a core of civil and political rights, including the rule of law, independence of the judiciary and the right to a constitutional remedy. It therefore set out a narrow, liberal model, emerging within a colonial framework that had been characterized by a bifurcated system (colonial rulers–'natives') and lack of separation of powers. This legacy notwithstanding, the Statute, in its 1956 version, served as the default constitution until 1973. A largely top-down, elitist process of independence, a lack of a shared political vision on the identity of the country (Egypt–Sudan; the status of Islam; secularism) and short-lived political regimes resulted in a lack of agreement on a Sudanese constitution during that period. The system, in so far as the protection of rights was concerned, largely functioned on the basis of the model carried over from colonial times. While some commentators have praised the legal system of this period for its respect for the rule of law, it was equally characterized by elitism and limited access to formal justice mechanisms.[23] It took the Nimeri dictatorship to adopt a constitution, ambitiously called the Permanent Constitution, in 1973, which granted a range of rights, including economic, social and cultural rights reflecting the socialist nature of the regime at the time. However, the constitution had not been based on broad constitutional debates, and was not embedded in a political framework that would have ensured the protection of human rights. Instead, the Nimeri regime came to be characterized by reforms that undermined the vestiges of the rule of law, and by the increasing

23 See further Mark Fathi Massoud, *Law's Fragile State: Colonial, Authoritarian, and Humanitarian Legacies in Sudan* (CUP 2014) 44ff.

influence of the Islamists, which succeeded in taking *Shari'a* beyond the narrow scope of family laws to which it had been consigned since the Anglo-Egyptian condominium.[24] The 'Islamization' of laws and the so-called September laws, particularly the introduction of the Basic Rule Judgment Act, 1983, significantly transformed Sudan's legal system in all domains (criminal, civil, personal laws). *Shari'a* became the new 'common law' of Sudan against which all laws, including customary laws and English common law are measured.[25] Since 1989, *Shari'a* law has become the main reference point against which the legitimacy of the constitutional framework and human rights are judged as the constitution should not contradict or be inconsistent with it.

The 1973 Permanent Constitution was anything but as it was abrogated following the fall of the Nimeri regime in 1985. The democratic period lasting from 1985 to 1989 witnessed a flourishing of debates surrounding constitution-making, law reform and human rights, including the ratification of key international human rights treaties such as the International Covenant on Civil and Political Rights and the International Covenant on Economic, Social and Cultural Rights.[26] The period exposed a number of weaknesses of the political parties, including their inability to act decisively to undertake reforms, such as the abolition of the 1983 September laws. However, negotiations surrounding a peace process had been advanced when the military coup brought the democratic interlude to an abrupt end.[27] The period since 1989, particularly the 1998 constitution, the 2005 INC (largely based on the CPA), and post 2011 developments, already referred to above, form part of broader historical constitutional developments in Sudan and the region. This includes aspirations for change and greater participation in decision-making processes through constitution-making as well as liberal peace agreements such as the CPA-based model of a 'constitution in a post-conflict society'.

Sudan's constitutions have been largely imposed by governments that lacked democratic credentials (1953, 1973, 1998 and, as part of the peace agreement, 2005). There is a parallel history of democratic constitution-making, which has, however, due to the overthrow of democratic regimes, not resulted in the adoption of any constitutions other than amendments or transitional constitutions. This history accounts for the lack of respect for constitutions and the limited rights protection in Sudan's constitutions. The Bill of Rights in the 2005 INC,

24 Ibid 102–18.

25 Mohamed Abdelsalam Babiker, 'Customary Law and Courts in the Context of Sudan's Legal Pluralism: Marginalized or Empowered under English Common Law and Islamic Law' in Barbara Casciari and Mohamed Babiker (eds), *Anthropology of Law in Muslim Sudan: Land, Courts and the Plurality of Practices* (Brill 2018).

26 Abdelsalam Hassan Abdelsalam and Amin M Medani, 'Criminal Law Reform and Human Rights in African and Muslim Countries with Particular Reference to Sudan' in Oette (n 19) 49–50.

27 Douglas H Johnson, *The Root Causes of Sudan's Civil Wars: Peace or Truce* (Rev Edn, James Currey 2011) 84–5.

which was the result of negotiations, including that of regional and international actors, is noteworthy for making international treaties binding on Sudan an integral part of the Bill, vesting the Constitutional Court with a potentially strong mandate to rule on the constitutionality of laws, and the belated setting up of a Human Rights Commission. In practice, however, it has been of limited value in enhancing human rights protection in Sudan as the CPA, and the INC, did not result in the envisaged democratic transformation of the country. Similar developments are also evident in the context of South Sudan. This is a salutary and important lesson 13 years on, as it demonstrates the insufficiency of relying on legalistic approaches in the absence of more far-reaching structural reforms, and respect for the rule of law and constitutionalism in the two Sudans (Sudan and South Sudan) which are prerequisites for any viable constitution-making process.

Considering this political, cultural and legal background, it is perhaps unsurprising that Sudan has produced some of the most influential constitutional and human rights thinkers on the continent. Abdullahi Ahmed An-Na'im and Francis Deng in particular have set out visions for constitution-making that hold important lessons. Both have emphasized the need for a contextual approach to constitutionalism that draws on indigenous traditions and experiences.[28] An-Na'im has provided important insights on Islam, *Shari'a* and constitutionalism, particularly on the contingent role of Islam. For him, the 'notion of an Islamic state as a political institution is conceptually incoherent, historically inaccurate, and practically not viable today'.[29] This has an important human rights dimension, including in the Sudanese context, where Mahmoud Taha and the Republican Brothers adopted their own constitutional vision and version of 'liberal' Islam, and denounced slavery and gender inequality that had been justified with reference to *Shari'a*.[30] An-Na'im builds on this legacy, and seeks to find common ground between universal human rights and Islam by way of Islamic reformation[31] and a cross-cultural dialogue.[32] Notwithstanding the undoubted appeal of this approach, there are areas where *Shari'a* law and international human rights norms appear irreconcilable, such as concerning *hudud* punishments, apostasy and freedom of religion, the rights of religious minorities and the status of women which all pose a challenge, and await clarification in any future Sudanese constitution. Francis Deng has focused on the importance of the right to self-determination, particularly 'the management of diversities through various *forms*

28 See for a good overview of their work (and that of Yash Ghai and Upendra Baxi), William Twining, 'Human Rights: Southern Voices' (2005) 11 *Rev Const Stud* 203.

29 An-Na'im (n 6) 104.

30 See further Edward Thomas, *Islam's Perfect Stranger: The Life of Mahmud Muhammad Taha, Muslim Reformer of Sudan* (IB Tauris 2010) 142–65 (discussing particularly Taha's 'The Second Message of Islam').

31 Abdullahi Ahmed An-Na'im, *Toward an Islamic Reformation: Civil Liberties, Human Rights, and International Law* (Syracuse University Press 1996).

32 Abdullahi Ahmed An-Na'im, 'Introduction' in An-Na'im (ed.), *Human Rights in Cross-Cultural Perspectives: A Quest for Consensus* (University of Pennsylvania Press 1992).

and degrees of self-determination … and *cultural contextualization* through the application of relevant indigenous norms within a framework that recognizes both peculiarities and commonalities'.[33] South Sudan's independence was an exercise of this right but has not closed the issue. In Sudan, there are many regions, such as Darfur, the Nuba Mountains, Blue Nile and eastern Sudan, whose people may claim a measure of self-determination or autonomy, or at least a stronger protection of minority rights. In South Sudan, and to a large extent in Abyei (as a contested region in Sudan), self-determination is closely related to federalism and increasing 'tribalism', which raises important issues of how the relationship between various groups and territorial units in South Sudan could, and should be, reflected in a new Constitution.

As set out above, this book takes a contextual approach to the constitutional protection of human rights in the Sudans, examining it in its historical, political and societal setting(s). Following this introduction, the first part delineates the multifaceted challenges for peace, human rights protection and constitutionalism in the Sudans. Oette's chapter 'Power, Conflict and Human Rights in Sudan' provides an analysis of the nexus of power, conflict and human rights protection in both countries. Drawing on a range of literature on the structural factors contributing to political instability and conflict in Sudan, he charts the adverse human rights impact of key features characterizing Sudan's historical development, particularly the centre–periphery divide; discrimination based on race, class and gender; resort to violence; and lack of respect for democracy and the rule of law. Against this legacy, he calls for an approach to constitution-making and human rights in the Sudans that is based on a structural transformation of modes of governance, and thereby moves beyond liberal models of constitutional human rights protection.

Babiker and Fadlalla's chapter 'In Search of Constitution and Constitutionalism in Sudan: The Quest for Legitimacy and the Protection of Rights' charts the history of constitutions and constitutionalism in Sudan from the time of the colonial condominium to the present. Drawing on the rich body of Fadlalla's work, particularly in the 1980s, and Babiker's contemporary writings, it critically assesses the underlying conceptions of State and society, constitution-making processes and rights protection. They identify a fundamental paradox in Sudan's history; while recurring debates evince a keen interest in key constitutional questions and rights protection, the unstable political system following independence and authoritarian politics has largely thwarted the expectations and promise that constitutionalism has held for human rights protection in Sudan. The chapter argues that Sudanese constitutions have been used as 'ideological instruments' to realize the vision of the regime in power. Colonial law reflected the common law ethos

33 Francis Deng, *Identity, Diversity, and Constitutionalism in Africa* (United States Institute of Peace 2008) 5 (emphasis in original). See also joint publication, Abdullahi Ahmed An-Na'im and Francis Deng, 'Self Determination and Unity: The Case of Sudan' (1997) 18 *Law & Soc* 199.

and values while subsequent constitutions represented the ideologies of socialism, Islamism and liberal peace.

David K. Deng's chapter 'Constitutionalism Under Siege: Constitutional Standoffs in South Sudan and Their Implications for the War-torn Nation' identifies similar challenges in the short history of constitution-making and constitutionalism in South Sudan. It shows how the failure to address adverse legacies of the lack of constitutionalism contributed to the conflict shortly after independence. Recent moves, such as the removal of state Governors, the extension of the government's mandate and the proliferation of states have further undermined a political culture in which constitutionalism can flourish, in addition to leading South Sudan towards an authoritarian system. Approaches to constitution-making as part of the peace process instil little confidence that they will result in greater human rights protection, accountability and justice.

The second part of the book examines several core dimensions of the constitutional protection of human rights in Sudan. The issues and rights addressed are fundamental to Sudan's identity, State and society, and have proved to be particularly critical in the context of protection against human rights violations. Babiker's chapter 'Human Rights Protection in Sudan's Constitutions: A critique of Bills of Rights' questions the extent to which the Bills of Rights in Sudan's constitutions have provided an adequate level, and effective mode, of human rights protection. He identifies a series of gaps, particularly in respect of the protection of economic, social and cultural rights (ESCR) throughout Sudan's constitutional history. This applies equally to the 2005 Bill of Rights which, although considered particularly progressive in the Sudanese context, has several shortcomings, and has been undermined both by the lack of effective institutional implementation and a series of constitutional amendments adopted since 2011. The chapter further argues that constitutional bills of rights and international human rights norms have limited impact in the context of Sudan's hybrid legal system (i.e., Islamic, customary, common and continental law). In this context, it highlights the lack of clarity surrounding the incorporation of international human rights law in Sudan's legal system before calling for respect for constitutionalism, rule of law and effective institutional mechanisms as major prerequisites for human rights protection in Sudan.

Assal's chapter 'Citizenship, Statelessness and Human Rights Protection in Sudan's Constitutions and post South Sudan Secession Challenges' combines a sociological and anthropological approach with a legal analysis of the recognition of citizenship rights in Sudan's constitutional and legal order, focusing particularly on the challenges posed by the 2011 secession/independence of South Sudan. He finds that the constitutional recognition of nationality and citizenship rights is flawed and insufficient, particularly in view of a descent-based, and gendered, approach to nationality that does not adequately reflect the realities of Sudan as a multi-ethnic and multi-cultural State. In this context, the chapter examines the interrelated question of multiculturalism and rights protection, and calls for a fundamental change in approach towards inclusive citizenship in any forthcoming constitution.

The chapter by Noha Ibrahim Abdelgabar, Mohamed Abdelsalam Babiker and Lutz Oette, 'Constitutional Dimensions of Minority Rights and the Rights of Peoples in the Sudans', takes Sudan's plurality as a point of departure. It finds that its constitutions, particularly the INC, and peace agreements that had a constitutional dimension, such as the CPA or the Darfur Peace Agreement, provide a degree of recognition and protection. However, they do not add up to a satisfactory minority rights regime judged by international standards, particularly in respect of the rights of religious minorities, which are undermined by a plethora of laws and practices against which the legal system affords inadequate protection. The right to self-determination has featured prominently in the case of South Sudan but its recognition and exercise is far less certain, and ensured in the context of the various regions of and peoples in Sudan, such as in respect of Darfur, the Nuba mountains and Abyei, and in South Sudan itself.

Ebtisam Sanhouri Elrayh's chapter 'Women's rights in Sudan: Constitutional Recognition and Lived Experiences' charts the historical development of women's rights in Sudan's constitutions before examining in-depth how the 2005 INC guarantees such rights. She identifies a lack of clarity between the position of *Shari'a* law and customary law on the one hand and women's rights on the other, and poor drafting of the rights guaranteed as major shortcomings. The constitutional recognition of women's rights is also undermined by the non-ratification of relevant international treaties, such as the Convention on the Elimination of All Forms of Discrimination against Women and the Protocol on the Rights of Women in Africa (Maputo Protocol). Combined, these factors, together with inadequate institutional protection (judiciary, commissions), explain how legislation, such as the Personal Status Law of Muslims, and public order laws and criminal laws, which are demonstrably incompatible with, and detrimental to, women's rights, remains in force. In light of these experiences, she calls for a holistic approach to women's rights, both in any future constitution and across the various areas of Sudanese law.

The appendix provides the text of the human rights provisions of the constitutions of Sudan and South Sudan for ease of reference. It also sets out brief summaries of selected constitutional cases in which the highest Sudanese courts have upheld, or articulated, constitutional rights. It does not refer to the considerable body of cases in which the courts have done the opposite, or did not render a decision within a reasonable time. The selection only covers cases decided before 2013, as Constitutional Court decisions have not been published since, contrary to the requirements stipulated in the Constitutional Court Act of 2005.

Part I

The challenges for peace, human rights protection and constitutionalism in the Sudans

1 Power, conflict and human rights in Sudan

Lutz Oette

1 Introduction

Sudan's dismal human rights record, particularly since 1989, and its role in a series of armed conflicts is common knowledge, as a result of decades of monitoring, documentation and litigation.[1] A conventional approach to human rights protection in any amended, or new constitution in Sudan, and this applies *mutatis mutandis* to South Sudan, would be to set out a substantive list of rights, add a provision that ensures adherence to international human rights standards and strengthen the institutional protection of rights. Indeed, this very approach is reflected in the Bill of Rights of the 2005 Interim National Constitution (INC) that was adopted as part of the implementation of the 2005 Comprehensive Peace Agreement (CPA) between the Government of Sudan and the Sudan People's Liberation Movement/Army (SPLM/SPLA). Over the last decade, it has become increasingly apparent that this Bill of Rights model has, on its own, largely failed to guarantee the effective constitutional protection of human rights. While there are some shortcomings in the way the Bill of Rights has been drafted,[2] its lack of implementation points to a deeper malaise in the system, and the limits of liberal, legalistic and pro forma institutionalized approaches. The absence of a suitable political and legal system in which Sudan's myriad challenges could be

1 See for the period from 1989–2000 in particular Human Rights Watch/Africa, *Behind the Red Line: Political Repression in Sudan* (1996); Amin M. Medani, *Crimes against International Humanitarian Law in Sudan: 1989-2000* (Dar El Mostaqbal El Arabi 2001). For the last two decades, there has been a large number of reports by the United Nations (UN), such as the 2005 International Commission of Inquiry Report on Darfur, and reports by the Special Rapporteur (now Independent Expert) on the situation of human rights in the Sudan; the African Commission on Human and Peoples' Rights (ACHPR); the Prosecutor of the International Criminal Court (ICC) to the UN Security Council; as well as national, regional and international NGOs. There is also a growing body of cases against Sudan before the ACHPR, see e.g. Lutz Oette, 'Litigation before the African Commission on Human and Peoples' Rights and the struggle against torture in Sudan' (2016) 54 *Sud Stud S Sud & Sud* 20.

2 See contributions in Mohamed Abdelsalam Babiker and Lutz Oette (eds), *The Constitutional Protection of Human Rights in Sudan: Challenges and Future Perspectives* (REDRESS; Faculty of Law, University of Khartoum; Sudanese Human Rights Monitor January 2014); Noha Ibrahim, 'The Sudanese Bill of Rights' (2008) 12 *IJHR* 613.

satisfactorily addressed has spawned several protest movements as well as political opposition, including armed movements. Increasingly, a number of these actors have identified addressing Sudan's deep-seated governance problems as a fundamental prerequisite for an end to Sudan's human rights crisis.[3]

This chapter, drawing on the burgeoning literature on Sudanese history, politics and the economy, as well as a substantial body of human rights reports and cases, examines both structural and ideational factors that have contributed to a legacy of human rights violations and weak rule of law. This includes Sudan's history of constitution-making, which has been aptly described as one 'in search of a constitution'.[4] The chapter locates these factors in the process of State formation and 'State building' in the Sudans, focusing on the colonial periods (1820–81 and 1898–1956), the *Mahdiyya* (1881–98) and developments since independence in 1956 (and 2011 in the case of South Sudan). The historical perspective taken does not suggest that developments have been uniform and constant. This applies in particular to the period after 1989, in which many of the policies and practices of the new regime aggravated existing problems and created new ones. Nonetheless, the dominance of certain interrelated themes in the discourse on the Sudans suggests a broadly shared understanding of what has been referred to as 'root causes' of conflict and violations.[5] This includes the centre–periphery divide and gendered and racial hierarchies, which form part of the fundamental question of Sudanese identity; lopsided governance and the repressive and arbitrary exercise of State power; an unbalanced and corrupt economic system; resort to repression and violence as a means of establishing/maintaining power and settling disputes; and weaknesses in the legal system, including lack of transparency and accountability. These features can be attributed to persistent patterns of modes of exercising power[6] in a State that is both weak and fierce,[7] particularly as a 'practitioner of violence',[8] a characteristic that Sudan shares with a number

3 See e.g. Sudan Call: *A Political Declaration on the Establishment of a State of Citizenship and Democracy* (3 December 2014), www.sudantribune.com/spip.php?article 53263, accessed 10 June 2018.

4 Ali Suleiman Fadlalla, 'Constitution-making in the Sudan: past experiences' (Advisory Council for Human Rights, with support from United Nations, Constitution-making Forum: A Government of Sudan Consultation, 24–25 May 2011). See further Abdel Salam Sidahmed and Alsir Sidahmed, *Sudan* (Routledge 2005) 46–50; Babiker and Oette (n 2); Kristine Mo, *Contested Constitutions: Constitutional development in Sudan 1953–2005* (Chr Michelsen Institute 2014).

5 See Douglas H Johnson, *The Root Causes of Sudan's Civil Wars: Peace or Truce* (Rev Edn, James Currey 2011).

6 Justin Willis, 'The ambitions of the State' in John Ryle et al (eds), *The Sudan Handbook* (James Currey 2011).

7 Nazih Ayubi, *Over-stating the Arab State: Politics and Society in the Middle East* (IB Tauris 1995 (2009 reprint)) 449–50.

8 Term used by Franz Neumann, *Behemoth, The Structure and Practice of National Socialism, 1933–1944* (OUP 1942, 1944) 458, with reference to Nazi Germany.

of other African States.[9] Unsurprisingly, these features have resulted in a series of human rights violations and, more broadly, in a lack of respect for the rule of law. These violations have been integral to the exercise of power in Sudan, particularly since 1989. Many violations, such as those committed during the war against the Nuba in the mid-1990s,[10] bear the hallmark of what has in a different context been termed 'planned misery'.[11] This includes both deliberate violations and the 'logic of particular socio-economic arrangements'.[12]

This chapter argues that, in order not to become trapped in the cycle of past failings, the constitution-making process must move beyond a narrow focus on legal components and form part of broader reforms at multiple levels.[13] This process requires addressing the causes and factors perpetuating abuse of power, which in turn places a considerable burden on Sudan's elites and other powerful actors to fundamentally alter their way of doing politics. The SPLM's experience is highly instructive in this regard. Its erstwhile leader, John Garang, identified many of the structural problems that produce and reproduce human rights violations, but his authoritarianism was highly problematic from a human rights perspective.[14] The SPLM now rules South Sudan and is embroiled in both repressive politics and abuses forming part of an internal power struggle. Sudanese elites and powerful actors have become skilful in manoeuvring if not manipulating various forms of regional and international engagement.[15] Such engagement is therefore permanently at risk of becoming part of the problem, inadvertently fostering the status quo. This applies equally to initiatives in the Sudans by several United Nations (UN) and African Union (AU) agencies or joint missions, forming part of broader international 'rule of law promotion'.[16]

Ultimately, therefore, any change will have to be driven by a sufficiently strong cross-section of Sudanese actors to overcome the structural weaknesses and biases of what remains a highly unstable State (which equally, if not more so, applies to the new State of South Sudan). A number of protest movements,

9 See further Jeffrey Herbst, *State and Power in Africa: Comparative Lessons in Authority and Control* (2nd edn, Princeton University Press 2014).

10 African Rights, *Facing Genocide: The Nuba of Sudan* (African Rights 1995).

11 Susan Marks, 'Human rights and root causes' (2011) 74 *MLR* 57.

12 Ibid 75.

13 See on critical constitutionalism, brief overview in Scott Newton, *The Constitutional Systems of the Independent Central Asian States* (Hart 2017) 5–10.

14 See John Young, *The Fate of Sudan: The Origins and Consequences of a Flawed Peace Process* (Zed Books 2012) 44–74.

15 See e.g. Daniel Large and Luke A Patey (eds), *Sudan Looks East: China, India and the Politics of Asian Alternatives* (James Currey 2011).

16 Richard Zajac Sannerholm, *Rule of Law after War and Crisis: Ideologies, Norms and Methods* (Intersentia 2012). Recent policies pursued by the European Union (EU) and EU States to build the capacity of States in the Horn of Africa, including Sudan, to combat human trafficking and smuggling are the latest example of engagement to strengthen local capacity, albeit one that is driven by strong policy interests to 'better manage migration'. See Lutz Oette and Mohamed Abdelsalam Babiker, 'Migration control á la Khartoum: EU external engagement and human rights protection in the Horn of Africa' (2017) 36 *RSQ* 64.

civil society and political opposition groups have emerged in Sudan since 2005 which provide the nucleus for change.[17] Many actors have identified the need for change but there is a considerable degree of wariness, given that several opposition leaders and movements appear to engage in the very mode of doing politics that needs changing. Even if new political forces were to come to power, the challenges of building a viable, peaceful State based on respect for the rule of law would be formidable. The spectre of the failed democratic intervals following successful uprisings inevitably looms large, and serves as warning against any facile assumptions or complacency that equates political change with a solution to Sudan's structural problems.[18] Heeding An-Na'im's call for a contextual approach to constitution-making that draws on indigenous concepts and experiences will be an important element of addressing these challenges.[19] This applies equally to Sudan's new neighbour. South Sudan has, notwithstanding some marked differences (such as an emerging tribalist ideology), inherited a number of Sudan's problems, exacerbated by decades of conflict and neglect. Many of the human rights violations there follow a pattern set in Sudan over two centuries of conflict and repression. As the chapter will highlight, a better understanding and acknowledgment of these deep-seated challenges that takes the legacy of human rights violations seriously offers an important basis on which to develop policies and approaches that stand a better chance of succeeding than previous efforts. Any constitution-making process and newly adopted constitution in Sudan will need to address these underlying factors, lest it risks sharing the fate of its predecessors.

2 Structural factors

2.1 Hegemony and inequality

Hegemony, understood as dominance by means of coercion and/or ideology, and inequality – i.e. the uneven distribution of, and access to wealth, power and other goods based on criteria such as race, gender and class – characterize Sudanese politics and society.[20] An analysis of these structural factors therefore provides the key to an understanding of patterns of victimisation.

17 See e.g. Khalid Medani, 'Understanding the prospects and challenges for another popular intifada in Sudan' *Jadaliyya* (27 June 2012), www.jadaliyya.com/Details/26390/Understanding-the-Prospects-and-Challenges-for-Another-Popular-Intifada-in-Sudan, accessed 10 June 2018, and, particularly on comparing the 1985 uprising with recent protest movements, Alex de Waal, 'Sudan's elusive democratization: civil mobilization, provincial rebellion and chameleon dictatorships' (2013) 31 *J Cont Afr Stud* 213.

18 WJ Berridge, *Civil Uprisings in Modern Sudan: The 'Khartoum Springs' of 1964 and 1985* (Bloomsbury 2015).

19 Abdullahi Ahmed An-Na'im, *African Constitutionalism and the Role of Islam* (University of Pennsylvania Press 2006) 1–8.

20 See in this context the discussion of the notion of repressive State apparatus and ideological State apparatus in Louis Althusserl, *On the Reproduction of Capitalism: Ideology and Ideological State Apparatus* (Verso 2014) 65–93.

2.1.1 The centre–periphery divide and systemic discrimination

The African Union High Level Panel on Darfur aptly described what is happening in that region as 'Sudan's crisis in Darfur'.[21] It set out what can by now be regarded as a widely shared understanding of the factors that underpin Sudanese conflicts, the principal of which is the divide between the centre and the periphery.[22] This structural ordering of the Sudanese State is based on a centre dominated by the riverine groups at the expense of other, marginalized ones. The dominant groups have pursued a discourse and policies that privileges an 'Arab', monocultural identity,[23] which is presented as the status quo, over a plural one that by necessity includes other Sudanese identities. They have also succeeded in largely controlling political and economic power, as laid out in the 'Black Book'.[24] This development can be traced to the process of colonial State formation. The *Turkiyya*, 1820–81,[25] and later the Anglo–Egyptian Condominium, 1898–1956,[26] brought disparate political units such as Sennar, Darfur and the southern kingdoms and other territories together in what eventually became the Sudan. The *Turkiyya*, from its newly established political centre in Khartoum,[27] pursued a racist and exploitative policy aimed at extracting profits from the slave trade (at least in its early period), gold and ivory, and taxation. It largely governed by recourse to force and a measure of co-optation predominantly in the central areas of today's Sudan, with slave raids (first by the State, later privatized) and punitive expedition to other parts of Sudan, particularly the South.[28] The *Mahdiyya*, in place from 1881–98, was an indigenous, proto-nationalist movement that replaced the colonial rulers. It was itself characterized

21 *Darfur: The Quest for Peace, Justice and Reconciliation*, Report of the African Union High-Level Panel on Darfur (AUPD), PSC/AHG/2 (CCVII) (29 October 2009) 9.

22 Amir Idris, *Identity, Citizenship, and Violence in two Sudans: Reimagining a Common Future* (Palgrave 2013); Johnson (n 5); Willis (n 6); Noah Bassil, *The Post-Colonial State and Civil War in Sudan: The Origins of Conflict in Darfur* (IB Tauris 2012).

23 See on the construction of national identities, without specific reference to Sudan, Benedict Anderson, *Imagined Communities: Reflections on the Origin and Spread of Nationalism* (New edn, Verso 1998).

24 Anonymous, *Black Book of Sudan: Imbalance of Power and Wealth in Sudan* (2000). See also Abdullahi Osman El-Tom, 'Review article: Black Book of Sudan: Imbalance of Power and Wealth in Sudan' (2003) 1 *J Afr Nat Aff* 25.

25 Richard Hill, *Egypt in the Sudan 1820–1881* (OUP 1959); Richard Gray, *A History of the Southern Sudan 1839–1889* (OUP 1961).

26 Muddathir Abdel-Rahim, *Imperialism and Nationalism in the Sudan: A Study in Constitutional and Political Development, 1899–1956* (Clarendon Press 1969); Peter Woodward, *Sudan, 1898–1989: The Unstable State* (Lynne Rienner Lester Crook Academic Publishing 1990) 13–93.

27 See Bushra El Tayed Babiker, *Khartoum: Past, Present and the Prospects for the Future* (Working Paper, University of Durham Centre for Middle Eastern and Islamic Studies 2003).

28 PM Holt and MW Daly, *A History of the Sudan: From the Coming of Islam to the Present Day* (6th edn, Routledge 2011) 33ff.

by autocratic rule based on its understanding of Islam.[29] The British, who effectively ruled during the Condominium with extremely limited personnel, brought their own racial views, shared by local elites, which proved influential in creating Sudanese 'subjects' and establishing social divisions. They privileged 'Arabs' and tribal leaders who were the main beneficiaries of the (limited) education opportunities made available, primarily to educate mid-level elites.[30] Members of riverine elites also benefited from economic policies pursued by the British, particularly the Gezira scheme, while other parts of the country remained underdeveloped.[31] The political and economic power was centred in Khartoum, with the remainder of the Sudan subject to what was referred to as native administration and closed district ordinances in various parts of the country, particularly South Sudan, which reflected British views of the latter's nature.[32] While these structures did not translate into a situation of one directional top-down control,[33] it is equally clear that areas outside the centre suffered from even more neglect than Sudan as a whole. The bias in favour of the riverine elite was evident on the eve of independence among Sudanese actors when key political figures were drawn from a small circle.[34] The newly independent State was seen as having modern institutions at its centre and as being culturally 'Arab' and Muslim (though the status of Islam was contentious, including in Sudan's constitution), with groups outside the centre having limited if any voice in these debates.[35] It is against this background unsurprising that Sudanese politics since independence have been dominated by the centre. This perpetuated colonial discourses and mind-sets, creating a dichotomy between advanced, 'civilized' (politically, culturally, economy) parts of Sudan, self-referred to as 'Arab', and other 'backward' parts of the country, which were either seen as 'tribal' (Muslim but uneducated/'African') or inherently inferior (southern Sudanese). This proclaimed or assumed superiority was challenged by the erstwhile leader of the SPLM/SPLA John Garang in his vision of a new Sudan and helped fuel opposition by various regional groups to riverine hegemony.[36] While the various conflicts in Sudan have multiple causes, the fight against political and societal inequality is at their heart.

29 PM Holt, *The Mahdist State in the Sudan: 1881–1898: A Study of its Origins, Development and Overthrow* (2nd edn, OUP with Clarendon Press 1977).
30 Heather J Sharkey, *Living with Colonialism: Nationalism and Culture in the Anglo-Egyptian Sudan* (University of California Press 2003) 138–41.
31 See for a brief overview of colonial economic policies, Ibrahim Elnur, *Contested Sudan: The Political Economy of War and Destruction* (Routledge 2009) 10–15.
32 MW Daly, *Empire on the Nile: The Anglo-Egyptian Sudan 1898–1934* (CUP 1986) 396–419; further, O. Collins, *Shadows in the Grass: Britain in the Southern Sudan, 1918–1956* (Yale University Press 1983).
33 Cherry Leonardi, *Dealing with Government in South Sudan: Histories of Chiefship, Community and State* (James Currey 2013); Chris Vaughan, *Darfur: Colonial Violence, Sultanic Legacies & Local Politics, 1916–1956* (James Currey 2015).
34 Holt and Daly (n 28) 109–112; Sharkey (n 30) 91–94.
35 See further Woodward (n 26) 97–135.
36 John Garang, *The Call for Democracy in Sudan* (Kegan Paul International 1992).

Regional hegemony and inequality is mirrored, and complemented by deep inequalities based on group membership. As highlighted in a number of studies and by various actors, Sudan's society is still marked by a considerable focus on status-based factors such as race, ethnicity, religion and gender.[37] The ensuing stratification translates into relationships of dominance that frequently result in exploitation, oppression and denial of rights.

Status differences based on race found their starkest expression in the practice of slavery. This practice, which subsided under the Condominium, with the British pursuing ambivalent policies, and resurfaced during the civil war in the South, has profoundly shaped relationships and perceptions, and hence identities, in Sudan.[38] In its most extreme form, often influenced by cultural and religious stereotypes, it views 'Arabs' as free, worthy and educated, and 'non-Arabs' as the opposite, perceptions that were reinforced during colonial times.[39] Notions of race and religion, or simply race (in terms of colour and/or ethnicity) did not only result in discrimination but also in targeting and dehumanization. In the context of the armed conflicts in the North–South civil war, the Nuba Mountains, Blue Nile and Darfur, there is considerable evidence that international crimes, including war crimes, crimes against humanity and possibly genocide, have been committed against members of certain groups on the basis of race, ethnicity or religion.[40] It is telling that a foundational human rights report made this link explicit, showing how the then Government of Sudan, in 1987, exploited ethnic tensions and became complicit in serious large-scale violations committed against Dinkas in Dhein (located in southern Darfur).[41]

Discrimination of members belonging to ethnic and religious minority groups, particularly southern Sudanese, Nuba from the Nuba Mountains, Darfurians and the Beja from eastern Sudan has been systemic, flowing from elite and group-based policies that marginalize other communities in Sudan.[42]

37 Idris (n 22).

38 Amir Idris, *Sudan's Civil War: Slavery, Race, and Formational Identities* (Edwin Mellen Press 2001); Ahmad Alawad Sikainga, *Slaves into Workers: Emancipation and Labor in Colonial Sudan* (University of Texas Press 1996); Jok Madut Jok, *War and Slavery in Sudan* (University of Pennsylvania Press 2001); Abbas Ibrahim Muhammad Ali, *The British, the Slave Trade and Slavery in the Sudan*, 1820–1881 (Khartoum University Press 1972); Mohamed Ibrahim Nugud, *Slavery in the Sudan: History, Documents and Commentary* (Palgrave Macmillan 2013).

39 Sharkey (n 30) 36–39.

40 See *Report of the International Commission of Inquiry on Darfur to the United Nations Secretary-General* (25 January 2005); *Sudanese Civilians in South Kordofan and Blue Nile (represented by REDRESS, SDFG, HRW and the Enough Project) v Sudan*, Comm 420/12 (joined with 402/11), pending before ACHPR; African Rights (n 10); Samuel Totten (ed.), *Conflict in the Nuba Mountains: From Genocide by Attrition to the Contemporary Crisis* (Routledge 2015); M. W. Daly, *Darfur's Sorrow: A History of Destruction and Genocide* (CUP 2007); Gerard Prunier, *Darfur: A 21st Century Genocide* (3rd edn, Cornell University Press 2008).

41 Ushari Ahmad Mahmud and Suleyman Ali Baldo, *Human Rights Abuses in the Sudan 1987: The Dhein Massacre-Slavery in the Sudan* (Sudan Relief and Rehabilitation Association 1987).

42 See 'issues of concerns and recommendations' in Committee on the Elimination of Racial Discrimination, *Concluding Observations on the Combined Twelfth to Sixteenth Reports of Sudan*, UN doc CERD/C/SDN/CO/12-16 (15 May 2015) paras 6–33.

Poverty, underdevelopment, lack of affirmative action and precarious status, particularly of internally displaced persons (IDPs) due to the armed conflicts, have combined to lead to a lower realization of economic, social and cultural rights.[43] Members of these groups, particularly those suspected of being opposed to the Government of Sudan, have also been exposed to torture and other ill-treatment as well as a series of other violations, including unfair trials.[44] Others are especially vulnerable due to their lower status (lower levels of education, fewer resources, less influential connections) and limited access to justice.[45] In some instances, these factors have been aggravated by government policies and laws, such as the disenfranchisement of persons with South Sudanese links in 2011, which stripped them of civil and political rights based on citizen status.[46]

Viewing the military coup in 1989 and subsequent Islamist project[47] in a broader, historical perspective raises the question whether it represented an intensification of existing patterns or a radical rupture, which not only introduced a number of changes but also a radical, culturally alien political project to Sudan.[48] In fact, it appears to have combined the two, imposing an Islamist ideology fused with a strong military–security complex and neoliberal and high modernist development projects.[49] *Shari'a* law served a dual function in this regard, providing ideological legitimacy and serving as instrument of repression, while inscribing 'Muslim' – as defined by the regime – hegemony into the legal order.[50]

43 See e.g. *Report of the Special Rapporteur on the Human Rights of Internally Displaced Persons, Chaloka Beyani: Mission to Sudan*, UN doc A/HRC/23/44/Add.2 (25 June 2013).

44 REDRESS and ACJPS, *Sudan's Human Rights Crisis: High Time to Take Article 2 of the Covenant Seriously: Submission to the UN Human Rights Committee ahead of its Examination of Sudan's Fourth Periodic Report under the International Covenant on Civil and Political Rights* (June 2014) paras 44–120, www.redress.org/downloads/publications/140613SubmissionSudanHRC.pdf, accessed 10 June 2018.

45 Ibid.

46 Mike Sanderson, 'Statelessness and mass expulsion in Sudan: a reassessment of the international law' (2014) 12 *Northwest. JIHR* 74. See also Chapter 5 in this collection.

47 Alex de Waal and AH Abdel Salam, 'Islamism, State power and jihad in Sudan' in Alex De Waal (ed.), *Islamism and its Enemies in the Horn of Africa* (Hurst & Co 2003).

48 See on changes made, Sidahmed (n 4) 60–62; and, on the Islamic State, Abdullahi A Gallab, *The First Islamist Republic: Development and Disintegration of Islamism in Sudan* (Ashgate 2007); Charles Tripp, 'Sudan: State and elite: review essay' (1997) 67 *Africa* 159, 172–3.

49 Roland Marchal and Einas Ahmed, 'Multiple uses of neoliberalism: war, new boundaries, and reorganization of the government in Sudan' in Francisco Gutiérrez and Gerd Schönwälder (eds), *Economic Liberalization and Political Violence: Utopia or Dystopia?* (Pluto Press and International Development Research Centre 2010); Elnur (n 31) 64–90; Harry Verhoeven, *Water, Civilisation and Power in Sudan: The Political Economy of Military-Islamist State Building* (CUP 2015), particularly 83ff.

50 Abdelsalam Hassan Abdelsalam and Amin M Medani, 'Criminal law reform and human rights in African and Muslim countries with particular reference to Sudan' in Lutz Oette (ed.), *Criminal Law Reform and Transitional Justice: Human Rights Perspectives for Sudan* (Ashgate 2011) 45–8, 54–5.

One of the key causes for persistent conflicts since 1989 has been the denial of the right to self-determination and minority rights.[51] The lack of adequate recognition of political and cultural difference has been compounded by the twin denial of both civil and political rights as well as economic, social and cultural rights stemming from a radicalization and racialization of politics, abusive development projects and a crackdown on protests. The UN Committee on Economic, Social and Cultural Rights captured and highlighted the consequences of these structural inequalities and policies in its concluding observations on Sudan's second State party report. It noted

> with concern the significant disparities in the enjoyment of economic, social and cultural rights among the constituent States of the State party, with States in the eastern Sudan, Darfur and Kordofan being particularly disadvantaged, as extreme poverty remains widespread there and access to education, health services and drinking water is limited. The Committee is further concerned that disadvantaged States do not receive federal resources proportionate to their needs.[52]

The UN Human Rights Committee, for its part, was concerned

> at reports of serious human rights violations, including rape, torture, arbitrary detention, large-scale displacements and extrajudicial killings, which have been and continue to be committed in conflict-affected areas, in particular Darfur, South Kordofan and Blue Nile, and lack of accountability for these crimes. The Committee is further concerned at reports indicating that State party authorities have at times arbitrarily denied the timely access of life saving humanitarian assistance for civilian populations in some conflict-affected areas, particularly those controlled by rebel groups.[53]

The Committee on the Elimination of Racial Discrimination highlighted the ethnic dimension of conflicts, the lack of minority representation and abusive development projects. It noted

> with concern the persistence of old and the emergence of new conflicts with strong ethnic dimensions in different parts of the State party, notably in the Darfur region, as well as in South Kordofan and Blue Nile States. The Committee is also concerned that ethnic tensions could intensify in other parts of the Sudan, including in the Nuba region in the north and in the

51 See Chapter 6 in this collection.

52 *Concluding Observations on the Second Periodic Report of the Sudan*, UN doc E/C.12/SDN/CO/2 (27 October 2015) para 21.

53 *Concluding observations on the Fourth Periodic report of the Sudan*, UN doc CCPR/S/SDN/CO/4 (19 August 2014) para 8.

eastern areas of Red Sea and Kassala States, which are predominantly inhabited by ethnic minority groups.[54]

The Committee regretted

> the absence of available data on political representation of minority groups in the public administration, the police and the army. The Committee is further concerned about their reported limited political participation and representation ...[55]

and expressed its concerns about

> reports indicating that the Government plans to resume the construction of the Kajbar dams on lands traditionally occupied or inhabited by the Nubian people. The Committee is concerned that the dam, if constructed, may lead to the displacement of thousands of Nubians who, according to the State party's delegation, have been living on those lands for more than 8,000 years, and to the destruction of many archaeological sites with historical and cultural significance for Nubians. The Committee is also concerned that the amendment to article 43 of the Interim Constitution, empowering the President to allocate and confiscate land for investment purposes without restriction, may further contribute to the above-mentioned consequences for Nubians.[56]

These concerns are echoed in the regular reports published by the Independent Expert on the situation of human rights in the Sudan, which have repeatedly highlighted the lack of effective remedies.[57] Recurring conflicts, uprisings and local protests against development policies, such as dam projects resulting in the destruction of culture and forced evictions, and other rights violations are the manifestation of a system that fails to accommodate diversity and offers no effective institutional mechanisms to address grievances and resolve conflicts. Political actors such as the ruling National Congress Party (NCP) have sought to repress and/or buy off communities protesting against the status quo and specific policies and projects. This strategy has succeeded in terms of keeping the NCP in power but has come at the price of embedding violence at the centre of governance and perpetuating a highly unstable State.

54 *Concluding Observations on the Combined Twelfth to Sixteenth Reports of Sudan*, UN doc CERD/C/SDN/CO/12-16 (12 June 2015) para 6.

55 Ibid para 18.

56 Ibid para 21.

57 The reports are available at www.ohchr.org/EN/HRBodies/SP/CountriesMandates/SD/Pages/IESudan.aspx, accessed 10 June 2018.

2.1.2 Lack of gender equality

Gender relations in a country as diverse as Sudan are doubtlessly complex. Yet, it is widely acknowledged that Sudanese society has been male dominated, with such domination grounded in, and justified with reference to, custom and religion.[58] Moves towards greater gender equality suffered a considerable setback from 1989 onwards when discrimination against women was openly practiced, and even legislated for.[59] A version of *Shari'a* was invoked to inscribe male dominance into the legal order. Discriminatory laws abound, with personal status law in particular enshrining dependency and inferior rights for women compared to men.[60] Public order laws have targeted women disproportionately to enforce male moral standards of acceptable female conduct, such as dress codes.[61] This discrimination is aggravated for women from marginalized backgrounds who have frequently suffered multiple (intersectional) discrimination based on ethnicity, class and gender.[62] For example, southern Sudanese women selling *Marissa* (beer) in Khartoum are disproportionately represented in Omdurman's women's prison.[63] The institutionalized discrimination has also adversely affected women's economic, social and cultural rights. The UN Human Rights Committee noted with concern

> the discriminatory provisions affecting women, religious minorities and lesbian, gay, bisexual, transgender and intersex persons that are still in force in the State party, including those contained in the Criminal Law Act, the Personal Status Act, the Public Service Regulations, the Social Insurance Act and the Sudanese Nationality Act. The Committee is also concerned at the lack of legislation to implement the constitutional and Covenant provisions on non-discrimination. Moreover, the Committee is particularly concerned at reports of discrimination of individuals on the basis of religion and of sexual orientation and gender identity.
>
> (art. 2)

58 See Equal Rights Trust and SORD, *In Search of Confluence: Addressing Discrimination and Inequality in Sudan* (2014); Nada Mustafa Ali, *Gender, Race, and Sudan's Exile Politics: Do We All Belong To This Country?* (Lexington Books 2015).

59 Equal Rights Trust ibid; Asma Abdel Halim, 'Gendered justice: women and the application of penal laws in the Sudan' in Oette (n 50); Liv Tønnessen and Samia al-Nagar, *Women and Girls Caught between Rape and Adultery in Sudan: Criminal Law Reform, 2005–2015* (Chr Michelsen Institute 2015).

60 Equal Rights Trust (n 58) 31–244; CCPR/C/SDN/CO/4 (n 53) paras 10 and 12; *Report of the Special Rapporteur on Violence Against Women, its Causes and Consequences on her Mission to the Sudan*, UN doc A/HRC/32/42/Add.1 (18 April 2016) para 84.

61 See ibid paras 82, 85; SIHA, *Beyond Trousers: The Public Order Regime and the Human Rights of Women and Girls in Sudan* (A Discussion Paper, Submission to the 46th Ordinary Session of the African Commission on Human and Peoples' Rights, Banjul, the Gambia 12 November 2009).

62 Ibid and SIHA and REDRESS, *Criminalisation of Women in Sudan: A need for Fundamental Reform* (December 2017).

63 Ibid.

> The Committee is concerned at the inferior status of women in the family and in the society in the State party, which is reflected in several legal provisions limiting their rights. It is also concerned at the negative impact of this status on women's access to education, employment, health (including women's autonomy in regard to their health) and vulnerability to violence. It notes in particular that women are primarily employed in low-skilled jobs and in the informal economy.
>
> (art. 3)[64]

Beyond institutionalizing discrimination, Sudan's law has also inadequately protected women against sexual violence, particularly against rape, which until February 2015 had been defined as involuntary adultery, thereby exposing women to the risk of prosecution where they failed to prove coercion.[65] This lack of protection, which also manifests itself in the absence of effective investigations and prosecutions, has an eminently political dimension. Rape and sexual violence as international crimes have been widely documented in Sudan's civil wars, particularly in Darfur. This is reflected in the fact that charges in this regard form part of the arrest warrants issued by the International Criminal Court (ICC) against Ahmad Muhammad Harun, Ali Kushayb, Omar Hassan Ahmad Al Bashir and Abdel Raheem Muhammad Hussein.[66]

The persistence of discrimination and gender-based violence reflects women's limited participation in political decision-making and public life. In the CPA, which was essentially negotiated and drafted by men, women's concerns were dealt with incidentally, rather than forming an integral part of a positive peace and broader democratic transformation.[67] This includes the INC. While it enshrines formal equality between men and women,[68] it equally retains provisions on the role of *Shari'a* that may be used to legitimate inequality and does not provide for any measures aimed at redressing existing structural inequalities.[69]

This account does not mean that women lack agency in Sudan, far from it. Several women's groups, such as No to Women Oppression, have responded to negative discourses, systemic discrimination and exclusion by staging public protests, such as in Lubna Hussein's case, and in respect of the video showing a woman flogged by policemen.[70] Women have also spoken out, such as Safia Ishag Ibrahim against her rape alleged to be at the hands of Sudan's National Intelligence and Security Service (NISS).[71] Women's organizations and

64 CCPR/C/SDN/CO/4 (n 53) paras 19, 29.

65 See African Centre for Justice and Peace Studies, *Sudan's New Law on Rape and Sexual Harassment: One Step Forward, Two Steps Back?* (8 March 2016) on remaining concerns.

66 See for further information on these cases, www.icc-cpi.int/darfur, accessed 10 June 2018.

67 Halim (n 59) 228–9.

68 Arts 31 and 32 INC.

69 See further Elrayh, Chapter 7.

70 See on these cases, REDRESS and Sudanese Human Rights Monitor, *No More Cracking of the Whip: Time to End Corporal Punishment in Sudan* (March 2012) 15–16, and on the women's movement (n 58–9).

71 *Safia Ishaq Mohammed Issa (represented by REDRESS) v Sudan*, Comm 443/12, case pending before ACHPR.

government bodies have advocated law reform, in particular with regard to rape and adultery laws as well as penalizing female genital mutilation and child marriage.[72] As important as these struggles are, if anything they highlight the lack of legal and institutional protection, and the need to consider women's rights in Sudan in a more holistic fashion. This includes identifying where, and how, law and institutional, cultural and religiously justified practices create, perpetuate or help to justify discrimination and violence against women.

2.2 Governance, violence and the rule of law

2.2.1 Patronage, skewed development and abuse of power

The Sudanese State shares a number of features of States in the region more generally.[73] In contrast to the archetypical Weberian State based on notions of rationality and formal legal orders, the Sudanese State is characterized by a strong, often highly personalized, executive. It is marked by its capacity and willingness to (ab)use State power with institutional impunity if it serves the interest of the ruling elites. Government operates by co-opting individuals, groups and communities and providing patronage rather than by developing and implementing policies within a framework of independent institutions, space for political opposition and a vibrant civil society.[74] In the absence of democratic legitimacy and avenues that could either effectively challenge or provide alternatives to patronage and co-optation, groups excluded from the feast frequently resort to protest and armed insurrection.

This mode of governance is part of embedded structures in as much as many of its elements are carried over from pre-colonial and colonial States whose governments represented and benefited elites (whether national or foreign), lacked democratic legitimacy, had no accountability *vis-à-vis* the electorate and used the State apparatus to repress, pacify and/or exploit the populace. The Condominium government introduced a bifurcated system of a light modern State, with its primary focus on Khartoum, and of native administration, a delegated 'tribal' exercise of power that constituted a form of patronage.[75] Abuses of power were ripe, including by chiefs, with limited protection provided by central government or the judiciary, which, though independent, had limited coverage and operated within the existing colonial order.[76] Government was largely seen as hostile, rather than as an entity that represents the people or a significant part

72 See Tønnessen (n 59).

73 This is not to say that these problems are unique to Sudan or the region, and are not, at least to some degree, a feature of political systems worldwide.

74 See further Alex de Waal, *The Real Politics of the Horn of Africa: Money, War and the Business of Power* (Polity 2015) 69–90.

75 See further Willis (n 6); Woodward (n 26); Vaughan (n 33); Leonardi (n 33); Idris (n 22); Nesrine Malik, 'Khartoum: the most selfish city?' *Guardian* (19 September 2014).

76 Mark Fathi Massoud, *Law's Fragile State: Colonial, Authoritarian, and Humanitarian Legacies in Sudan* (CUP 2013) 44–84.

thereof.[77] This perception was – and has since been – particularly strong in the marginalized areas.[78]

The failure to create a stable and democratic State following Sudan's independence is well-known.[79] Alternating between weak and exclusive (*vis-à-vis* the South in particular) parliamentarian regimes on the one hand and authoritarian regimes on the other, the period from 1956–89 has been characterized by the dominance of central executive power. However, this power was not unchallenged; the judiciary largely retained its independence until the 1970s and Sudanese civil society was twice able to mobilize and overthrow authoritarian regimes.[80] Yet, parliamentary regimes were unable to address broader power imbalances, such as between the centre and the periphery, and inequalities, also because they themselves partook in Sudanese elite politics. The project of building an Islamist State after the 1989 coup, instead of redressing structural imbalances and providing stability, gave way to executive, unaccountable policies married with patrimonialism and corruption.[81] The discovery of oil, together with neo-liberal policies and co-operation with authoritarian regimes, such as China, Malaysia and several States in the Middle East, has resulted in a skewed and non-transparent economic system.[82] Instead of pursuing a sustainable development policy, including in the field of agriculture,[83] which would have included much needed investment in infrastructure, education, skills and institutional capacity, the regime has used a large part of its revenues for military and security purposes or its members appropriated available resources.[84] The main beneficiaries of these policies have been individuals belonging to, or close to, the regime, particularly in the security sector, and a small middle class, primarily in Khartoum, as well as groups supporting the government in the peripheries.[85] Inhabitants of rural areas and the poorer urban strata have largely lost out. This applies particularly in respect of practices

77 See further chapter 2 in this collection, particularly on the use of martial law and repressive legislation.

78 See Gérard Prunier, 'Why did South Sudan blow up in December 2013 and what is likely to happen as a result?' (2015) 51 *Sud Stud S Sud & Sud* 7.

79 Woodward (n 26).

80 Berridge (n 18).

81 See further de Waal and Abdel Salam (n 47), and Girogio Musso, 'The Islamic movement and power in Sudan: from revolution to absorption into the State' in Barbara Casciarri, Munzoul AM Assal and François Ireton (eds), *Multidimensional Change in Sudan (1989–2011): Reshaping Livelihoods, Conflicts and Identities* (Berghahn 2015).

82 Jemera Rone, *Sudan, Oil, and Human Rights* (Human Rights Watch 2003); Siddig Umbadda, *Towards Institutional Reform and Economic Policies Supporting Stability (after Political Reconciliation)* (Sudan Democracy First Group, Institutional Reform Series Paper No 3, Consultation meeting on Institutional Reform in Sudan – Nairobi 15–17 September 2014); and various chapters in Large (n 15).

83 Umbadda ibid; Verhoeven (n 49) 198–207.

84 Umbadda ibid; Suliman Baldo, *Khartoum's Economic Achilles' Heel: The Intersection of War, Profit, and Greed* (Enough Project 2016).

85 Edward Thomas, 'Patterns of growth and inequality in Sudan, 1977–2017' (Working Paper, Institute for Middle East and Islamic Studies, Durham 2017).

such as dam projects, which have caused destruction and displacement,[86] and land grab.[87] The January 2015 constitutional amendments portrayed expropriation of land as part of broader investment policies.[88] In practice, however, these policies facilitate a sell out to rich foreign investors speculating on land that have disrupted local communities without providing them with tangible benefits.[89]

The armed conflicts in (the then) southern Sudan, Darfur, South Kordofan and Blue Nile have had a devastating impact on livelihoods, resulting in large-scale displacement.[90] The main response has been the provision of – largely foreign – humanitarian aid, where it could be delivered without impediment, rather than any concerted reconstruction.[91] Following the separation of South Sudan, the underlying weaknesses in Sudan's economy, and lack of economic policies, have been exposed. These conditions have resulted in hardship and recurring street protests against austerity policies imposed by the regime, which met with repression and the violation of the rights of freedom of expression and assembly.[92]

In view of the political dynamics and expected gains, political parties have frequently been more interested in capturing (a share of) power and wealth. This has come at the expense of an interest in representing their constituents and strengthening their rights, which limits the ability of citizens to participate in the political process through intermediaries. The limited focus on policy-making has inhibited both broader debates and the development of institutions capable of addressing Sudan's multiple governance problems. The institutions that have benefited from investment, particularly the military and the security apparatus, have reinforced lopsided governance in which the State's administrative capacity is primarily used for self-serving purposes.[93] The population, unless it belongs to

86 Harry Verhoeven, 'Sudan's hydropolitics: regional chess games, national hegemony and local resistance' in Casciarri (n 81); *Ali Askouri and Abdel-Hakeem Nasr (on Behalf of Persons Affected by the Construction of the Merowe and Kajbar Dam) v Sudan*, Comm 452/13, pending before ACHPR.

87 Liz Alden Wily, *Making Peace Impossible? Failure to Honour the Land Obligations of the Comprehensive Peace Agreement in Central Sudan*, A Resource Paper (September 2010), www.mokoro.co.uk/wp-content/uploads/making_peace_impossible_land_obligations_in_central_sudan.pdf, accessed 10 June 2018; Siddig Umbadda, 'Agricultural investment through land grabbing in Sudan' in Jörg Gertel, Richard Rottenburg & Sandra Calkins (eds), *Disrupting Territories: Land, Commodification & Conflict in Sudan* (James Currey 2014); and contributions in Barbara Casciarri and Mohamed A Babiker (eds), *Anthropology of Law in Muslim Sudan: Land, Courts and the Plurality of Practices* (Brill 2018).

88 Revised art 186, see further analysis in Nabil Adib, Mohamed Abdelsalam Babiker, and Lutz Oette, *Constitutional Reforms, Governance and Human Rights Protection: Sudan's 2015 Constitutional Amendments* (unpublished, on file with author 2015).

89 See further Gertel (n 87).

90 SR report on IDPs (n 43); Elnur (n 31) 93–110 on the economic implications.

91 Umbadda (n 82). See on humanitarian aid the regular reports on Sudan by the UN Secretary-General.

92 See on 'human rights violations during the September 2013 demonstrations' in particular *Report of the Independent Expert on the Situation of Human Rights in the Sudan, Mashood A Baderin*, UN doc A/HRC/27/69 (4 September 2014) paras 32–41.

93 See further Baldo (n 84).

the relatively small strata of persons who are affluent and/or well connected or otherwise benefit from the regime, including business elites, is therefore largely excluded from political processes, particularly outside Khartoum.

Since 1989, despite the proliferation of armed conflicts and the weak exercise of State power in parts of the periphery, Sudan is not what has been called a failed State.[94] Instead, it can be described as a flawed State where the ruling elite has captured the State, sought to impose an ideology, by means of violence if necessary, and focused on strengthening institutions of interest (security, economy) while neglecting or undermining others, such as an independent judiciary and other rule-of-law institutions, including supposedly independent bodies created under the CPA. The latter includes the Human Rights Commission, the National Judicial Service Commission, the National Constitutional Review Commission and the National Commission for the Allocation of Resources.[95] The CPA and INC set out limited institutional reforms, such as of the NISS, which were, however, not (adequately) implemented.[96] The CPA's vertical model left power structures intact; in the absence of a genuine democratic process, the lack of transparency and accountability has remained the status quo which allowed practices of abuse of power to persist and thrive. South Sudan's self-determination, rather than change this situation, has created conditions that perpetuate the flawed State in rump Sudan and allow it to flourish in South Sudan. The major casualties in the political process have been political parties and civil society. Constituting influential forces prior to 1989, they have since been systematically emasculated. Against this background, Sudan has witnessed increasing resort to communal identity-based politics, often taking the form of armed insurrection and protest, which are in turn met with further repression.

2.2.2 Violence

Resort to violence as a means of establishing and maintaining power, and of settling disputes, has been a recurring theme in Sudan's history, to the point that it has been called endemic.[97] The *Turkiyya* and the British during the Condominium used considerable armed force at various points, including punitive expeditions to subdue rebellions, such as in South Kordofan, Darfur and South Sudan.[98] The formation of the Sudanese State was therefore built on violence, as was Sudan's Statehood, the terms of which were immediately contested by southern Sudanese and met with violent responses. The 1970s and 1980s witnessed acts of violence

94 See Daniel Thürer, 'The "failed State" and international law' (1999) 81 *IRRC* 731.

95 See arts 129, 140, 142 and 198 INC.

96 See REDRESS and SORD, *Security for all: Reforming Sudan's National Security Service* (September 2009).

97 See e.g. Abdullahi A Gallab, *A Civil Society Deferred: The Tertiary Grip of Violence in the Sudan* (University Press of Florida 2011).

98 See Vaughan (n 33), and Justin Willis, 'Violence, authority, and the State in the Nuba Mountains of Condominium Sudan' (2003) 46 *Hist J* 89.

by the Nimeri regime against political opposition and a radicalization after 1983, both in terms of the North–South conflict and tensions in Darfur, and legislatively sanctioned violence to enforce *Shari'a* law.[99] The latter culminated in the execution of Mahmoud Mohamed Taha, including for a crime, i.e., apostasy, that was at the time not even recognized in statutory law.[100] Following the overthrow of the Nimeri regime, the democratic government harnessed 'tribal' violence in the North–South conflict and was complicit in massacres.[101]

Under the current regime, the use of armed force and other forms of violence have become a mode of governance. The 1989 coup was followed by the persecution of political opponents, student movements, trade unions, other civil society groups and individuals or groups with different beliefs, and the dismissal of judges, academics and civil servants. This persecution was carried out by means that included extrajudicial killings and torture in the infamous ghost houses.[102] Its long aftermath has been characterized by an intensification of armed conflict in the South and violent campaigns, including the commission of large-scale international crimes to crush opposition to the ruling government in the Nuba Mountains, Darfur, again in the Nuba Mountains and Blue Nile, as well as to a lesser degree in east Sudan.[103] The government has both institutionalized State violence, particularly through the NISS, and relied on individuals and groups whose potential for violence can be instrumentalized where necessary, such as the 'Arab' tribes in Darfur.[104] Recent developments have witnessed a convergence of the two, with non-State actors and tribal militias, including the *Janjaweed* (in Darfur) and the Rapid Support Forces (RSF) being incorporated into the security and armed forces.[105] This practice has been underpinned by the militarization of education and a rhetoric of violence, which often draws on Islam, that openly threatens the infliction of harm.[106]

The absence of legal and political restraints, including a measure of effective regional self-government rather than weak decentralization, and lack of independent institutions capable of opposing or restraining the politicized use of violence,

99 Aharon Layish and Gabriel Warburg, *The Reinstatement of Islamic Law in Sudan under Numayrī: An Evaluation of a Legal Experiment in the Light of its Historical context, Methodology, and Repercussions* (Brill 2002); Abdelsalam (n 50) 46–48.

100 Abdullahi An Na'im, 'The Islamic law of apostasy and its modern applicability: a case from the Sudan' (1986) 16 *Religion* 197. See also Abdullahi Ali Ibrahim, *Manichaean Delirium: Decolonizing the Judiciary and Islamic Renewal in Sudan, 1898–1985* (Brill 2008) 273–321.

101 See Mahmud (n 41).

102 See in particular Medani, and Human Rights Watch (both n 1).

103 See Johnson (n 5); Totten (n 40); Prunier (n 40).

104 Alex de Waal, 'Counter-insurgency on the cheap' (5 August 2014) 26 *LRB* 25.

105 Akshaya Kumar and Omer Ismail, *Janjaweed Reincarnate: Sudan's New Army of War Criminals* (Enough Project June 2014), www.enoughproject.org/files/JanjaweedReincarnate_June2014.pdf, accessed 10 June 2018.

106 Iris Seri-Hersch, 'Between ideological security and intellectual plurality: "colonialism" and "globalization" in Northern Sudanese educational discourses' in Casciarri (n 81).

have resulted in a climate of impunity. The capacity to use violence selectively to ensure its survival has therefore become the hallmark of the current regime.

2.2.3 Law

Sudan's legal system traditionally consisted of a mixture of statutory law, Islamic law and customary law in the North, and customary law in the South.[107] During the Condominium, the British introduced a bifurcated system, which combined colonial criminal law and common law on the one hand and *Shari'a* law (personal status) on the other, while transforming customary law through the system of British-appointed native chiefs.[108] Following independence, Sudan grappled with colonial legacies in its legal system. A significant (re)turn to customary law was – other than in some areas, particularly the South – difficult largely because of the political and social changes that had marginalized it. This left *Shari'a* as a strong candidate for an indigenous legal system and, for historical reasons, Egyptian law until the 1970s.[109] However, even at independence, a number of challenges were apparent. The experience of *Shari'a* law under the *Mahdiyya* had been idiosyncratic and often cruel; the population had showed limited appetite for (personal status) Islamic law;[110] and a considerable part of the population was non-Muslim, particularly in the South.[111]

Prior to the Nimeri regime, many parts of the colonial system had survived, including an independent and sophisticated judiciary, at least at the apex level.[112] However, after some experimentation with legal reforms that had mixed outcomes, Nimeri introduced the *Shari'a* September laws of 1983.[113] This move was seen as a means to placate the Islamists and to shore up the flailing authority of the regime. Together with the subsequent implementation of the law, including through the Judgments and Basic Rules Act, 1983, it firmly enshrined *Shari'a* law as an overtly political project. Following the coup in 1989, *Shari'a* law and punishments were part of a broader reform in which laws served a dual function of establishing a new order, with whatever coercion necessary, and of entrenching it in several areas of governance.[114]

107 Abdelsalam (n 50) 38–9.

108 Francis M Deng, *Customary Law in the Modern World: The Crossfire of Sudan's War of Identities* (Routledge 2010) 27–32. See also Zaki Mustafa, *The Common Law in the Sudan: An Account of the Justice, Equity and Good Conscience* (Clarendon Press 1971).

109 GA Lutfi, 'The future of the English law in the Sudan' (1967) *SLJR* 219; Carolyn Fluehr-Lobban, *Islamic Law and Society in the Sudan* (Frank Cass 1987).

110 See Abdelsalam (n 50) 46, and, for an account of how the *qadis* were made to have a lesser status, Ibrahim (n 100) 97–108.

111 Abdelsalam ibid 43–46.

112 Ibid; Massoud (n 76) 102–10. See on the struggle between civil judges and quadis in the course of decolonization, Ibrahim (n 100) 49–113.

113 See Amin M. Medani, 'A legacy of institutionalized repression: criminal law and justice in Sudan' in Oette (n 50).

114 Massoud (n 76) 119–54, and Lutz Oette, 'Book review: Carolyn Fluehr-Lobban, Shari'a and Islamism in Sudan: conflict, law and social transformation', London and New York, I.B. Tauris, 2012, 343p. in M Lau and E Cotran (eds), *Yearbook of Islamic and Middle Eastern Law* 17 (2011–12) (Brill 2015).

Since 1989, criminal, anti-terrorism and public order laws have been adopted that provide for an arsenal of harsh punishments. The Criminal Procedure Act, 1991, the Police Act, 2008, and the National Security and Intelligence Act of 2010 (and previous acts of 1994 and 1999), as well as emergency laws vest the authorities with broad repressive powers subject to extremely limited constraints.[115] At the same time, the law does not adequately criminalize and punish serious human rights violations. Instead, it grants officials (conditional) immunity, and thereby fails to provide a suitable framework for accountability.[116] While the Bill of Rights of 2005 set out a number of internationally recognized rights,[117] a series of laws were maintained or subsequently enacted that – with few exceptions – squarely fall short of the INC's requirements, and constitute or facilitate violations of a series of rights.[118] Notwithstanding the commitments to law reform made in the CPA and sustained protests by national and international actors, the Government of Sudan has made only limited changes to the multiple repressive and discriminatory provisions characterizing Sudan's legal system. It has instead used the law primarily to entrench its power, providing for selective protection of rights only in those areas that by their nature carry less threat to its modes of exercising power. Reforms by way of adoption or amendment of laws have often been employed strategically, such as to respond to the ICC's investigation of the Darfur situation and to appeal to international actors in the area of migration law.[119]

These legislative developments have been accompanied by significant institutional changes. Judges were summarily dismissed in large numbers following the 1989 coup and largely replaced with new cadres, many of which had been trained in the newly established Islamic law.[120] The judiciary and the legal profession lost their independence, and bodies tasked with protecting human rights are either part of the government or institutionally weak.[121] While complaints systems are in place to resolve disputes, there are no effective oversight systems, be it by parliament, independent bodies or the judiciary, and no effective recourse or redress for victims in case of violations involving officials.[122] The media is subject

115 Medani (n 113).

116 Mohamed Abdelsalam Babiker, 'The prosecution of international crimes under Sudan's criminal and military laws: developments, gaps and limitations' in Oette (n 50).

117 See in particular its Bill of Rights and especially its art 27(3).

118 See REDRESS (n 44).

119 See amendments to the Criminal Act in 2008 and to the Armed Forces Act, 2007, on war crimes, crimes against humanity and genocide, and the Combating Human Trafficking Act of 2014 and Asylum Regulation Act of 2014. Further reforms include the Child Act of 2010 and the 2015 amendments of the Criminal Act of 1991 provisions pertaining to rape and sexual harassment.

120 Dr. Amin Mekki Medani, in Deng (n 108) 294; Massoud (n 76) 130–4; African Centre for Justice and Peace Studies, *The Judiciary in Sudan: Its Role in the Protection of Human Rights During the Comprehensive Peace Agreement Interim Period (2005–2011)* (2012).

121 This includes the Human Rights Commission set up in 2010.

122 See e.g. *Monim Elgak, Osman Hummeida and Amir Suliman (represented by FIDH and OMCT) v Sudan*, Comm 379/09 (2014) paras 47–71.

to censorship and civil society is subject to restrictions if not reprisals. These measures have stifled public and political debate about the numerous violations in Sudan.[123] The government or those close to it portray violations as unfounded, unwarranted political attacks.[124] This doubly silences victims who, in addition to seeing their rights side-lined and frustrated in the legal system, are denied any recognition in public.

The combination of these developments has resulted in a system of wide powers and lack of restraints and accountability that provides broad scope for abuse and arbitrariness. It is therefore the very antithesis of the rule of law. Undertaking reforms to ensure the compatibility of the law with Sudan's human rights obligations is overdue. The main question is, though, how the fundamental reforms needed, both of the law and its institutions, can be carried out against the backdrop of colonial legacies, a confused hybrid system and three decades marked by a lack of respect for the rule of law and constitutionalism.

3 Evaluation and prospects

The political crisis in Sudan characterized by recurring conflicts and serious human rights violations has prompted both international (including regional) and domestic responses. The 2005 CPA has been the most important development. It provided a template for Sudanese peace agreements by addressing the dominance of the centre and the denial of the right to self-determination and minority rights by means of a power and wealth-sharing formula. The agreement incorporated a Bill of Rights based on international human rights standards in the INC of 2005. It also set out a series of institutional reforms, both to strengthen institutions such as the judiciary and to reduce the power of the NISS against the background of its notorious record of repression. Together with political reforms towards a multiparty democracy and free elections, the CPA envisaged the democratic transformation of Sudan as a guarantee for a united Sudan. Ultimately, the outcome of the 2011 referendum signalled the rejection of a united Sudan and vindicated South Sudan's right to self-determination, albeit at a heavy price as subsequent developments in both countries showed.[125]

The CPA failed to bring about substantial reforms because it left power structures intact and enshrined difference rather than setting out a viable model to

123 See for example Human Rights Watch, '*Good Girls Don't Protest': Repression and Abuse of Women Human Rights Defenders, Activists, and Protesters in Sudan* (23 March 2016).

124 Kevin Sieff, 'Washington Post interview with Sudanese President Omar al-Bashir' *Washington Post* (23 December 2014), www.washingtonpost.com/world/washington-post-interview-with-sudanese-president-omar-al-bashir/2014/12/23/65a42040-0505-46e8-9926-aa1f153a7243_story.html, accessed 10 June 2018.

125 See further Francis Mading Deng, in collaboration with Daniel J Deng, *Bound by Conflict: Dilemmas of the Two Sudans* (The Center for International Humanitarian Cooperation and the Institute of International Humanitarian Affairs, Fordham University 2015).

accommodate diversity and ensure democracy. While acknowledging formal equality, the CPA created, in the absence of early free and fair elections, two spheres of one-party influence in their respective territories, thereby foreshadowing the eventual separation of Sudan. This top-down mode of 'liberal peacemaking' has several problematic features.[126] It was not based on a broader debate following a participatory, gender inclusive model that would have gone beyond the armed actors in a conflict, and left the State and its political system unreconstructed. In Sudan, the CPA did not challenge the primacy of the centre and of the newly ruling elites, dominated by the NCP. Instead, the latter retained its dominance in parliament and other key institutions, thereby enabling it to control the six-year CPA implementation period, and respond to any demands challenging its power by the threat of, or use of coercion or violence. This included keeping the judiciary weak, if not using it to combat its enemies, maintaining the power of the repressive State apparatus, particularly the NISS, and manipulating the political process.

The CPA and other peace agreements made some concessions, particularly in relation to the treatment of southern Sudanese, which were excluded from the application of *Shari'a* law, political and economic power-sharing and formal equality of treatment.[127] Beyond its focus on the South, the CPA did not set out an effective system protecting minority rights or a federal model paying closer heed to the rights and concerns of marginalized groups. The formal equality and minority rights provision provided in the 2005 Bill of Rights[128] proved insufficient to offset these shortcomings. This outcome was predictable, given the absence of structural and effective institutional reforms that would link greater local, regional powers with development and affirmative action, and strengthen rule of law institutions, which would be in a position to effectively protect rights in the first place. The formula therefore failed to create non-discriminatory citizenship bolstered by adequate political processes and judicial and other bodies.

A number of international actors engaged with Sudan on the issue of human rights protection and rule of law promotion. Confrontational approaches, such as criticism of Sudan's human rights record, requesting Sudan to improve the situation, setting up a UN International Commission of Inquiry and referral of the Darfur situation to the Prosecutor of the ICC have largely failed to bring about systemic changes due to Sudan's intransigence. The latter's position was facilitated by political support from a number of countries in the broader region. It also benefited from the contradictory and fragmented foreign policy of several European

126 Young (n 14) 1–17. This critique was echoed in the *Final Report of the African Union Commission of Inquiry on South Sudan* (15 October 2014) paras 45 and 102.

127 See Chapters I–III of The Comprehensive Peace Agreement Between the Government of The Republic of The Sudan and The Sudan People's Liberation Movement/Sudan People's Liberation Army (2005).

128 Arts 31 and 47 INC. See also Abdelgabar, Babiker and Oette, Chapter 6.

States and the USA,[129] and the lack of a strong domestic political constituency in the face of repression of civil society and political opposition. Co-operative approaches, such as rule of law promotion by UNDP, including as part of the constitution-making process, and capacity building and technical cooperation forming part of the revised mandate of the Independent Expert on the situation of Human Rights in Sudan, have yielded some positive outcomes, such as limited legislative reforms. However, they are ultimately contingent on the willingness of Sudan to engage. As its response to the Universal Periodic Review shows, a number of critical areas are beyond reforms.[130] The lack of political freedoms and an open democratic process was evident in the National Dialogue launched by President al-Bashir in January 2014. This dialogue, rather than creating space for political participation and genuine reforms, was widely seen as an attempt by the NCP to gain time to deal with mounting challenges to its survival.[131] The Sudan Call, which was issued by opposition and civil society groups and set out the magnitude of challenges and prerequisites for transition to democracy, went unheeded.[132] In response to the Call, the government detained two of its signatories, the late Dr. Amin Mekki Medani and Farouk Abu Issa.[133] Given these developments, there is no prospect of a fundamental change resulting in greater human rights protection and respect for the rule of law in the current political set-up.

A political transition is therefore a necessary precondition but no guarantee for greater human rights protection considering the systemic challenges that Sudan faces. Equally, legislative reforms aimed at strengthening human rights compliance, while important and overdue, are by themselves unlikely to provide a lasting foundation for change without broader political, economic and institutional transformation. This applies equally to any new constitution, particularly if it is not based on a democratic process that is already part of any such transformation. Such process would need to reflect both learning from past shortcomings and developing visions for a different, less conflict-ridden, violent and divisive future.

Initially forming part of broader debates on how to respond to the legacy of dictatorships in Latin America, transitional justice is widely seen as a process best suited to address past violations, also with a view to preventing future

129 See for example in relation to the national dialogue initiated by the Government of Sudan, International Crisis Group, *Sudan: The Prospects for 'National Dialogue'*, Crisis Group Africa Briefing No108 (11 March 2015).

130 *Report of the Working Group on the Universal Periodic Review: Sudan*, UN doc A/HRC/33/8 (11 July 2016) paras 138–41.

131 Elshafie Khidir Saeid, *Sudan's National Dialogue Conference: The Permissible Questions* (Berghof Foundation February 2017).

132 *Sudan Call: A Political Declaration on the Establishment of a State of Citizenship and Democracy* (3 December 2014).

133 A third man, Farah Alagar, was also arrested by the NISS. See *Report of the Independent Expert on the situation of human rights in the Sudan, Aristide Nononsi*, UN doc A/HRC/30/60 (24 August 2015) para 17.

ones.[134] Transitional justice measures, including mechanisms to ensure criminal accountability, reparation, truth and reconciliation, as well as legislative and institutional reforms have already formed part of responses to the North–South conflict and the war in Darfur.[135] These measures, which were either external, such as the ICC, or included in various peace agreements, have largely failed in the absence of a genuine political transition. This 'shadow' transitional justice can be dismissed for having discredited the notion in Sudan, exposing its political malleability. However, such narrow reading would ignore that the notion, and the various measures associated with it, has become part of broader political debates in Sudan, and thereby provides a yardstick for legitimacy.

A truth and reconciliation commission (TRC) may by its nature be best placed to address systemic factors, i.e. root causes, and provide victims with a voice so as to challenge misperceptions and redress power imbalances.[136] TRCs have become important sites of testimony and visions for change. However, they also have inherent constraints. This includes their mandate, composition, time frame and the need for political support to implement their recommendations, which invariably open them to a degree of political compromise if not manipulation. Any such measures, including TRCs, are against this background an important part of any transition. They are critically important in Sudan where previous political transitions have been marked by their failure to satisfactorily address structural legacies. However, these measures need to be complemented by, and underpinned by broader political and societal changes that result in respect for laws, institutions and processes based on equality in diversity as well as individual and collective rights. A constitution, by setting a framework in which to address these issues, is uniquely suited to capture and reflect such context. Participatory constitutional processes and broad support across society that strengthens a constitution's legitimacy are essential prerequisites in this regard.[137]

Agreeing on, and adopting, such a constitution will be an immense challenge, having to address a number of highly contested issues. It is the ultimate litmus test for Sudan's political classes and elites to articulate a lasting political vision and structures for the country. While regional and international actors can support this process, it is important that it is open to a range of Sudanese voices and represents a truly national outcome. An alternative, elite driven process, including processes that draw on external, technical support, may itself distort the content of the constitution by favouring, even if inadvertently, certain outcomes and thereby replicating problematic patterns of governance.

134 See in this regard particularly the work of the UN Special Rapporteur on the promotion of truth, justice, reparation and guarantees of non-recurrence.

135 See discussion in AUHLP report (n 21).

136 See further Priscilla B Hayner, *Unspeakable Truths: Transitional Justice and the Challenge of Truth Commissions* (2nd edn, Routledge 2010).

137 See for detailed suggestions on a 'participatory constitution-making framework', Balghis Badri, 'A critical analysis of the evolution of constitutions in Sudan' (2014) 31 *AhfJ* 3, 13–15.

4 South Sudan

South Sudan invariably shares several of the legacies discussed above, having been part of Sudan until 2011. A number of Sudan's problems have been exacerbated in South Sudan due to the nature of external rule, both by foreign entities and within the Sudanese State. This rule, and the legacy of conflict and rebel forces military governance, has resulted in weak State structures, underdevelopment and a high propensity for violence to settle disputes. The opportunity provided by the CPA to address structural issues was not seized in South Sudan.[138] The legacy of war crimes, crimes against humanity and violations committed by the rebel groups in the course of conflict in South Sudan was equally not addressed, resulting in a culture of impunity.[139] Also as a result of these developments, South Sudan is increasingly grappling with a politically driven 'ethnicization' of conflict, stemming from unaddressed 'longstanding south-south grievances and problems',[140] manipulation by political actors and the lack of national government structures and institutions to solve disputes and mediate conflict.[141] The SPLM/SPLA, for its part, has proved to be highly authoritarian, replicating modes of governance, including lack of democracy, accountability, transparency, neo-patrimonialism, corruption and human rights violations, that it ostensibly fought against when in opposition.[142] This is partly due to the legacy of military struggle, which meant that the SPLM/SPLA has replicated the experience of post-colonial one-party States. In addition, South Sudan has not developed a participatory mode of governance. During the armed struggle, the SPLM/SPLA was largely externally oriented, relying on humanitarian aid rather than building on self-reliance.[143] Subsequently, during the CPA and following independence, it has assumed the features of a gatekeeper State, relying on oil and foreign entrepreneurs. This approach has largely neglected development policies, particularly by means of investment in infrastructure and economic participation of the broader population.[144]

Since independence, South Sudan's human rights record has been poor. It has been characterized by discrimination based on ethnicity and gender, a lack of

138 See *Final Report of the African Union Commission of Inquiry on South Sudan* (15 October 2014) paras 44–60, and *A Separate Opinion*, Professor Mahmood Mamdani, Commissioner, Member, African Union Commission of Inquiry on South Sudan (20 October 2014). See further Deng (n 125).

139 Final report, ibid paras 69–80.

140 Ibid para 46.

141 See ibid paras 44–60.

142 Mamdani (n 138) para 89, commented that '[t]he political order created under the CPA was not a dictatorship of a single party; rather, it was a dictatorship of all armed groups'. See further Alex de Waal, 'When kleptocracy becomes insolvent: brute causes of the civil war in South Sudan' (2014) 113 *Afr Aff* 347, and Clemence Pinaud, 'South Sudan: civil War, predation and the making of a military aristocracy' (2014) 113 *Afr Aff* 192.

143 Young (n 14).

144 Edward Thomas, *South Sudan: A Slow Liberation* (Zed Books 2015).

progressive realization of economic, social and cultural rights, and serious violations, including arbitrary arrests and torture. The absence of an adequate legal and institutional framework, a sound administration of justice and respect for the rule of law were repeatedly exposed by the arbitrary exercise of power, which culminated in open conflict.[145]

South Sudan therefore faces similar challenges to Sudan, albeit in an even more taxing context of nascent State building in a fragile and hostile environment. This challenge was dramatically highlighted in the civil war that erupted in December 2013, which exposed and amplified existing fault lines. The South Sudan peace agreement of 17 August 2015, in addition to providing for a transitional government, ceasefire and security arrangements, as well as humanitarian assistance and reconstruction, sets out a number of areas critical for structural reforms.[146] This includes resource, economic and financial management arrangements, and a series of transitional justice mechanisms, including a Commission for Truth, Reconciliation and Healing, a Hybrid Court and a Compensation and Reparation Authority.[147] The peace agreement has a section on 'Agreed Principles for Transitional Justice'.[148] However, rather than setting out the context, guiding principles and goals of a transitional justice process, the section focuses on institutional arrangements. It states that the bodies to be established 'shall independently promote the common objective of facilitating truth, reconciliation and healing, compensation and reparation in South Sudan',[149] without, however, defining these notions further. The peace agreement also stipulates the 'Parameters of Permanent Constitution' that spells out in some detail the principles on which the constitution-making process shall be based. This includes

> a federal and democratic system of government that reflects the character of South Sudan in its various institutions taken together, guarantees good governance, constitutionalism, rule of human rights, gender equity and affirmative action … peoples participation in the governance of the country … respecting ethnic and regional diversity and communal rights … ensuring the provision of the basic needs of the people … regional and international cooperation … peaceful resolution of national issues.[150]

These provisions, which follow the failure of the 2011 transitional constitution to provide a suitable framework for democratic governance and conflict resolution, are pivotal for a sustainable peace and respect for human rights in South Sudan.

145 AU Commission of Inquiry Report (n 138); de Waal (n 142).
146 *Agreement on the Resolution of the Conflict in the Republic of South Sudan*, Addis Ababa, Ethiopia (17 August 2015).
147 Chapters IV. and V. ibid.
148 Chapter V. 1 ibid.
149 Chapter V. 1.3 ibid.
150 Chapter VI. 1 ibid.

They provide both a challenge and test for the ability of South Sudanese actors to forge a more sustainable political order.

5 Conclusion

Participation has become a common yardstick to determine the legitimacy of constitution-making processes. The lack of adequate participation, in peace agreements and other constitution-making processes in both Sudan and South Sudan, has underscored the importance of making the population a leading actor in any efforts aimed at drafting new constitutions. Ultimately, it is their voice that is meant to be reflected and their rights that are to be protected in the constitutional order. Such participation is not only imperative as an exercise of democratic rights but also to avoid a repeat of past failures, which the history of Sudan's ephemeral constitutions embodies. Participation, besides being subject to the risk of manipulation, is not a guarantee for a constitution that succeeds in satisfactorily addressing the governance and human rights challenges facing both Sudan and South Sudan. The structural legacies, and histories of abuse of power, need to be central to the way a new constitution is drafted. This calls for a holistic approach that pays careful attention to key issues. These issues include the power granted to various entities, the question of federalism, the rights of citizens, political entities and anyone within Sudan's and South Sudan's jurisdiction, the legislative and institutional framework of governance and rights protection, and the gendered nature of institutions and society. The status of marginalized groups, the question of land rights, economic policies and institutions, as well as the settlement of disputes are also pivotal. Sudan's constitutional history and the legacy of conflict hold a clear lesson. Any attempts to impose orders that violate Sudan's and/or South Sudan's diversity and ignore the need for a more sustainable, and particularly more peaceful, political dispensation are doomed to perpetuate the chronic state of instability with all its attendant, detrimental consequences.

2 In search of constitution and constitutionalism in Sudan

The quest for legitimacy and the protection of rights

Ali Suleiman Fadlalla and Mohamed Abdelsalam Babiker

1 Introduction

Since the time of the Mahdi in the late nineteenth century, the history of Sudan has been one of a country in search of a constitution. Now, more than sixty years since its independence, it seems that perennial search for a constitution has not, yet, been successfully concluded. A close scrutiny of past endeavours in Sudan's constitution-making shows that previous constitution-making processes have been so flawed that the structure that they sought to build could not withstand the test of time.

This chapter is largely based on the Sudanese experience in constitutional developments, which is not only of interest in its own right. Sudan represents, in the eyes of many observers, a microcosm of Africa in terms of geography and population, and cultural, ethnic, linguistic and religious diversity. This factor makes it possible to draw some general conclusions from the Sudanese experience that might be of broader application. With this in mind, the chapter examines the history of constitution-making and constitutions in Sudan, charting developments of various constitutions from the time of the colonial condominium (the Self-Rule Statute of 1953) to the short-lived constitutions (1956, 1964, 1973, 1985) and the present Interim National Constitution (INC) of 2005 with its subsequent amendments after the secession/independence of South Sudan (2011, 2015, 2016, 2017 amendments). This historical inquiry is followed by a detailed examination of the INC 2005, i.e. its genesis, content and scope of application, also with a view to drawing lessons for the current review process and analysing in-depth both its current process (actors, inclusivity, participation) and content. The chapter ends with an assessment of Sudan's constitutional development, identifying critical factors needed to bring about a legitimate and durable constitutional order.

Although this chapter is largely based on developments in Sudan, it also reflects on the debate on African constitutionalism, situating the Sudanese experience as a reflection of constitution-making processes at the heart of the African continent. The quest of many States in the region for constitutional development and adaption of a system of government that is more suitable to their needs is an important one and requires serious debate.

The chapter argues that Sudanese constitutions have been used by subsequent regimes as ideological instruments and as a tool of social control to 'indoctrinate the nation' with the vision or ideology of the regime in power. The Self-Government Statute of 1953 during the colonial time reflected the common law ethos and values while latter constitutions (i.e. the 1973 Permanent Constitution, the 1998 Constitution, the INC 2005) represented the ideologies of socialism, Islamism and a liberal peace constitution-making model of power and wealth sharing respectively. It is unfortunate, but unsurprising, that these constitutions, which bear the marks of certain constitutional ideologies, have failed to attract the consensus of all Sudanese.

Sudan has had a number of constitutions but has experienced neither democratic processes of constitution-making nor respect for constitutions in force. This lack of respect for successive constitutions in Sudan reflects a broader disregard for fundamental constitutional principles and the rule of law. The chapter concludes that it is imperative for Sudan in the years to come to agree on best modalities on how to choose an appropriate constitution-making process and to reach a consensus on the 'substantive' norms of a new constitution. It also concludes that there is a need for Sudan to break away from the 'evil cycles' of adopting short-lived interim constitutions and to condemn the path of 'traditional constitution writing processes' which lacks ownership, effective participation and ultimately has failed to attract true allegiance of the Sudanese populace. In terms of substantive constitutional debate any future constitutional review process should address key challenges including respect of the supremacy of the constitution, circumscribing the powers of the President, control of emergency powers and enhancing parliamentary oversight over the executive branches of government.

2 Constitution-making

Constitutions embody the fundamental principles of a political order. Constitutions can be created through different methods and devices. They can be the work of a clandestine group of experts through a legislative enactment or through the deliberations of a constituent assembly, especially elected for such a task. They may also be the result of a special constitutional convention that seeks to find solutions to all the political ills of the country. And, in the past as in most recent times, constitutions can be created through popular initiatives, in which the public play a direct role in expressing its views on all aspects of a constitution. This popular initiative can at times be limited to putting up the constitution for approval through a public referendum or plebiscite which must be preceded at the drafting stage or after, by a series of public discussions, of the constitutional proposal as it will otherwise lack genuine legitimacy.[1]

1 BO Nwabueze, *Constitutionalism in the Emergent States* (C Hurst 1973).

Indeed, it could be argued that the process of constitution-making might just be as important as the component parts of the constitution itself.[2] Where the process does not reflect sound and transparent participatory mechanisms, it is unlikely that the institutions created as a result of such an exercise will last for long. And even if they did, they are unlikely to capture the imagination of the people or win their support. Sudan's short-lived peace agreements – Comprehensive Peace Agreement (CPA), Darfur Peace Agreement (DPA), Doha Document for Peace in Darfur (DDPD) and East Sudan Peace Agreement (ESPA) – constitute the foundation of the current constitutional framework and created various institutions of governance. However, they have failed due to their duality, combining peace agreements with constitution-making. The agreements created transitional constitutions which were later incorporated into Sudan's current constitutional framework based on a model of liberal peace of power and wealth sharing.[3] This model is flawed, as it lacks transparency, public participation and ownership. Most of the Sudanese people have participated neither in the peace-making nor in the constitution-making processes. It thereby forms part of a broader historical trajectory. Sudan has embarked on constitution-writing processes rather than proper constitution-making, and such processes were constantly manipulated by military and civilian governments and supported by elites. In what follows, we intend to offer a quick historical account of constitution-making in the Sudan, beginning with its colonial experience.

2.1 Colonial legacy

The modern history of what is now Sudan is usually traced back to what the Sudanese referred to as the 'Turkish' administration of Mohamed Ali, the then ruler of Ottoman Egypt, which began in 1821. Turkish rule, generally accepted to be oppressive, was over-run by the *Mahadist* 'revolution' in 1885. The *Mahdiyya* used its call for the revival of Islam and the fight against oppression to build up support for its newly established regime based on the fraternity of Islam, which went beyond tribal or ethnic affiliations.[4] The short-lived *Mahdiyya* (1885–99) left no constitutional documents or influence on constitutional thought in Sudan but it adhered to Islamic law as a fundamental tenet of Sudan's political and legal order.[5]

2 See generally, Charles M Fombad, *Separation of Powers in African Constitutionalism* (OUP 2016); Sotirios A Barber, Robert P George (eds), *Constitutional Politics: Essays on Constitution Making, Maintenance, and Change* (Princeton University Press 2001).

3 John Young, *The Fate of Sudan: The Origins and Consequences of a Flawed Peace Process* (Zed Books 2012).

4 See Mohamed Saeed Al-Gadal, *The Mahdi: A Portrait of a Sudanese Revolutionary* (Khartoum University Press 1986).

5 See Mohamed Mahjoub Malik, *The Internal Resistance of the Mahdi Movement* (Dar-Algeel 1987) (Arabic); Mohamed Mahmoud Al-Souroji, Studies on the Modern and Contemporary History of Sudan and Egypt (Alexandria University 1998) (Arabic).

As is well known, Sudan was a Condominium, the co-domini being Egypt and Britain. The new administration formed as a result of the Anglo-Egyptian treaty of 1899 turned Sudan, in reality though not in designation, into a British 'colony'.[6] The country was ruled by a British governor-general who had all the powers of government in his hands: legislative, executive and judicial. Under the terms of the 1899 treaty, Sudan was placed under martial law with the governor–general as the sole and absolute ruler assisted by a few British officials. For the first quarter of a century or so the British administration remained military in nature and various military expeditions were sent to different parts of the country to subdue any rebellions. Although martial law was not regularly resorted to, it was often reaffirmed whenever the need arose and remained on the statute book at least until 1926.[7] Penal codes, based on those of India, were adopted almost at the dawn of colonial rule, which contained many restrictions on individual liberty, notably in the area of freedom of expression that allowed little room for the exercise of any meaningful criticism of the Government.[8] There was also an array of legislative enactments such as the Press Ordinance (allowing for censorship) and the Closed District Regulations (limiting freedom of movement), that added to the repressive armoury at the disposal of colonial rulers.[9] If we add to these the fact that institutional guarantees provided by the Common Law, such as trial by jury and the writ of *habeas corpus*, were lacking in Sudan, we can begin to understand the restrictive nature of colonial administration in the country. Also, the apparent lack of preventive detention legislation did not deter colonial rulers from relying on such measures in practice.[10] This in turn may explain, though not excuse, why national leaders, post-independence, found it rather convenient to add even more to the arsenal of legal rules at their disposal. These rulers were 'brought up' in a colonial society and inherited its legal administration superstructure at independence.[11] Yet they found its logic increasingly indispensable – so they added their own restrictive measures to the statute book, even though they may have been voted into office by promising to dismantle all repressive colonial structure.[12]

6 See Waleed Mohamed S Al-Aatami, *Sudan in the British Secret Documents: Abboud Military Coup of 1958: A Study on the Secret British Documents Declassified on 1/1/1989 in London* (Publications and Distribution of International Library-Iraq 1990) (Arabic).

7 Ali Suleiman Fadlalla, *African Constitutionalism and the Quest for Legitimacy and Protection of Rights*, presented at faculty of law, University of Khartoum conference on 'Constitutionalism and Political Development in Africa', Khartoum, Grand Hotel (14–17 December 1987).

8 Abdelsalam Hassan Abdelsalam and Amin M Medani, 'Criminal Law Reform and Human Rights in African and Muslim Countries with Particular Reference to Sudan', in Lutz Oette (ed.), *Criminal Law and Transitional Justice: Human Rights Perspectives for Sudan* (Ashgate 2011) 49–50.

9 Al-Aatami (n 6).

10 Ibid.

11 Ibid.

12 See Mohamed Ahmed Mahjoub, *Democracy in the Scale in Sudan* (Khartoum Publications of the Capital of Arabic Culture 2010) (Arabic reprint).

Unsurprisingly, against this background, the independence years often saw frequent recourse to declarations of emergency and preventive detention as the order of the day.

By 1922 Sudan's colonial government resorted to 'indirect rule' and reliance on tribal leaders and chiefs, for the maintenance of law and order. Where no leaders existed, they had to be created, and tribalism, despite the fatal blows of the *Mahdiyya*, was revived. The tribal leaders were tasked with the administration of large areas but their powers were not unfettered. As elsewhere in Africa, a British presence was always maintained in the person of district commissioners, the awe-invoking, 'self-righteous' symbols of colonial rule.[13] They combined all legislative, executive and judicial powers which were not separated in the practice of governments in most of the colonial period in Africa.[14]

A more heinous aspect of the policy of indirect rule was the creation of 'closed districts' over large areas of Sudan, in an attempt to develop various parts of the country differently, purportedly on account of their different levels of development. A most notable example of this was the adoption of the 'Southern Policy', officially inaugurated in 1930, but whose beginnings in fact can be traced to the early years of the condominium.[15] In 1943, a consultative council for the North was created, largely through the pressure of educated nationalists who, through the Graduates Congress, started to agitate for self-determination. By 1948, the British Administration had created a Legislative Assembly and Executive Council for the whole country; the Southerners had accepted to participate as a result of the recommendation of the Juba Conference in 1947. In 1948 a few Southerners, selected on indirect franchise, became members in Sudan's first Legislative Assembly, the successor to the Northern Advisory Council created in 1945. However, the abandonment of the Southern policy in 1946, just a few years before self-government, allowed hardly any time for bridging the gulf in development, leaving the country to reap the whirlwind of this colonial legacy in years of bitter strife.[16]

In March 1951, a constitution amendment commission was convened under the chairmanship of Mr. Justice Stanley-Baker. Its membership was composed of some thirteen members of the Legislative Assembly, four others were brought

13 Ibid.

14 Ibid.

15 See Mohamed Omer Basheir, *Southern Sudan* (University of Khartoum Press 1971). Under this policy the whole of the Southern Sudan was declared a 'closed district' and the access of 'northerners' to the South was limited. Southerners were also prevented from moving to the north. Arabic, the only lingua franca that existed, was discouraged and English was promoted as a substitute. The rationale which the Sudan Government advanced for its Southern policy was that it sought to protect the Southerners from domination by the more articulate and educated Northerners until the Southerners achieved a sufficient level of development and progress, so as to enable them to decide their own future. The result was the uneven development of the two parts of the country, and distrust.

16 Peter Woodward, 'Sudan Fragile State: 1956–1989', in John Ryle et al. (eds), *The Sudan Handbook* (James Currey 2011).

into the discussions when the electoral rules were considered. When Egypt suddenly and unilaterally abrogated its treaty with Britain in 1953, and purported to extend its rule over Sudan, some members of the commission wanted Sudan to be placed under an international commission to resolve the issues of contested sovereignty over Sudan. When they failed, they eventually resigned. But, the chairperson of the commission managed to compile a summary of the various recommendations and to submit his report to the Governor-General. An interesting feature of the work of this commission was that its chairperson submitted his report to a British academic, Professor Vincent Harlow, the Beit Professor of the History of the British Empire at Oxford University, who made elaborate comments on the commission's work. To mention just one very useful result that came out of Professor Harlow's comments, the professor suggested that the amended constitution should include, as part of the chapter on fundamental rights, a comprehensive provision on the 'Rule of Law'. Though his recommendation might not have been fully implemented, the final outcome of the Self-Government Statute 1953 that resulted from the constitution amendment commission contained an important article, article 8 on 'The Rule of Law'.[17] In 1953 the country became self- governing under a Self-Government Statute that created a parliamentary system on 'The Westminster Model'. By January 1956, that Statute was amended to provide Sudan's first constitution. It lasted a mere two years, with General Abboud's coup of 1958 setting a precedent for Sudan, which signalled the unstable nature of its political system and concomitant constitutions. As elsewhere in Africa, the sudden shift from colonial authoritarianism to parliamentary democracy was a factor that underscored the fragility of the new institutions of government and eventually contributed to their demise. This certainly belies any claim of legitimacy by colonial regimes. The fact is that leaders who were brought up by colonial governors and their aides under an authoritarian and illiberal regime were expected almost overnight to set in motion a liberal parliamentary system. It is no surprise that this expectation has for the most part been disappointed. Not only were most of the parliaments dissolved or reduced to parlous existence, but we still witness basic, recurring debates that would have been concluded during the period of colonial tutelage if the political aim of colonialism had been the creation of viable democratic values. [18]

2.2 Independence and After: 1956–64

The Anglo-Egyptian Agreement of 1953, the self-determination agreement, paved the way for self-government in the Sudan through the holding of a free

17 The article states: 'All persons and associations of persons, official or otherwise, are subject to the law as administered by the Court of Justice, saving only the established privileges of parliament.'

18 Ali Suleiman Fadlalla, 'Constitution-Making in the Sudan: Past Experiences 1956–2005' (Advisory Council for Human Rights, With Support from United Nations, Constitution-Making Forum: A Government of Sudan Consultation, 24–25 May 2011) 72–9.

general election for a bicameral parliament. The election resulted in the winning of a majority by the National Unionist Party, a body composed of several pro-Egyptian political groups. This period was supposed to be followed by a constituent assembly that would decide the future of the country to consist either in some form of union with Egypt or independence. Instead, independence was declared from within the parliament itself and the country became independent on the first of January 1956. The Self-Government Statute was hurriedly amended and 'approved by parliament' as Sudan's Transitional Constitution of 1956. It provided for a 'Westminster model', with a cabinet government subject to the control of a bicameral parliament, an independent judiciary and a reasonably well-staffed bureaucratic system. The constitution also enshrined certain fundamental rights that had first appeared in the Self-Government Statute, including the right not to be arrested, or deprived of the use of their property, and the protection of their freedom of religion, opinion and association, their right to constitutional remedy, independence of the judiciary and rule of law.[19]

The first Constituent Assembly was elected in 1957. Under it, a national commission was appointed to draft a constitution for the country, composed of 46 members, all men. These men, however, were drawn from a wide circle of academics, lawyers, politicians, representatives of workers and farmers. This commission opted for a parliamentary system of government and Sudan was declared a democratic parliamentary republic. Attempts to insert 'Islamic' after the word parliamentary and before republic were not conceded by the national commission. However, Islam was to be the 'official religion of the State' and 'Arabic' its official language. The Southern members of the Assembly had withdrawn from the national commission when it failed to endorse their claim for federalism. In December 1955 the southern Members of Parliament agreed to vote for independence, and thus maintain unanimity, only after parliament had passed a resolution stipulating that any future constitution should take into consideration the views of the southerners.

The government of Ismail Al-Azhari, the first Prime Minister, fell shortly after independence and with members frequently crossing floor, it was soon clear that an unstable coalition would be the basis of government. This contributed to the lack of policies for the development of the country, and the major issue which came to pre-occupy parliament was the adoption of a Permanent Constitution. Following the 1958 election, the Constituent Assembly set up a national committee to draft the constitution. It spent its time debating the merits of the British and American systems of government and whether the State should be secular or Muslim in its future orientation. No agreement had been reached when the army, under its commander-in-chief, Major General Abboud, took over in November 1958. Abboud's reign was the shortest among the military regimes that assumed power in the Sudan (1958–64). The 'revolutionary' armed command stayed at the apex of the executive power, sharing legislative powers with the central

19 See arts 5–10 of the Bill of Rights of the Self-Government Statute 1953.

council. Two other successful military coups were to take place subsequently in May 1969 and June 1989. However, the hands of civilians, and their connivance were clearly present in instigating these military coups.[20]

2.3 Parliamentary democracy 1958–69

Abboud's downfall at the hands of a popular movement, the October revolution of 1964,[21] was followed by the re-adoption of the transnational constitution of 1964 as an interim solution, and Sudan returned again to search for a Permanent Constitution. Eventually a draft was completed in January 1968 and presented to the Constituent Assembly for discussion. This time, a national commission was appointed, helped by a technical committee, which was composed of legal experts and politicians conversant with constitutional matters. The technical committee conducted its business through a series of papers, prepared by members of the committee, detailing the various options. Once agreed to, members were selected to present the options on any particular topic before the national commission. Eventually, the national commission settled for the draft that came to be known as the 'Islamic constitution' of 1968. The draft constitution of 1968 opted for a presidential rather than parliamentary system of government;[22] this was seen as more likely to safeguard the executive from the frequent upheavals that it had experienced during the first years of independence when the national unionist government faced a vote of censure immediately before and after the declaration of independence. The critics of a presidential system, however, feared that such a President would effectively be beyond the control of the democratically elected representatives, and the country would soon degenerate into a civilian dictatorship. The advocates of a presidential system argued that it was the only means to secure the stability of government, and maintain national unity, if one considered the volatile nature of Sudanese politics. An executive President would be able to carry on with the business of government unaffected by the ever-changing condition and political grouping within the Assembly, and the exercise of his powers would be subject to the constitution and the law.[23] The draft constitution also included other salient features. It vested executive powers in the President who was to be directly elected by the people for a period of five years but who could not hold office for more than two consecutive periods. The President was to exercise his (the President was presumed to be male) powers subject to the law and the constitution, assisted by a Prime Minister and a Council of Ministers who were to be collectively and individually accountable to the national assembly. The President himself could be removed from his office by a two-thirds majority of the Assembly. The assembly, like the President, would continue for a period of five

20 Woodward (n16); Fadllala 2011 (n18).

21 See Hayder Ibrahim et al (eds), *50 Years since the Sudanese October Revolution (1964–2014): Sudan's Early Uprising* (Sudanese Studies Center 2105) (Arabic).

22 Arts 43, 59.

23 See Fadllala 1987 (n 7).

years and was not subject to dissolution.[24] Another dilemma in the constitution-making processes in Sudan was the question of secularism, religion and the State. Should Sudan be declared a Muslim State in deference to the religious beliefs of the majority of its citizens? Or would it be better to leave it as a secular State in deference to the state of national integration and religious harmony? The Draft Constitution adopted a slightly modified version of the first option. The State was to be a 'democratic, socialist republic based on the guidance of Islam' which is declared the 'official religion'.[25] In this way Islam enjoyed the status of an established religion. But the constitution went further, enjoining the State to 'strive to spread religious enlightenment among citizens, and eradicate atheism, all kinds of corruption and moral turpitude'.[26] Not unnaturally, many non-Muslims were alarmed. Southern politicians in particular had argued for a secular constitution that would depoliticize the issue of religion and thus would be more conducive to national unity. For their part, supporters of the draft pointed out that this would be tantamount to subjecting the majority of Muslims to the views of the minority. Besides, the draft constitution did not abandon the religious interests of minorities as it clearly stipulated that 'the State shall guarantee freedom to religious minorities to establish their educational institutions and to administer such institutions in accordance with the law'.[27] Moreover, religious freedom was a fundamental right guaranteed to people still enjoying freedom of religion, opinion and conscience and the right to profess their religious beliefs subject to such reasonable limitations in the interest of the majority, health or public order as may be imposed by law.[28]

It may indeed 'seem fairly straightforward for a country which is about 60 percent Muslim in population to enrich the position of Islam in its constitution'.[29] Yet in the climate of conflict that prevailed, and the religious dimensions which it sometimes assumed, it was inevitable that southern Christians and other minority groups would feel disturbed. They were not alone in this, as the communists, more than anybody, felt directly threatened by these provisions of the draft constitution. At the time, the communists had emerged as an effective political group after 1964, with eleven representatives in the Constituent Assembly, who, despite their limited numbers, proved to be very vocal, and, in the eyes of the government, an irksome opposition.[30] On the pretext that communist students had uttered some blasphemous remarks about the prophet, the government

24 Arts 59, 45, 48, 50, 66, 76, 108, 109.
25 Arts 1 and 3.
26 Art 14.
27 Art 19.
28 Art 32.
29 George Gretton, 'The Law and the Constitution in the Sudan' (1968) 24 *World Today*, 314, 321.
30 See Fouad Matar, *The Sudanese Communist Party: Slaughtered or Committed a Suicide?* (Dar El Nihar for Publication 1971) (Arabic); Abdullahi Ali Ibrahim, *The Massacre of the Presidential Palace: 1971* (Al-Musawarat for Printing and Publication 2017) (Arabic).

secured from the Consitutent Assembly a constitutional amendment that allowed it to outlaw any communist activity. The amendment was challenged before the High Court which declared, in *Joseph Garang and Others v Supreme Commission and Others* that the amendment was unconstitutional.[31] Despite the fact that the decision was subject to an appeal, the government reacted in a manner that suggested its lack of concern for the rule of law, dismissing the decision as being merely declaratory and insisting that it would not abide by it. The government subsequently obtained reaffirmation from the Constituent Assembly of its initial decision, and sought to pre-empt any future challenges by outlawing communist activities. Thus, article 33(1) of the draft constitution on freedom of expression and the press was subject to the proviso that, 'no person shall be allowed to propagate or seek to propagate communism or atheism or it overthrows or call to overthrow the system of the government by force or by coercion or by unlawful means'. Such powers raised concerns because they could easily be utilized by a party in power to curtail the freedom of action of its critics.[32]

The draft constitution of 1968 contained an impressive list of non-justiciable directive principles of State policy enjoining the State to work for the promotion of ethnic harmony, and strive to achieve social justice and self-sufficiency, and endeavour to abolish economic exploitation and endeavour to abolish economic exploitation and inequitable distribution of national income among citizens. Moreover, it embodied a chapter on fundamental rights and freedoms which, apart from the restrictions imposed on freedom of expression to make unlawful the propagation of communism or atheist ideas, sought to protect most of the usual civil and political rights of citizens subject to 'reasonable limitation' imposed by law.[33]

The draft constitution of 1968 advocated for a regional system of government, in an effort to resolve the conflict in the south, and to 'arrest' the increasing regional agitation in the north which manifested itself in the proliferation of new political groups such as the Beja Congress in the east and the Nuba Mountains Union in the west.[34] Under the proposed draft constitution each of the existing nine provinces, including the three southern provinces, was to be established in a separate region with an elected regional council and presided over by a governor, appointed by the President of the republic in accordance with specified procedures. Other provinces sought to regulate the relationship between national and regional laws, giving primacy to national legislation.[35]

From this brief review of the draft constitution of 1968, it can be seen that it contained enough to have merited serious debate and could, but for the futility of party politics in Sudan, have provided the country with a reasonable framework

31 *Joseph Garang and Others v Supreme Commission and Others,* (1986) *Sudan Law Journal and Reports (SLJR)* 1.

32 Fadllala 1987 (n 7).

33 For a thorough discussion on fundamental rights and freedoms, see chapter 5 on Bills of Rights in Sudanese constitutions.

34 Arts 8–24.

35 Arts 163–79.

of government. All this, however, came to an end when a group of army officers, led by [the then] Lt. Col. Nimeri, took over power on 25 May 1969.

2.4 The Nimeri Era: 1969–85

The 'October Revolution' put an end to the rule of Abboud's junta in 1964. Yet five years later the people were ready to receive the young army officers of the Nimeri military regime of 1969. Unlike the first military, the Nimeri regime attempted to build a constitutional system based on a one-party structure, headed by the leader-President, the embodiment of the will of the nation, in the hope that the new charismatic leadership, and the enormous powers at the disposal of the Executive-President would be used to enhance the causes of nation-building and development. But, as we shall emphasize later, sixteen years of such personal rule eventually spelt disaster for the country. Nimeri and his followers initially depended on the support of communists and others on the political left. When he finally fell out with the communists, in the aftermath of a coup attempt against his regime in 1971, he tried to reach out for a wider base of support through the building of a one-party structure, the socialist union, based on the Egyptian model.

Nimeri put himself up for election as President, thereafter dissolving the revolutionary command council. The People's Assembly was appointed in 1972 to adopt a constitution prepared by the government. The Assembly was divided into ten committees, each of which was to give its own report on all aspects of the draft constitution. Substantial changes were made to the draft, many of which the regime accepted, including a whole chapter on procedural aspects of the rule of law.[36]

2.4.1 The Permanent Constitution of 1973

Nimeri's regime began with 'revolutionary' objectives, but later primarily focused on institutionalizing itself, and strengthening its position through the establishment of Sudan's first Permanent Constitution in 1973. Although Sudan was already more authoritarian than it had been under the earlier civilian governments, the new People's Assembly, which included many who had been discredited by the regime in its first two years, did play a role in assessing the new constitution.

Admittedly, some of the basic issues that had thwarted previous efforts to agree on a Permanent Constitution were settled before the convening of the People's Assembly. Sudan already had an executive presidency operating within the framework of a sole political organization – the Sudan Socialist Union (SSU) – and the southern Sudan was by then enjoying autonomous status following the

36 Mansour Khalid, *The False Dawn: Nimeri and the Tampering with Sharia* (Dar-El Hilal 1978) (Arabic).

1972 Addis Ababa Agreement.[37] But this must not be taken to mean that the constitution-making process amounted to no more than the rubber-stamping of government plans. As is clear from the debates the draft was subject to candid and open discussion and many changes were made. Even as regards the presidency, attempts were made to contain some of the excesses foreseen by the leader of the Assembly, and to create some sort of balance between the necessity of granting wide and effective powers to the President and the need for adequate guarantees to ensure that the system would not degenerate into the rule of an absolute individual.[38]

Under the 1973 Permanent Constitution, the President was both the head of the government and the head of State. All executive powers were vested in his hands and he also enjoyed extensive legislative powers. He was also the Supreme Commander of the Armed Forces, head of the public service and he appointed all the judges, on advice from the High Council of the Judiciary. He was indeed the pivot around whom the whole constitutional and political set-up revolved; the symbol of sovereignty and national unity and the representative of the people's will. As such he was made responsible for protecting the victories of the May revolution, the achievements of the people and the preservation of freedom, justice and the welfare of the people. Though such articles may have initially been intended to add to the charismatic appeal of the President, we shall see that its amendment in 1975 increased the powers of the President to such an extent that the whole constitutional balance was greatly impaired.[39]

The President was nominated by the SSU and was elected to office through public plebiscite, for a term of six years, but with no limitation as to the number of times he could present himself for re-election. Here, despite the clear demand made by many of the drafting committees for a two-term limit, Sudan followed the example of many other one-party States in Africa. The absence of any limitation on the number of times a person could stand for re-election had adverse results for the whole political system; not only did it breed cynicism but it also encouraged the ambitious to resort to unconstitutional means to oust the President.[40]

Another cause for concern was the role of the President in the legislative process, where his participation was not limited simply to initiating and assenting to bills. He was also empowered when the People's Assembly is not sitting or in cases of importance and urgency to make provisional orders which had the force of law immediately when made, subject to their future endorsement by the Assembly. This practice became the usual method of legislating in the country:

37 Ibid.

38 Ibid.

39 Arts 80, 82, 99, 188, 191 of the Permanent Constitution of 1973.

40 The People's Assembly Report in the Committee and the suggestions of the Coordination Committee on the constitution summary of proceedings stated that 'the general thinking in all committees, with the exception of two, is that the presidency should be for two terms each terms 6 years', 14th meeting, 62 (Arabic). See Fadllala 1987 (n 7).

there were no adequate checks on its exercise and the normal legislative process was undermined by it. Since, according to its procedure, the Assembly could only approve or disapprove of a provisional order, it was often reluctant to disturb such an order once made. And since what was urgent or important was left entirely to the executive, it could clearly manipulate the legislative process, by bringing out laws first as provisional orders, with the unlikely, indeed remote, possibility of their being reversed by the Assembly.[41] The President also enjoyed wide treaty-making powers, and though he could declare war only with the assent of the Assembly, he could send troops on any mission abroad if 'the public interest or the country's obligations so demand'.[42] Furthermore, the President exercised wide powers whenever he declared a state of emergency. This could occur whenever he was satisfied that a danger was threatening the independence of the country or the integrity and safety of its territory or its economy, the republican organs of the State and its constitutional institutions, the fulfilment of its international obligations or the achievements of the people – whenever there was a necessity to prevent the threatened danger.[43]

During the debate on the constitution some members warned against treading the thin line that separates wide and effective powers from absolute or dictatorial ones. And even though the doctrine of the separation of powers was rejected, some effort was made towards setting a limit on the activities of the executive, to be exercised by the Assembly. An important example was provided by article 118 of the constitution, when it stated that the Assembly was to approve the general plan for development and the general budget, and exercise a control over the executive. However, although it was envisaged that the budget should receive the approval of the Assembly, that approval had to be given within 45 days otherwise the President could bring out the budget by a provisional order which would have effect as if passed by the Assembly. Such a presidential power made illusory any real prospect of control, and the debate on the budget was but an occasion to vent some criticism of the government's plan that had little effect in practice.

Although the Assembly had certain theoretical rights over the executive, in practice the constitution gave control over it to the President. First, its composition was controlled by law and the practice of making provisional orders extending to laws governing election to the Assembly. In this way the executive could affect whatever changes it wished in the composition of the Assembly. Secondly, by the constitution, the President was empowered to appoint up to 10 per cent of the members of the Assembly. A combination of these two powers, coupled with the presence of a 'sole political organization', made the possibility of an Assembly opposed to the government highly unlikely. It was due to such factors

41 SHM El Effendi, *Legislation in the Sudan under the Permanent Constitution of 1973* (LLM University of Birmingham 1980, unpublished).

42 Art 105 of the Permanent 1973 Constitution.

43 Art 111 ibid.

that under the constitution the Assembly could not be regarded as independent of the government.[44]

2.4.2 *The 1975 constitutional amendments: a retreat from constitutionalism*

Despite its limitations and the fact that it was operating within a one-party structure, a modicum of constitutionalism was arguably created by the Permanent Constitution of 1973. Admittedly the President exercised wide powers, but these were ultimately subject to the constitution itself and although the political process was based upon the activities of a sole political organization, every effort was made to woo outsiders to either join it or participate in its activities. The constitution had provided for the protection of human rights and fundamental freedoms.[45] Indeed, in the first constitutional case decided under this constitution, the *Sol Nasr* case, the Supreme Court ruled that the trial of civilians before military tribunals, using a penal law that had retroactive effect, offended the 'the letter and spirit' of the constitution.[46] However, just as that court was about to deliver another decision, this time on the unconstitutionality of preventive detention, an attempted *coup d'état* took place on 5 September 1975 against the regime. The regime then used the incident as a pretext for far reaching amendments to the constitution, which sought, *inter alia*, to greatly enhance the powers of the President and ensure the constitutionality of preventive detention and special criminal courts. The constitutional amendments were made with retrospective effect. From then on the constitution became what the President thought it should be.[47]

In the same year, Nimeri used his enhanced power to amend the 1972 Addis Ababa Agreement that had created the regional government for the South. Even the solid 'good' act that could count as the regime's basic achievement, namely the establishment of autonomous self-government, was greatly undermined by a decision in 1983 (in violation of Addis Ababa Agreement) in which the South was further divided into three other regions in a manner that was not strictly in conformity with the constitutional rules that sought to entrench the Southern Sudan Regional Government Act, 1972. Many observers saw this step as a means of weakening the South, and began to resist it as such.[48] And all would agree that constitutionalism was given a serious blow.

44 Khalid (n 36).

45 See Babiker, Chapter 4 for a detailed analysis of the Bill of Rights of the 1973 Permanent Constitution.

46 This case, though unpublished in the SJLR, was included in the book of the Sudanese Judge Henry Riyad, *The Most Famous Political Trials in Sudan: Exploitation of Power, Smuggling of the Flasha, Political Assassinations and Preventive Detention* (Beirut Dar al-Jil 1987) (Arabic).

47 Fadllala 2011 (n 18).

48 See Abel Alier, *Southern Sudan: Too Many Agreements Dishonored* (Ithaca 1990).

In the wake of Nimeri's departure on 6 April 1985, Sudan was left once more to try and return to civilian rule, and write a new constitution, but of 'what kind'? Despite ideological differences between the military governments that have ruled over Sudan, their systems of government are not much dissimilar from each other. They all start with a decree that suspends the existing constitution, orders the dissolution of the government and the national assembly and curtails political freedom. Slowly they seek to shed away their Khaki and assume civilian garb and institutions. The Nimeri regime (1969–85) ended by another popular revolution.[49] A transitional military administration, assisted by a civilian council of ministers, shared power under the transitional constitution of Sudan 1985, based on the initial transitional constitution of 1956 and its later amendments, as well as the 1973 constitution. An elected constituent assembly and a civilian cabinet assumed power in April 1986.[50] A Permanent Constitution was to be prepared by this new constituent assembly. But until the demise of this regime by the forces of the so-called national salvation military regime on 30 June 1989, the constituent assembly and the government failed even to set up any institution to support the process of constitution-making. The new military regime finally decided in 1998, after almost ten years of ruling through presidential decrees, to adopt the 1998 constitution for the Republic of Sudan. To this end, the pattern adopted in 1968 was followed. A national commission was appointed, assisted by a technical committee. The final report of this body was submitted to the President. It was soon discovered that the version that was passed to the National Assembly for approval was fundamentally different from the initial document that had been sent to the President. In fact, the constitution that was submitted to the Assembly was a leaner version than the one that had been adopted by the national commission. The language used in the drafting was also different, carrying the hallmark of style of writing of Dr. Turabi, the foremost lawyer of the Islamist movement in Sudan. A controversial provision on *tawali*, translated into English as 'freedom of association' was a particular cause for concern, with some observers seeing it as an attempt for perpetual rule of the governing party. The Islamic character of the constitution was also emphasized through a provision declaring sovereignty to God alone.[51]

3 Post-conflict transitional constitutions: the INC 2005 and the CPA as flawed models of constitution-making

The Interim National Constitution of 2005 (INC 2005) is based on the CPA, negotiated over many years by the government of Sudan and the Sudan People's Liberation Movement/Army (SPLM/SPLA). The details of the INC 2005 are to be found in the various accords relating to the distribution of power and wealth

49 See WJ Berridge, *Civil Uprisings in Modern Sudan: The 'Khartoum Springs' of 1964 and 1985* (Bloomsbury 2015).
50 Woodward (n 16).
51 Fadlalla 2011 (n 18).

agreed to in Nivasha, Kenya. Its final wording was prepared by the National Constitutional Review Commission (NCRC) and endorsed by an appointed national assembly, in which the government and the SPLM had 80 per cent of the seats.[52] The CPA provisions form an integral part of the INC 2005, and, at least on paper, included many impressive provisions such as the Bill of Rights (BoR), and the measures adopted to curtail the presidential powers, particularly in relation to provisional orders.

The CPA sets out a blueprint for major constitutional, legislative and institutional reforms. However, it is based on a model which resulted in entrenching the authority of the ruling forces to share wealth and power. This model, which is neither transparent nor participatory, underpins an era of transitional constitutions in post conflict societies. It was tainted with failures, divisions and disintegration in both Sudan and South Sudan as well as creating weak and manipulated institutions. The CPA and the INC 2005 created new commissions, such as the National Constitutional Review Commission (NCRC), a commission on the treatment of non-Muslims in the Capital, the National Human Rights Commission (NHRC), the Land Commission and the National Judicial Service Commission (NJSC). Some of these commissions, despite the enactment of the statutes supporting them, are not functioning, and certainly not independently in the face of a manipulative executive branch of government. The executive carefully manipulated the appointment or selection of the commissions' members and their operational independence was compromised. Although they were tasked with undertaking key reforms, they were weak and played a limited role in initiating institutional reform. For example, the constitution guarantees the independence of the judiciary under NJSC. However, this commission, which has been dominated by ruling National Congress Party (NCP) members, has focused on technical issues rather than substantive issues of judicial reform. This includes avoiding the hegemony of the Presidency and adoption of clear procedures with regard to the appointment of judges to the Constitutional Court, the Chief Justice and his deputies, judges of the High Court and other judges. It has also not taken any measures with regard to frequently raised concerns relating to the independence of the judiciary. This comprises the judicial competence over judicial work, the interference of the Ministry of Justice in the work of the judiciary in staying or dismissing legal proceedings, the role of the judiciary with regard to special courts, immunities granted to law enforcement officials, reform of the court system, lustration and vetting of judges, and initiating a transparent system of case allocation.[53]

52 Art 2.2.5 of the CPA.

53 See African Center for Justice and Peace Studies, *The Judiciary in Sudan: Its Role in the Protection of Human Rights During the Comprehensive Peace Agreement Interim Period: 2005–2011* (ACJHR 2012). For a historical background on the development of the Sudan's judiciary see Mohamed Ibrahim Mohamed, *The History of the Sudan Judiciary: between Two Eras 1899–2005* (Currency Printing House 2007) (Arabic).

Other commissions such as the NHRC mandated to deal with victims of human rights violations have not played their supposed role in supporting victims to access justice and to help them in any reparation for the harm suffered including reparation for violations related to armed conflicts.[54] Both the CPA and the INC 2005 were silent on reparations or accountability for past human rights violations while other commissions created under the Doha Document for Peace in Darfur (DDPD) (i.e. Truth, Justice and Reconciliation Commission, Property Claims Commission, Compensation Commission) have remained ineffective. The lack of a transitional justice mechanism in the current constitutional framework and peace agreements is due to the fact that the liberal peace constitutional models adopted as part of the CPA and the DDPD did not put in place any mechanism to ensure accountability and reparations for mass victimization. The current constitutional framework lacks constitutional or institutional mechanisms which provide avenues for victims' rights. Instead, those who concluded the peace agreements were shielded from any kind of accountability for previous atrocities. Most notably, both parties to the CPA reportedly agreed not to prosecute any crimes committed, reflecting the primacy of the political over the law.[55] This is evident as the CPA and the INC 2005 do not include any specific provision on accountability or transitional justice. Subsequent efforts towards ensuring accountability in the Darfur context have equally failed. Numerous justice initiatives, from the International Criminal Court to the African Union High Level Panel on Darfur, have been ignored.[56] Thus, the constitutional framework is not responsive to victims' rights and communities' demands for justice. The lack of effective 'transitional justice' measures, such as on truth, justice, reparation and guarantees of non-recurrence,[57] has deepened grievances and serves to perpetuate conflict.

In addition to the flawed CPA and INC 2005 peace model, there are substantive concerns over the incompatibility of a number of laws with the INC 2005 and international human rights standards which have remained largely unaddressed.[58] The legal system is riddled with laws that enshrine deep-seated power

54 See Mohamed Abdelsalam Babiker, 'Victims Access to Justice in Sudan: At the Mercy of the State and Impotence of Global and African Justice Mechanisms', in Thomas Obel Hansen (ed.) *Victims and Post-conflict Justice Mechanisms in Africa* (Kenya Human Rights Commission, LawAfrica 2017).

55 Lutz Oette and Mohamed Abdelsalam Babiker, *The Rule of Law and Human Rights in Sudan: Challenges and Prospects for Reform* (Sudan Democracy First Group, Institutional Reform Series 2 2014).

56 See African Union High-Level Panel Report on Darfur (AUPD) (29 October 2009) PSC/AHG/2(CCVII).

57 See in this regard the work of the UN Special Rapporteur on the promotion of truth, justice, reparation and guarantees of non-recurrence, Mr. Pablo de Greiff, www.ohchr.org/EN/Issues/TruthJusticeReparation/Pages/Index.aspx, accessed 1 July 2018.

58 During this period repressive legislation enacted included the National Security and Intelligence Act 2010, Trade Unions Act 2010, Press and Printed Materials Act 2009, and the Regulation of Voluntary and Humanitarian Work Act 2006.

imbalances, discrimination – particularly based on gender (personal status law, criminal law, evidence) – and lack of human rights protection. Institutions tasked with the criminal justice system are both overly powerful and lack accountability (e.g. immunities, special courts, punishments).[59] Since South Sudan's independence in July 2011, law-making is in the hands of an NCP-dominated parliament and the President (decree-making power), and emergency powers and the ongoing armed conflicts have affected the operation of the rule of law and governance.[60] Opportunities for civil society to broaden its advocacy on the constitutional review and legislative reform processes are constrained, as there is limited space for public debate to effectively engage local constituencies and raise issues including discussion of democratic and participatory constitutional review and law reform process and their implementation in the Sudanese context. Current debates surrounding the 'National Dialogue' and forthcoming 2020 elections provide no possible openings; instead, they have been utilized by the NCP seeking to legitimize existing power structures, and above all, to replicate the CPA's flawed model of peace-making.

4 Constitutionalism and constitutional ideology in Sudan: from common law to autocracy, socialism and Islamism

Constitutional development in the emergent African States in the post-colonial era, including Sudan, was a quest for constitutionalism, a quest for appropriate restraints upon the power of the government in the interest of individual liberty.[61] Scholars tended to see constitutionalism largely in terms of Western liberal articulation of that concept, summed up neatly in a much used quotation from De Smith, in which constitutionalism would only be identified in a country[62] where the government is accountable to an entity or organ distinct from itself, where elections are freely held on a wide franchise of frequent intervals, where political groups are free to organize and to campaign in between as well as immediately before elections with a view to presenting themselves as an alternative government, and where there are effective legal guarantees of basic civil liberties enforced by an independent judiciary.[63]

Very often constitutional development in Africa tended to be assessed in terms of a Western concept of constitutionalism[64] which presupposes a highly

59 Oette and Babiker (n 55).
60 Ibid.
61 BO Nwabueze, *Presidentialism in Commonwealth Africa* (C Hurst 1974) 234–5.
62 Referred to in Robert B Seidman, *The State, Law and Development* (Heineman 1978) 378–9; Karl Lowenstein, 'Reflections on the Value of Constitutions in our Revolutionary Age', in Arnold J Zurcher (ed.), *Constitutions and Constitutional Trends since World War II: An Examination of Significant Aspects of Postwar Public Law with Particular Reference to the New Constitutions of Western Europe* (New York University Press 1951) 192.
63 Nwabueze (n 61) 10.
64 Ibid.

normative system, with substantial limitations on the exercise of power whether by the legislature or the executive.[65] However, the above liberal approach is not without its critics and various reactions were advanced.[66] First, the operation of a multi-party system of government is not in conformity with African traditional polities of consensus. Second, the idea of liberal constitutionalism was never reflected in the authoritarianism of colonial rule, and that is why perhaps most systems of liberal democracy that were hurriedly assembled on the eve of independence in Africa have easily crumbled.[67] Third, it was not conducive to the real interests of Africa at this juncture in its history; what Africa in contrast needed most was a considered effort of rapid development and national cohesion to be taken by strong governments with extensive powers that enables them to undertake enormous tasks which require accelerators and not brakes, to expedite the pace of development. Fourth, religious and philosophical foundations upon which Western constitutional democracy was based cannot be found in many of the countries concerned. Most of the communities that have adopted the constitutions in this century are neither solely, or even primarily Christian, nor do they share the heritage of Roman law and Greek philosophy. The very thought processes upon which Western constitutionalism rests are part of this tradition.[68] On the other hand, there are those who would criticize the De Smith's approach to constitutionalism as seeking to suggest that constitutions merely provide a neutral framework of government for the containment of social strife whereas in reality rules of constitutional law, like other norms, must favour some and not others.[69] Thus constitutions, rather than being neutral, reflect certain values and preferences, and are in fact important weapons of social control.[70]

In post-colonial Sudan, constitutions and laws have been used as an instrument for ideological or political purposes and as a means of control and repression. Looking at Sudan's constitutional developments it is obvious that various constitutions were used by subsequent regimes as a tool of social control to 'indoctrinate the nation' with the vision or ideology of the regime in power. When closely reading Sudanese constitutions it is evident that they bear the marks of certain constitutional ideology. The Self-Government Statute of 1953 during the colonial time reflected the common law ethos and values. The 1973 Permanent Constitution represented socialist ideology while the September laws of 1983 and the 1998 constitution reflected an Islamic ideology with its 'Islamic civilizational mission'. This 'civilization project' was initiated with the Islamization of laws in Sudan in September 1983, when *Shari'a* law became the new common law of the Sudan, and not the constitution, as constitutions and laws should comply and not contradict *Shari'a* law; otherwise, they would be regarded as null and

65 Yash Ghai, 'Constitutions and the Political Order in East Africa' (1972) 21 *ICLQ* 403.
66 Fadlalla 1987 (n 7).
67 Ibid.
68 Ibid.
69 Seidman (n 62).
70 Fadlalla 1987 (n 7).

void. This process of Islamization of constitutions and laws dominated the political and legal discourse with varying degrees but has intensified since the 1989 Islamist military coup.[71] The current constitutional framework and subsequent liberal peace agreement ushered in a new model of power- and wealth-sharing, enshrining a new era of post-conflict constitutions, namely the INC 2005 which is derived from bilateral flawed model of peace agreements lacking inclusivity and representation of the majority of the Sudanese populace. Hence, the CPA and its subsequent incorporation in the INC 2005 represent a unilateral agreement (signed between the Islamists and the so-called 'freedom fighters' of the SPLM/SPLA during the liberation struggle but doomed to failure simply because the peace deal and the current constitutional framework was ultimately designed at the exclusion of other segments of the society and, unfortunately, endorsed by the international community). Eventually both Sudan(s) retreated from constitutionalism and the two countries' fate were ransomed to 'thug' dictatorship and autocracy, i.e. systems of government in which supreme power (social and political) is concentrated in the hands of one person, whose decisions are subject to neither external legal restraints nor regularized mechanisms of popular control.

Hence, by examining the constitutional developments in Sudan, and indeed, many African countries, one can trace at various times the ideological and political nature of the aforementioned constitutions. In the post-colonial era Sudan turned away from a multi-party system of parliamentary government inherited at independence in favour of a one-party presidential system.[72] This form of government has been presented as the most suitable framework for the achievement of the twin goals of development and national integration since it sought to eschew divisions and mobilize all efforts towards these cherished aims with the charismatic leader-President, the embodiment of the will of the people. Yet the experience of many countries in Africa testify to the disparity between the theory and the practice with the system transformed into something of a presidential monarchy, perpetuating the rule of one individual, who is often larger than all the other constitutional and political structures within the State, and is able to manipulate the entire system.[73] Theoretically this fact alone should not be a hindrance to development since the leader-President could utilize his immense powers to realize the cherished goals after a full debate.[74] In practice, however, because of the lack of proper channels for communication and criticism inside and outside the party, there is little room for any meaningful or constructive opposition,

71 Abdel Salam Sidahmed, 'Islamism & the State', in Ryle (n 16).

72 Fadlalla 1987 (n 7).

73 Wai speaks of the 'shrinking political arena in Africa caused by the authoritarian practices of presidential monarchs', see Dunstan Wai, 'Revolution, Rhetoric and Reality in the Sudan' (1979) 17 *J Mod Afr Stud* 71, 71. See also Robert H. Jackson and Carl G. Rosberg, *Personal Rule in Black Africa: Prince, Autocrat, Prophet, Tyrant* (University of California Press 1982).

74 Fadlalla 1987 (n 7).

and policy decisions often take the form of a monologue, rather than being the outcome of genuine dialogue.[75]

Again, in Sudan, in recent years – since the singing of the CPA – constitutional developments lacked such genuine dialogue and popular participation. The current process of the so-called National Dialogue initiated by the current *Ingaz* military regime was a shallow exercise which tries to legitimize 'fake' processes. Its main objective is to manipulate constitution-making processes in a hostile and unconducive environment in which a democratic society, rule of law and constitutionalism barely exist. The recent constitutional amendments of 2011, 2016 and 2017 violated the federal system by concentrating powers in the hand of the President in terms of removing elected governors, control of land for investment and introducing a mixed parliamentary–presidential system but without giving actual powers to the parliament to have real oversight over the executive branches of government.

Thus, constitution-making processes in Sudan have serious drawbacks as they were constantly manipulated. The latest constitutional amendments post 2011 serve as a particularly pertinent illustration of the concentration and manipulation of powers in the hands of the President and his ruling party. Yash Ghai usefully suggested that we would learn more from the constitutional development of a country if one adopted 'a manipulative view of the constitution' that looks upon the constitution not as a neutral framework for political competition but rather as a weapon in the political struggle itself, so that the constitution becomes, or more precisely is made, a handmaiden of the party in power, as a means of the retention of power.[76] The trouble with such a manipulative view of the constitution, in as much as it undermines the notion of permanence attached to a constitution, is that the value of a constitution as a fundamental law may lose its significance. If the basic goals of African States for which they need to manipulate constitutional norms are rapid development and national cohesion, such goals will be ill-served by an instrument that is often distorted to accommodate the needs of a ruling clique or party. For the symbolic role of the constitution as the main gestation of the ideas and the hopes of a nation will be greatly diminished and when that happens the constitution's utility as means to unify and mobilize the nation's effort for development and national unity will be drastically limited.

5 Concluding remarks

Constitutions are pivotal for any legal system. We have attempted in this chapter an analysis of the constitutional developments in Sudan in terms of legitimacy and the protection of rights, using the concept of constitutionalism as a yardstick.

75 Ibid.

76 Ghai (n 65) 434, argues that the 'role of the constitution in political development is a subsidiary one'. However, he accepts that, if their use by those in power is seen as cynical and opportunistic by the people, then constitutions may lose the potential to confirm and consolidate political gains or developments.

The examination of the political history of Sudan and subsequent constitution-making processes from the colonial era to the INC 2005 suggest that the cause of constitutionalism and participatory constitution-making processes have indeed suffered. The desired equilibrium has not, as yet, been achieved. This is true not just of Sudan but also of many parts in Africa and the Middle East. Sudan, in particular, has had a number of constitutions but has experienced neither democratic processes of constitution-making nor respect for constitutions in force. The lack of respect for successive constitutions in Sudan therefore reflects a broader disregard for fundamental constitutional principles and the rule of law. Governance has, with few short-lived exceptions, been characterized by a system of executive hegemony insufficiently checked by the judiciary. Indeed, since 1989, the judiciary was systematically dismantled and rebuilt in a fashion largely subservient to government interests.

Future constitutional endeavours would be an important milieu to express visions and agree on principles and best modalities of how Sudanese could carefully agree on an appropriate constitution process as well as addressing key substantive constitutional principles. As outlined above, it is evident from Sudan's experience that constitutional reform and constitution-making processes are key for all Sudanese who should reach a consensus on both the 'substantive' norms of a new constitution as well as modalities of constitution-making processes to ensure transparent and full public participation. There is a need for Sudan to break away from the detrimental cycles of adopting short-lived interim constitutions and to condemn the path of 'traditional constitution writing processes' which lacks ownership and ultimately has failed to attract true allegiance of the Sudanese populace. The constitutional debate should therefore venture beyond the text of the constitution and find ways and means to advocate for credible and effective processes to ensure constitutionalism, effective participation and, above all, availability of institutional mechanisms to effectively afford protection of human rights and ensure the rule of law.

3 Constitutionalism under siege

Constitutional standoffs in South Sudan and their implications for the war-torn nation

David K. Deng

1 Introduction

More than four years since the start of the war in December 2013, conflict continues to rage in South Sudan. Fighting between the Government of South Sudan and various armed opposition groups has brought the August 2015 peace agreement to the brink of collapse, and caused widespread insecurity and economic hardship. The conflict has raised fundamental questions for the new nation. How did South Sudan find itself embroiled in a civil war just two years after celebrating independence? The conflict was triggered by political dispute in the ruling Sudan People's Liberation Movement (SPLM) party, but what underlying conditions have sustained it? What is needed to secure sustainable peace? As the nation struggles to find a solution to the crisis, questions such as these are at the forefront of people's minds.

Among the factors that have been identified as drivers of conflict in South Sudan are the weakness of constitutionalism in both its substantive and procedural sense. Substantively speaking, constitutionalism is based on a recognition that the constitution as enforced by the judiciary is a higher authority than the executive or parliament. In its procedural sense, constitutionalism presupposes the development of the constitution through participatory processes in which the broader citizenry has a sense of ownership over the outcome. Both these features of constitutionalism are lacking in South Sudan.

Recent years have witnessed numerous examples of the constitution being casually amended by the SPLM-dominated legislature or blatantly violated to suit the short-term interests of a small political elite. Examples include the President's removal of elected state governors in 2013 and 2015, the October 2015 presidential decree to create twenty-eight states (subsequently increased to thirty-two states) out of the existing ten states, and the March 2015 constitutional amendment to extend the term of the government, all of which are discussed further in this chapter. Acts such as these have served to undermine the constitution by changing the constitutional framework to serve the interests of the governing party.

This chapter examines the factors that account for the weak sense of constitutionalism in South Sudan. Three main themes emerge from this analysis.

First, the transitory nature of governance in South Sudan gives rise to conditions that are not conducive to a strong sense of constitutionalism. For more than a decade now, South Sudan has been mired in transitions within transitions. The signing of the Comprehensive Peace Agreement (CPA) and the adoption of the Interim Constitution of Southern Sudan (ICSS) in 2005 marked the start of the first transition that culminated in South Sudan's secession in 2011. With independence came the Transitional Constitution of the Republic of South Sudan (2011) and its promise of elections and a new Permanent Constitution by the end of a four-year transitional period. That process was derailed with the outbreak of violence in December 2013. The signing of the Agreement on the Resolution of the Conflict in South Sudan (ARCISS) in 2015 and the efforts of the Intergovernmental Authority for Development (IGAD) to 'revitalize' the peace agreement in 2017 are now setting the stage for yet another transition.[1]

These transitions have privileged peace processes as a predominant vehicle for constitutional change, resulting in a series of placeholder constitutions crafted by a small political elite for short-term purposes. The constitutions and the processes through which they were developed lack democratic legitimacy and do not reflect a South Sudanese worldview.[2] As a result, state actors can change the constitution to suit their interests or violate it altogether at very little political cost.

A second theme examines how historical factors have contributed to the weakness of constitutionalism in South Sudan. For much of the nineteenth and twentieth centuries, South Sudanese were denied self-determination; first by external rule under the Ottoman, Turko–Egyptian and British empires and subsequently by the Sudanese state and its governing elite in Khartoum. The Sudan People's Liberation Movement and Army (SPLM/A) was founded on a principle of self-determination for the marginalized peoples of Sudan. However, since assuming control of the Government of Southern Sudan in 2005, the SPLM's governance culture has displayed many of the characteristics of these previous authoritarian regimes. The notion of civilian control of the military is largely absent from the political culture of the SPLM, and there is little to restrain its leaders from pushing constitutional boundaries when it suits them. With independence in 2011, political leaders no longer had to concern themselves about whether South Sudan's nationhood would be internationally recognized and constitutional violations began to occur with greater frequency.

1 The ARCISS requires the government to enact a Permanent Constitution and hold elections in 2018. Intergovernmental Authority on Development (IGAD), Agreement on the Resolution of the Conflict in South Sudan (17 August 2015). In December 2017, IGAD brought the warring parties together under the auspices of the High-Level Revitalization Forum to discuss extending the timeframe for elections and other measures to rescue the peace agreement.

2 Remember Miamingi, 'Constitution making and the challenges of state building in South Sudan' in Amir Idris (ed.), *South Sudan: Post-Independence Dilemmas* (Taylor & Francis 2018).

The third theme focuses on the failure to provide for broad civic participation in constitution-making processes. One of the core demands of the SPLM/A since its founding was for a National Constitutional Conference to be held in which the governance system in Sudan could be debated by representatives of the people. However, when the SPLM assumed control of the regional government in 2005 and the newly independent state in 2011, it failed to honour its commitments regarding public participation in constitutional matters. The SPLM strictly controlled constitution-making in the country, including the process that led to the adoption of the Transitional Constitution at independence and the work of the National Constitutional Review Commission (NCRC) to develop a Permanent Constitution.[3]

The August 2015 ARCISS replicates the approach of the Transitional Constitution and does little to encourage greater citizen participation. Had it included a requirement that the constitution be subjected to a referendum, for example, the ARCSS could have helped to create space for more civic engagement in the constitution-making process. The timeframe in the ARCISS is also problematic as it requires the Permanent Constitution to be developed in just eighteen months. Considering the tense political and security environment that is likely to characterize any transition from conflict in South Sudan, the timeframe in the ARCISS would essentially preclude meaningful public participation in the constitution-making process. At the time of writing, the warring parties are meeting in the region to discuss adjustments to the ARCSS timeframe, but the talks are focusing on governance and security arrangements and are unlikely to result in substantive changes to the constitutional development process.[4]

Public participation in the constitutional development process is even more important in a young nation like South Sudan where people have not yet developed a strong sense of national identity and a common understanding of their values and aspirations.[5] In a country where only 27 per cent of adults can read

3 This feature of governance in South Sudan is similar to that of Sudan, where the ruling National Congress Party (NCP) in Sudan has also strictly controlled constitution-making processes.

4 Aly Verjee, 'South Sudan's high level revitalization forum: identifying conditions for success' (2017) 228 *USIP Peace Brief*, www.usip.org/sites/default/files/PB228-South-Sudan-s-High-Level-Revitalization-Forum.pdf, accessed 10 March 2018. The elite-driven nature of constitution-making processes in South Sudan raises parallels to peace processes in the country in the sense that neither prioritizes the involvement of the citizenry at large. For example, the same people were involved in the drafting of the Comprehensive Peace Agreement (CPA) in 2005, the Interim Constitution in 2005, the Transitional Constitution in 2011 and the ARCISS in 2015.

5 According to Jennifer Widner, the extent to which constitutions in post-conflict states can become self-enforcing instruments is an important metric of success: 'If citizens are engaged in the process through public consultation and civic education, they are more likely to know the rough parameters of accepted behavior under the new constitution, monitor the behavior of officials, and impede those who transgress.' Jennifer Widner, 'Constitution Writing in Post-conflict Settings: An Overview' (2008) 49 *Wm & Mary L. Rev* 1513, 1519.

and write, the notion of a written document serving as the foundation of the relationship between citizens and the state is itself an unfamiliar concept. The lack of participation in the constitution-making process further perpetuates the sentiment that the constitution and statutory laws are things that the government develops for itself, not for the people. This, in turn, ties into the broader colonial narrative of people's exclusion from political processes.

In exploring the three themes described above, this chapter tracks a series of constitutional standoffs in recent years and explains how each standoff has been associated with heightened tensions and in some cases, open conflict. A people-driven constitution-making process could help to strengthen constitutionalism and make an important contribution to nation-building efforts and sustainable peace in the longer term. The challenge for the SPLM and its various factions is to move beyond the rhetoric of participation and to invest the time and resources that are required to develop a constitution that genuinely reflects South Sudanese views and experiences.

This would require a fundamental shift in how both the governing elite and the society at large perceive constitution-making and peacebuilding. The focus would have to be placed on civic engagement and dialogue as a basis for agreement on a framework for conflict prevention and nation-building. To strengthen the participatory aspect of constitutionalism, the constitution could incorporate political practices and norms as they currently exist at the community level.[6] This approach would have more relevance to people than one based on abstract foreign models with little practical significance to their daily lives. Constitutional models that devolve power and resources to the local level and reinforce the power of local government relative to state and national governments could better account for the multiethnic composition of South Sudanese society. Perhaps the biggest challenge would be convincing the SPLM to cede some control over the process and allow space for other civic and political actors to participate, something which until now it has been unable or unwilling to do.[7]

6 Francis M Deng, *Identity, Diversity and Constitutionalism in Africa* (United States Institute of Peace Press 2008).

7 The chapter refers to the literature on constitutionalism in Sudan and South Sudan where possible. The literature on constitutionalism in South Sudan is generally lacking, which is not surprising given the scarcity of constitution-making processes in pre- and post-independence South Sudan. Nonetheless, important contributions have been made by a few South Sudanese scholars, such as Francis Deng and Remember Miamingi, and there is some evidence of increased engagement as people grapple with the question of how to resolve the ongoing conflict, ibid; Miamingi (n 2). See also Katrin Seidel and Timm Sureau (eds), 'Special collection: emerging South Sudan: negotiating statehood' (2015) 9 *J East Afr Stud*; Andreas Auer et al, 'The transitional constitution of the Republic of South Sudan 2011: an expert view from outside' *Centre for Research on Direct Democracy* (31 October 2011), www.news.uzh.ch/dam/jcr:00000000-15ea-d211-0000-000018ed8a24/SouthSudan2011.pdf, accessed 10 March 2018.

2 Constitution-making in South Sudan

Constitution-making in South Sudan is best understood through the lens of the broader Sudanese experience.[8] Sudan's entire constitutional history has revolved around the pursuit of a Permanent Constitution.[9] Since independence from British colonial rule in 1956, Sudan has effectively four constitutions, two of which were written after signing peace agreements with armed groups in southern Sudan.[10] These constitutions have focused on ushering in and legitimizing new political dispensations rather than setting out a long-term relationship between citizens and the state.[11] As discussed in the subsections that follow, similar dynamics are apparent in post-2005 constitutional changes in South Sudan.

2.1 Development of the Transitional Constitution of the Republic of South Sudan

South Sudan has had two constitutions since the end of the last war in 2005. The 2005 ICSS was largely derived from the peace agreement that ended the civil war. It gave expression to the 'one country, two systems' model, in which Southern Sudan was given regional autonomy and the right to decide after a six-year interim period whether it would remain united with Sudan or secede to create an independent nation in the south. The ICSS was developed by a small political elite from the two parties to the peace agreement – the SPLM and the Government of Sudan, dominated by the National Congress Party (NCP). The new constitution was a means of domesticating the peace agreement and legitimizing the new political order; the broader population was not involved in the process.

The ICSS was designed to withstand the constitutional implications of the referendum on self-determination to be held in 2011.[12] Article 208 stipulated that in the event of either a vote for secession or for unity, the ICSS would remain in force pending the development of a Permanent Constitution:

(6) Should the outcome of the referendum on self-determination confirm unity, the current system of governance established under this Constitution shall remain in force and all the institutions established under it shall continue

8 Compare to Miamingi's chronicle of constitution making in the Sudans, ibid 96–9.

9 Kristine Mo, *Contested Constitutions: Constitutional Developments in Sudan 1953–2005* (Chr Michelsen Institute 2014).

10 The two peace agreements adopted after signing peace agreements with armed groups in southern Sudan were the 1973 constitution adopted after the signing of the Addis Ababa Peace Agreement and the 2005 Interim Constitution adopted after the signing of the CPA.

11 Another feature of the constitution-making processes in Sudan and South Sudan is that they are approached as legal drafting exercises that focus on the text of the constitution rather than its meaning and relevance to the citizenry.

12 The ICSS was drafted and reviewed by a committee that was dominated by the SPLM. Miamingi (n 2) 97–8.

to function in accordance with the provisions thereof until a permanent Constitution is promulgated.

(7) If the outcome of the referendum on self-determination favours secession, this Constitution shall remain in force as the Constitution of a sovereign and independent Southern Sudan, and the parts, chapters, articles, sub-articles and schedules of this Constitution that provide for national institutions, representation, rights and obligations shall be deemed to have been duly repealed.[13]

Despite the presumption of the continuity of the ICSS, the SPLM proceeded to adopt a new constitution when South Sudan became independent. Like the ICSS, the adoption of the Transitional Constitution was driven by external events and the need to have a constitution to govern a new political order. On 21 January 2011, just a few weeks before the outcome of the self-determination referendum was officially announced, President Salva Kiir issued a decree establishing a technical committee to review the ICSS.[14] The body was initially comprised of twenty-three SPLM members and included just one member of an opposition party. After sustained public criticism from other political parties, faith leaders and civil society, the membership was eventually broadened to include representatives from these other constituencies, bringing the total number of individuals in the technical committee to more than fifty.[15]

The technical committee was given a very narrow mandate to recommend amendments to the ICSS that would become necessary if southern Sudanese voted to secede from Sudan. According to the presidential decree, its mandate was to:

> bring into effect and operationalize Article 208(5) and Article 208(6) or (7) of the Interim Constitution of Southern Sudan, 2005 … as may be appropriate based on the outcome of the Southern Sudan Referendum, and highlighting the transitional nature of the Constitution until a permanent constitution is promulgated. In the event of secession, it shall ensure the transition of the ICSS from a regional or sub-national constitution to a constitution of an independent state.[16]

13 Interim Constitution of Southern Sudan (ICSS) (2005) Pt 15, § 208.

14 While the President had legal authority to create *ad hoc* committees under art 103(2)(k) of the ICSS, to make changes to the constitution using such a committee arguably exceeded any powers that the President had the authority to delegate. Government of South Sudan, Office of the President, Presidential Decree 002/2011 (21 January 2011).

15 Government of Southern Sudan (GOSS), *Report of the Technical Committee to Review the Interim Constitution of Southern Sudan* (2011).

16 Presidential Decree 002/2011, Terms of Reference, Mandate, 1.1.

However, the committee went further to make extensive changes to the structures of governance.[17] It centralized the judiciary by placing state-level courts under the administration of the national government on the ground that 'the decentralization of the Judiciary was problematic during the Interim Period'.[18] The changes in the national legislature were even more far-reaching. The committee created a bicameral legislature consisting of a National Legislative Assembly and a Council of States, where the ICSS had stipulated a unicameral legislature consisting only of the Southern Sudan Legislative Assembly.[19]

Perhaps most concerning, and most relevant to the conflict that erupted shortly after independence, is the way the committee centralized power in the executive. Ostensibly to improve linkages between the central and state governments, it recommended granting the Office of the President the power to remove a state governor or to dissolve state assemblies, 'if the public interest so requires'.[20] As discussed in Section 3, the President's use of these powers in 2013 was among a series of decisions that sent the country into political turmoil and eventually full-scale armed conflict.

Most of the constitutional adjustments that were made on the eve of South Sudan's independence in 2011 served to concentrate power in the national government and the executive. This centralization of power contradicted the SPLM policy of 'taking towns to the people', in which the SPLM pledged to devolve power and resources to the lowest levels of government as a means of rewarding communities for supporting them during the long struggle.[21] Nonetheless, the political realities of independence and the SPLM's dominance of the legislature constrained the National Legislative Assembly from effectively scrutinizing

17 The constitutional changes were made under a provision of the decree that empowered the technical committee to 'evaluate and identify provisions in the ICSS that may need immediate modification or amendment to ensure effective governance, and present recommendations for such modifications to the President of the Government of Southern Sudan for consideration'. Ibid.

18 Report of the Technical Committee (n 15) 17. Executive institutions at the state and county level were known to interfere with the administration of justice in the courts during the interim period, even going so far as – as related by a member of the higher judiciary in a meeting in 2013 – to beat judges up in public for ruling against their interests. However, there was little evidence that centralizing these institutions did anything to strengthen their independence.

19 The reason for this change was, in large part, an effort to accommodate southern Sudanese who had been serving in the Council of States in the national government but lost their positions when southern Sudan opted for independence. The Transitional Constitution empowers the Council of States to address a range of state-level issues, including to 'initiate legislation on the decentralized system of government and other issues of interest to the states.' Pt 5, Ch I, § 59(a). Proponents of the bicameral system argue that it can help to empower states and promote federalism. However, as discussed in greater detail below, the central government has yet to devolve power and resources to state and local governance units, without which any effort to promote federalism is bound to fail.

20 Report of the Technical Committee (n 15) 18.

21 Speech of Dr. John Garang at the signing of the CPA in 2005, www.sudantribune.com/text-garang-s-speech-at-the,7476, accessed 10 March 2018.

the proposed changes to the constitutional framework. Although there is some question as to whether the qualified majority was reached when the Assembly voted on the Transitional Constitution, it was adopted as the foundational document of the new Republic of South Sudan amid the fanfare and celebration of independence.[22]

2.2 National Constitutional Review Commission

The process for developing South Sudan's Permanent Constitution started shortly after independence with the formation of the NCRC. From the start, the constitution-making process was deeply politicized. Exactly six months from independence, in accordance with the terms of the Transitional Constitution, the President issued a decree appointing forty members of the NCRC, the vast majority of whom were older male members of the SPLM.[23] As had occurred previously with the technical committee tasked to review the ICSS, the appointment of a SPLM-dominated NCRC sparked a series of public complaints by faith-based leaders and representatives of civil society. In response, the President appointed additional members bringing the total number to 55 by July 2012.

After its establishment, the work of the NCRC quickly stagnated. The Transitional Constitution provided the body a timeframe of one year to collect the views of various stakeholders and conduct its civic engagement activities. Had the NCRC used this time to engage the citizens of South Sudan on how they envisaged their relationship with the state, the process could have provided a nucleus of participatory constitution-making upon which to build a constitution. However, by the end of the first year the NCRC had only managed to conduct a couple of events and adopt a plan of action and internal rules of procedure.[24] Aside from the NCRC's lack of vision and independence from the SPLM, a lack of resources contributed to its slow progress.[25]

Political tensions in Juba steadily increased throughout 2013 as several SPLM political heavyweights, including then Vice-President Dr. Riek Machar Teny, expressed their interest in contesting for the party's chairmanship. The NCRC's work in developing a citizen-owned constitution took a back seat to political intrigue and grandstanding in the SPLM. The outbreak of large-scale conflict in

22 According to Auer et al: 'While some media reports asserted that the Assembly had actually rejected the draft, other sources indicate that the vote was 113 v 42 among the 170 members of the Assembly, the exact phrasing of the question being however unknown. If this be the case, the required qualified majority would have been missed by a one vote margin.' Auer (n 7) 25.

23 Government of South Sudan, Presidential Order, Appointment of full-time and part-time members of the NCRC, RSS/PD/J/03/2012 (9 January 2012).

24 Zachariah Diing Akol, 'A nation in transition: South Sudan's constitutional review process' *Policy Brief* (Sudd Institute February 2013).

25 'Amid conflict and crisis, what future for the South Sudan's permanent Constitution project? *ConstitutionNet* (30 January 2014), www.constitutionnet.org/news/amid-conflict-and-crisis-what-future-south-sudans-permanent-constitution-project, accessed 10 March 2018.

December 2013 brought the NCRC's activities to a halt. In December 2014, the NCRC's chairperson, the late Professor Akolda Man Tier, announced that the mandate of the body would expire without it completing its task due to a lack of funding.[26]

Several observations emerge from the events surrounding the work of the NCRC. First, the Transitional Constitution provided a central role for the President in the process of developing the Permanent Constitution. This approach reflects the trend towards centralization that was apparent in many of the changes that the technical committee working on the Transitional Constitution introduced at independence. The President was solely responsible for appointing the members of the NCRC. At every step of the process, from the preparation of a draft constitution by the NCRC to the review of the document by a National Constitutional Conference to the vote of the National Legislature, the President played a role in passing the draft text to the next institution. Finally, it is the President's signature that would bring the document into force. The centralized nature of the process in South Sudan is in marked contrast with that of other countries, such as Kenya, in which the draft constitution is subject to a referendum by the people to provide it with democratic legitimacy.[27]

Secondly, the SPLM strictly controlled the process from the outset and made no serious effort to open it to non-State actors or to receive input from the public. Indeed, the process of developing the Permanent Constitution was little more than an exercise in legal drafting, much like the process leading to the development of the Transitional Constitution. The little progress that was made on civic engagement was primarily the result of efforts by civil society actors outside of the formal process and over the objections of the political establishment.[28]

Lastly, the outbreak of armed conflict undermined any possibility of conducting the type of civic engagement that would be needed to secure broad public support for the constitution. This last point highlights the importance of an enabling environment for constitution-making processes. Political uncertainty and human insecurity preclude meaningful citizen participation. Proponents of the constitution-making process should therefore prioritize the establishment of political space for dialogue as a prerequisite to constitutional development, rather than pushing ahead with constitutions simply for their value as symbols of a new political order. The next section examines how the SPLM and its various factions

26 'Constitutional Review Commission to miss deadline' *Radio Tamazuj* (19 December 2014), https://radiotamazuj.org/en/article/constitutional-review-commission-miss-deadline, accessed 10 March 2018.

27 Jeffrey Gettlemen, 'Kenyans approve new constitution' *NY Times* (5 August 2010), www.nytimes.com/2010/08/06/world/africa/06kenya.html?mcubz=0, accessed 10 March 2018.

28 Justice Africa et al, 'Citizens' dialogues on the constitution conducted in the ten states of the Republic of South Sudan' (2014), http://cpn.nd.edu/assets/151041/report_citizen_s_dialogues_on_the_constitution_of_the_republic_of_south_sudan.pdf, accessed 10 March 2018.

repeated the mistake of rushing ahead with the development of a Permanent Constitution in the IGAD-led peace process, despite the distrust, fear and lingering insecurity that is bound to characterize any transition from the current conflict.

2.3 Agreement on the Resolution of the Conflict in South Sudan

As the conflict that erupted in December 2013 intensified, and the efforts of mediators under the auspices of IGAD repeatedly failed to secure a political settlement, the question of what was needed to achieve sustainable peace became an increasingly common topic of discussion in South Sudan. On 9 May 2014, the warring parties and other stakeholders agreed to open the mediation effort to a broader group of stakeholders, including a group of senior SPLM officials who had been detained at the start of the crisis and later forced into exile, other political parties, civil society and faith-based leaders. The agreement went on to state that 'these other stakeholders shall participate in negotiations on transitional governance, the Permanent Constitution, and any other items that concern the political future of the country and reconciliation of South Sudanese communities'.[29]

The new inclusive peace process was inaugurated with a stakeholder symposium in June 2014, followed by negotiations to develop a framework agreement outlining consensus positions and areas of disagreement across the various topics. Largely due to political machinations at the heads of state level, changes were introduced to the text at the last minute prior to an IGAD summit in August 2014 and the Sudan People's Liberation Movement-in-Opposition (SPLM-IO) and other stakeholders refused to sign the framework agreement.[30] Nonetheless, President Salva Kiir and the other IGAD heads of state signed the agreement and the Protocol on Agreed Principles on Transitional Arrangements Towards Resolution of the Crisis in South Sudan was published on 25 August 2014. With respect to the provisions on the constitutional development process, article 27 of the Protocol stated:

> The [Transitional Government of National Unity] to initiate and oversee a permanent constitution-making process, during the Transitional Period, based on the principles of federalism and taking into account unity in diversity, and to devolve more power to the states. The terms and parameters of this process shall be negotiated by the stakeholders in the negotiations.[31]

29 IGAD, Agreement to Resolve the Crisis in South Sudan, Addis Ababa (9 May 2014).

30 Among the provisions inserted at the last minute is that the President would have to approve the Opposition's nominee for prime minister and that candidate would not be eligible to contest elections, whereas no such restrictions were placed on Government positions. For more on the dynamics within IGAD, see Phillip Kasaija Apuuli, 'IGAD's Mediation in the Current South Sudan Conflict: Prospects and Challenges' 8 (2015) *Afr Sec* 120–45.

31 IGAD, Protocol on Agreed Principles on Transitional Arrangements Towards Resolution of the Crisis in South Sudan (25 August 2014).

Soon thereafter, the inclusive talks broke down and IGAD resorted once again to direct bilateral negotiations between the two warring parties. After a series of deadlines passed without the parties' agreement, in March 2015, IGAD rebranded itself IGAD-plus and enlisted the support of other states and intergovernmental organizations.[32] After months of arm-twisting, the two warring parties and other stakeholders finally signed the ARCISS in August 2015.

Chapter VI of the ARCISS, entitled, 'Parameters of Permanent Constitution', details the parties' plans for developing a new constitution during the thirty-month transitional period following the end of the conflict. Within the first six months, the Transitional National Legislative Assembly was to enact legislation to govern the constitution-making process, including the reconstitution of the NCRC. The remainder of the process appears remarkably similar to the process described in the Transitional Constitution.[33] There are some ambiguities concerning the timeframe, but article 4 of the Chapter VI suggests that all steps except for the last were to be completed no later than eighteen months into the transitional period.

At the time of writing in early 2018, with less than ten months remaining in the transitional period as provided for in the ARCISS, the South Sudanese government has not yet completed the first step of reconstituting the NCRC. The warring parties are currently meeting in regional capitals under the auspices of the IGAD-led High-Level Revitalization Forum to revisit timelines in the ARCISS, but it is not clear to what extent this process will address the shortcomings in the constitutional development process as outlined in Chapter VI.

Despite the uncertainties about the status of the peace agreement, the approach to the constitution-making process as described in Chapter VI shows that the political establishment in South Sudan remains committed to elite-driven political processes as vehicles for constitutional change. The eagerness to have a constitution in place prior to elections at the end of the transitional period greatly reduces the possibility for a genuinely people-driven constitution through the ARCISS process. Adding to the difficulties, the high level of distrust among the warring parties makes it difficult to envisage a conducive environment for a participatory constitution-making process in the short term.

If there is opportunity to revisit the constitution-making process moving forward, several changes could help to increase citizen participation in the process.

32 IGAD-plus included five other African countries, the AU, UN, the Troika (consisting of the US, UK and Norway), the EU and China. 'IGAD unveils new process to end South Sudan crisis' *Sudan Tribune* (11 March 2015), www.sudantribune.com/spip.php?article54254, accessed 10 March 2018.

33 According to the process laid out in Chapter VI of the ARCISS, the NCRC was to present the draft constitutional text to the President with an accompanying report, after which the President would hand the text over to a National Constitutional Conference whose composition was to be detailed in the legislation governing the constitution-making process. The Minister of Justice and Constitutional Affairs would then pass the draft constitutional text to a Transitional National Legislature that would transform itself into a Constituent Assembly three months before the end of the transitional period to adopt the Permanent Constitution.

First, the sequencing of the constitution-making process and elections could be reversed, such that the constitution would be developed under an elected government that enjoys greater legitimacy. As it is framed in the ARCISS, the parties would be campaigning alongside the constitution-making process, which would inevitably politicize the process and influence decisions that are made in favour of shorter-term political calculations. Extending the constitution-making process so that it takes place over several years would also allow for a genuine investment into civic engagement and the development of a citizen-owned constitution, rather than a simple revision of existing constitutions that were assembled by a small political elite. Second, the Permanent Constitution could be adopted through a referendum rather than a simple vote in the National Legislative Assembly reconstituted as Constituent Assembly.[34] Subjecting the document to the will of the people would mark a clear break with past constitution-making processes and could help to instil a sense of ownership over the document among the population. Lastly, the proponents of the constitution-making process could frame the process in such a way that it incorporates and builds upon South Sudanese political practices, institutions, cultures and norms. A constitution that reflects South Sudanese identities and experiences would engender greater support and ownership from the people. If properly nurtured, such a constitutional development process could provide a foundation for a national identity that finds strength in cultural diversity. This in turn could serve as a tool for conflict mitigation, in that people would have less incentive to resort to violence to protect their interests and the interests of their communities.

As the South Sudanese legal scholar Remember Miamingi observes, both the ICSS and the Transitional Constitution are built on liberal models that are not only foreign to the South Sudanese worldview, but also assume a common understanding of national identity, values and aspirations among the people of South Sudan. The political establishment adopted this approach even though they had fought a lengthy war against cultural homogeneity in the form of Arabization and Islamization in the Sudanese state. According to Miamingi:

> The state of South Sudan, as an artificial construct and a geographical expression, is disconnected from its history and from the values, norms, and traditions of its people. By running away from its ethnic diversities, it turned its ethnicity 'from a positive and inclusive form to negativity, exclusion and violence.' By contributing to imposing universal and liberal tendencies, the international community has encouraged a state that is centralizing in vision and monopolising in power and authority.[35]

34 In Kenya, for example, the constitution was first subject to a referendum in 2005 and was voted down by the people. After the 2007/08 post-election violence, a new constitution was approved through a referendum vote in 2010. Media Development Association and Konrad Adenauer Foundation, 'History of constitution making in Kenya' (2012), www.kas.de/wf/doc/kas_32994-1522-2-30.pdf?121206114608, accessed 10 March 2018.

35 Miamingi (n 2) 102.

To a certain extent, the discussion of federalism in the Sudans, discussed further in Section 3.3 below, may provide an entry point for restructuring the state to empower existing institutions at a more local level. Strengthening customary institutions, providing them with constitutional recognition and limiting the power of national and state governments relative to that of local government could help to bring the constitution into sync with existing realities. Admittedly, the Transitional Constitution does recognize South Sudan as 'a multi-ethnic, multi-cultural, multi-lingual, multi-religious and multi-racial entity where such diversities peacefully co-exist', and acknowledges the 'customs and traditions of the people' as sources of legislation.[36] The bill of rights also recognizes the rights of ethnic and cultural communities:

> Ethnic and cultural communities shall have the right to freely enjoy and develop their particular cultures. Members of such communities shall have the right to practice their beliefs, use their languages, observe their religions and raise their children within the context of their respective cultures and customs in accordance with this Constitution and the law.[37]

A greater devolution of power and resources to the local level could help give meaning to these clauses. The process by which the constitutional changes are made would also be an important factor. So long as the constitution-making process remains the exclusive enterprise of a small political elite negotiating in peace processes in foreign capitals, or drafting the constitution in isolation in Juba, it will not reflect the views and experiences of the people of South Sudan.

2.4 Transitional justice and nation-building

Another area in which the ARCISS attempts to address the crisis of national identity in South Sudan is with respect to transitional justice, or the range of processes and mechanisms that societies use to address legacies of conflict or authoritarian rule.[38] Such efforts are premised on the notion that divided post-conflict societies cannot truly reconcile without reckoning with past abuses and putting in place mechanisms to remedy those wrongs. Critical to the success of transitional justice programmes is their rootedness in the experience of the conflict-affected society

36 Transitional Constitution, § 4, 5(c).

37 § 33 ibid.

38 The United Nations defines 'transitional justice' as 'the full range of processes and mechanisms associated with a society's attempts to come to terms with a legacy of large-scale past abuses, in order to ensure accountability, serve justice and achieve reconciliation. These may include both judicial and non-judicial mechanisms, with differing levels of international involvement (or none at all) and individual prosecutions, reparations, truth-seeking, institutional reform, vetting and dismissals, or a combination thereof.' UN Secretary-General, 'The rule of law and transitional justice in conflict and post-conflict societies' UN doc S/2004/616 (23 August 2004).

and the degree to which people feel a sense of ownership over the effort. In this regard, the indicators of success in the field of transitional justice are not unlike that of constitution-making.[39]

Chapter V of the ARCISS, entitled 'Transitional Justice, Accountability, Reconciliation and Healing', lays out the terms of an ambitious transitional justice programme that focuses on three national-level institutions: the Hybrid Court for South Sudan (HCSS), the Commission on Truth, Reconciliation and Healing (CTRH) and the Compensation and Reparations Authority (CRA). Both the HCSS and the CTRH are conceived as 'hybrid' institutions, which would involve a combination of international and national staff and require a degree of cooperation between the Government of South Sudan and intergovernmental institutions, including the African Union (AU) and the United Nations.

As with the constitutional development process described in Chapter VI, the transitional justice institutions provided for in Chapter V have not yet been established. Towards the end of 2017, the Council of Ministers reportedly endorsed a memorandum of understanding and statute for the HCSS developed by the AU, and forwarded the document to the Legislative Assembly for ratification.[40] The Government of South Sudan has also established a technical committee to proceed with the development of legislation for the CTRH. The committee plans to conduct public consultations to inform the development of the legislation, but its ability to do so amid the prevailing insecurity remains in doubt.[41]

Aside from the high levels of insecurity, a central challenge with the transitional justice programme laid out in the ARCISS is that it presumes political will on the part of the Government of South Sudan to hold senior political or military actors who may be responsible for atrocity crimes criminally accountability for their actions.[42] The difficulty of embarking on these efforts in the absence of a

39 For more on the national consultations and the design of transitional justice mechanisms, see *Report of the Special Rapporteur on the Promotion of Truth, Justice, Reparation and Guarantees of Non-recurrence*, UN doc A/71/40827 (24 October 2016).

40 Ayen Bior, John Tanza, Dimo Silva, 'South Sudan inches closer to hybrid court on conflict's four-year anniversary' *VOA* (17 December 2017), www.voanews.com/a/south-sudan-inches-closer-to-hybrid-court/4167383.html, accessed 10 March 2018.

41 'Truth, Reconciliation and Healing Commission to conduct public consultations' *Eye Radio* (15 June 2017), www.eyeradio.org/truthreconciliation-healing-commission-public-consultations/, accessed 10 March 2018.

42 Human rights abuses by the warring parties have been extensively documented by the AU, UN and human rights organizations. Towards the end of 2016, Adama Dieng, the UN Special Adviser on Prevention of Genocide warned of potential genocide in South Sudan, and Yasmin Sooka, Chairperson of the UN Commission on Human Rights in South Sudan, said that ethnic cleansing was taking place. See 'South Sudan faces potential full-scale conflict as economy crumbles, secretary-general's special representative warns Security Council' *United Nations News* (17 November 2016), www.un.org/press/en/2016/sc12591.doc.htm, accessed 10 March 2018; 'UN human rights commissioner says international community has obligation to prevent ethnic cleansing in South Sudan' *United Nations News* (1 December 2016), www.ohchr.org/EN/NewsEvents/Pages/DisplayNews.aspx?NewsID=20970&LangID=E, accessed 10 March 2018; African Union Commission of Inquiry on South Sudan, *Final Report* (October 2014).

genuine political transition and while violence continues explains why these institutions have not yet been established.[43]

The few efforts made thus far to prepare the ground for transitional justice programmes have been made by South Sudanese civil society. Civil society groups have begun engaging citizens on the topic of transitional justice and conducting advocacy with regional and international actors to ensure that any transitional justice programme in South Sudan reflects the views and aspirations of the people.[44] National and international actors – including a Commission on Human Rights in South Sudan established by the UN Office of the High Commissioner for Human Rights – have also embarked on efforts to document atrocity crimes and preserve the evidence for use in future efforts to promote justice and accountability.[45]

If and when South Sudan stabilizes and large-scale violence subsides, efforts such as these could be scaled up to prepare people and institutions for a more robust effort to combat impunity and address legacies of past human rights abuses. Transitional justice and constitutional development could be mutually reinforcing in this regard. The transitional justice programme could help to build respect for rule of law and human rights that would make the constitution more effective in managing the relationship between citizens and the state. For its part, the constitutional development process could strengthen institutions and create an environment in which people can safely and confidently discuss their traumatic past without fear of destabilizing the post-conflict environment.

3 Constitutionalism under siege

In recent years, political leaders in South Sudan have engaged in several high-profile standoffs over controversial decisions that are seen to be in violation of constitutional norms. The frequency of these constitutional standoffs increased after independence, when the government no longer had to consider the implications that violations of the constitution would have for State legitimacy and the prospect of international recognition for the outcome of the referendum on self-determination. The government's shutdown of oil production in 2012 and the intensification of party politics that followed also provided incentives for the

43 Pablo de Greiff highlights the 'expansion of transitional justice mandates without sufficient sensitivity to functional and institutional requirements for success, or to basic features of the context of implementation' as a basic challenge confronting transitional justice processes globally. *Report of the Special Rapporteur on the Promotion of Truth, Justice, Reparation and Guarantees of Non-recurrence on his Global Study on Transitional Justice*, UN doc A/HRC/36/50/Add.1 (7 August 2017).

44 ReliefWeb, 'Transitional Justice Working Group', http://reliefweb.int/organization/tjwg-south-sudan, accessed 10 March 2018.

45 Office of the High Commissioner for Human Rights 'Commission on Human Rights in South Sudan', www.ohchr.org/EN/HRBodies/HRC/CoHSouthSudan/Pages/Index.aspx, accessed 10 March 2018.

President and other political actors to ignore constitutional constraints when it suited their political purposes.[46]

The weakness of constitutionalism is both a cause and consequence of insecurity and conflict in South Sudan. Unilateral decisions by the President and other state actors outside the boundaries of the constitution contributed to violent conflict, at least in part because the actors concerned did not have confidence in the independence of the formal court system and felt the need to pursue their cause through violent means.[47] Increased conflict in turn gave rise to increasingly authoritarian decision-making, as state actors felt a need to respond forcefully and decisively to the insurrection and were not overly concerned about constitutional constraints. The subsections that follow examine several of these constitutional standoffs in greater detail to better understand their significance for the new nation.

3.1 Removal of state governors

The way the Transitional Constitution concentrated power in the executive was among the first signals of an increasing tendency towards authoritarianism in post-independence South Sudan. Independence had greatly reduced the threat that Khartoum posed to South Sudan and with its newfound independence now secured, the SPLM was free to consolidate its position as the dominant political actor in the country. Circumstances changed in 2012, when the governments of Sudan and South Sudan were unable to agree upon terms to govern the future use of the Sudanese pipeline to the Red Sea and the Government of South Sudan unilaterally shut down oil production, sending the two countries into economic turmoil. The overnight loss of virtually all state revenue undermined the patronage system upon which the Government of South Sudan relied, and serious challenges to President Salva Kiir's position as Chairman of the SPLM and President of the Republic began to arise.[48]

The President's response was swift. With his newfound powers to remove state governors, the President removed the Governor of Lakes State in January 2013

46 In 2012, the Government of South Sudan shut down oil production over a dispute with Sudan about the use of its pipeline to the Red Sea. As South Sudan is entirely dependent on oil revenue for income, the shutdown sent the economy into a freefall and precipitated the political tensions that eventually culminated in the outbreak of violence in December 2013. See 'South Sudan to complete shutdown of oil production' *BBC* (28 January 2012), www.bbc.com/news/world-africa-16769935, accessed 10 March 2018.

47 As Widner (n 5) 1515 observes: 'The degree to which a constitution or a constitution-writing process displaces conflict from the streets and into institutions is an important measure of success.' Despite some efforts by other political parties to contest executive acts in the courts, the judiciary has not been able to provide a reliable check on executive overreach, as can be seen in the political interference in relation to a complaint submitted against the twenty-eight states decree (see 'Constitutionalism under siege' section below).

48 Alex de Waal, 'When kleptocracy becomes insolvent: brute causes of the civil war in South Sudan' (2014) 113 *Afr Aff* 347.

and the Governor of Unity State in July 2013, due to a suspicion that they might be supporting his political rivals. Although the Transitional Constitution permitted the President to remove a state governor and dissolve a state legislative assembly 'in the event of a crisis in the state that threatens national security and territorial integrity', the arguable absence of such a crisis in either location raised suspicions that the removals were intended to marginalize political rivals rather than to address insecurity.[49] Moreover, the constitutional requirement that elections be held within sixty days to elect a successor governor was not adhered to.[50] Indeed, the caretaker Governor in Lakes State served until December 2015 when he was removed to pave way for the new governors appointed to occupy gubernatorial positions after the decree to create twenty-eight states.

In this instance, the President's actions did not demonstrate a complete disregard for the constitutional order. To the contrary, the fact that the technical committee that drafted the Transitional Constitution took the opportunity to expand the President's powers arguably reflected the importance of acting within the colour of law for the government. As a new nation, the symbolic authority of the constitution and the legitimacy that it provided for the new State may have been a factor in how the decision was made. However, as subsequent acts would demonstrate, when political tensions increased, the pretence of a constitutional restraint on state power would soon give way to a system of rule by decree that belied the SPLM's origins as a revolutionary movement. Indeed, the removal of the governors of Unity and Lakes states in 2013 set the stage for additional removal of governors in 2015 and an attempt to unilaterally divide the country into twenty-eight states, largely along ethnic lines, in direct contravention of the Transitional Constitution.

3.2 Extension of the government's mandate

The armed conflict that erupted in December 2013 presented an obstacle to the transition envisaged in the Transitional Constitution. According to its timeline, the existing government would continue work for a four-year transitional period, during which a Permanent Constitution would be developed and elections would be held to inaugurate the first elected government in the new Republic.[51] By early 2015, it had become apparent that the ongoing, year-old conflict was likely to impede the timeline for national elections described in the Transitional

49 Government of South Sudan, Transitional Constitution, Pt 6, Ch II, § 101(r) (2011).

50 § 101(s) ibid.

51 Art 201(1) implicitly sets the start of the transitional period at independence on 9 July 2011, but the end date is not specified. The four-year time period is inferred from the mandate of the President, national legislature and state legislatures, which expire on 8 July 2015. Nor does the Transitional Constitution set a specific date for elections, though the four-year timeframe for executive and legislative mandates presumes that elections would take place at some point over the transitional period.

Constitution. Nonetheless, in January 2015, the National Elections Commission (NEC) announced that it would be conducting elections by 30 June 2015.[52]

The decision met with considerable opposition from various sectors of South Sudanese society, who decried the idea of conducting elections when nearly 20 per cent of the population was displaced from their homes and millions faced severe food insecurity.[53] Shortly after the announcement was made, an alliance of more than seventeen political parties opened a court case against the NEC arguing that the constitutionally required preconditions for elections, including the conduct of a national census and registration of political parties, had not yet taken place, and the elections could therefore not proceed. As Dr. Lam Akol, who was at the time the leader of the opposition Sudan People's Liberation Movement-Democratic Change (SPLM-DC) party, said in a press conference at the time:

> The National Alliance submitted this morning a constitutional suit to the Supreme Court seeking injunction against holding the elections on June 30, 2015 on the basis of Article 126 subsection (2) (c) and (k) of the Constitution, read together with Section 18 of the Civil Procedures Act 2008, for the violation of Article 194 of the Constitution and many sections of the National Elections Act 2012.[54]

The SPLM itself had only been registered in Khartoum during the interim period as the processes for party registration were not yet in place in South Sudan. Moreover, as the alliance's lawyer pointed out, the most important reason not to proceed with elections was 'the lack of conducive environment for these elections to be organized, because as you know the country is at war. So it is imperative peace is given utmost priority.'[55] In fact, the decision to conduct elections was made at a critical point in the peace process, where the mediators had given the warring parties an ultimatum to sign a peace agreement by March 2015 or face consequences, such as targeted sanctions or an arms embargo. The lawsuit by the opposition political parties was therefore as much about convincing the government to sign a peace agreement as it was about the constitutional issues that were raised.

52 'South Sudan vows to conduct credible elections' *Sudan Tribune* (17 January 2015), www.sudantribune.com/spip.php?article53684, accessed 10 March 2018; 'More than 2.25 million now displaced in South Sudan and across its borders' UNHCR (7 July 2015), www.unhcr.org/afr/news/latest/2015/7/559bdb0e6/225-million-displaced-south-sudan-across-its-borders.html, accessed 10 March 2018.

53 'South Sudan opposition says extending president's term illegal' *VOA* (25 March 2015), www.voanews.com/a/south-sudan-elections-tenure-mandate-extension-president-politics/2694329.html, accessed 10 March 2018.

54 'S. Sudan opposition parties petition electoral commission' *Sudan Tribune* (22 January 2015), www.sudantribune.com/spip.php?article53736, accessed 10 March 2018.

55 'Court case brought against holding South Sudan elections' *Radio Tamazuj* (23 January 2015), https://radiotamazuj.org/en/article/court-case-brought-against-holding-south-sudan-elections, accessed 10 March 2018.

On 15 February 2015, the government announced that it would be seeking a constitutional amendment to extend its term in office, presumably due to concerns about the political parties' lawsuit and the feasibility of conducting elections in the conflict environment.[56] In March 2015, the National Legislative Assembly voted on the proposed amendment. Despite allegations of irregularities in the vote, including that the required quorum had not been met, the mandate of the executive and legislature were extended to 9 July 2018.[57] The lawsuit by the opposition political parties became moot thereafter.

Perhaps the most curious aspect of the decision to extend the government mandate was that it was not a constitutional necessity. In fact, the Transitional Constitution foresaw a situation in which elections might not be held in time and put in place contingency measures. Article 102 describes the procedures to be followed if the Office of the President becomes vacant for five specified reasons, including 'expiration of the term of office'. According to article 102(2):

> If the office of the President of the Republic falls vacant prior to the conduct of the general elections, the post shall be assumed by the Vice President pending the filling of this position, within fourteen days from the date of the occurrence of the vacancy, by a nominee of the political party on whose ticket he or she was elected.

If this provision had been adhered to, Vice-President James Wani Igga could have assumed the presidency while the SPLM nominated a successor. The fact that this issue was never raised in the discussions surrounding the extension of the mandate suggests that none of the political actors involved saw it in their interest to have the SPLM appoint a successor to President Kiir. For the President and his supporters, it would have meant the loss of the presidency. For the opposition political parties, whose main goal was to push the government to accept the peace agreement and thereby avoid the need to extend their mandate, the risk that one of the hardliners in the SPLM would be appointed President outweighed any desire to see President Kiir step aside.

The politics surrounding the extension of the government's mandate notwithstanding, the way the judiciary and legislature emerged as key battlegrounds for the decision demonstrates a certain significance that the parties attached to the rule of law and its implications for state legitimacy. As was the case with the removal of state governors, the SPLM went to considerable lengths to give a

56 Peter Clottey, 'South Sudan leader seeks extension of mandate' *VOA* (15 February 2015), www.voanews.com/content/south-sudan-leader-seeks-extension-of-mandate/2644894.html, accessed 10 March 2018.

57 Denis Dumo, 'South Sudan parliament extends president's term by three years' *Reuters* (24 March 2015), www.reuters.com/article/us-southsudan-unrest-idUSKBN0MK1Z320150324; 'Irregularities in S. Sudan parliament vote' *Radio Tamazuj* (25 March 2015), https://radiotamazuj.org/en/article/irregularities-s-sudan-parliament-vote, both accessed 10 March 2018.

gloss of legality to its actions. This was only possible, of course, because the party dominated the legislature. The SPLM's hold over the courts was far more tenuous, as the government's withdrawal of a case against four high-profile political detainees had shown in April 2014.[58] However, as the war raged on and the high stakes of South Sudanese politics continued to increase, the SPLM's monopoly over the legislature would not suffice to guarantee outcomes in its favour. With the presidential decree to increase the number of states from ten to twenty-eight (and subsequently to thirty-two), the facade of legality surrounding SPLM decisions faded and the constitutional battle was decidedly won in favour of a form of rule by decree more reminiscent of a revolutionary movement than a nation-state.

3.3 Proliferation of states

Discussions of federalism in southern Sudan are as old as the Sudanese State itself. In the early 1950s, as Sudanese political leaders began to consider constitutional formulas in the event of independence from British colonial rule, the Liberal Party, Southern Sudan's first political party, articulated a possible separate self-determination for the south independent of what was being considered by the north.[59] According to the historian Douglas Johnson, the notion of federalism surfaced in southern Sudanese political thought for the first time as a condition for Southern Sudan's participation in a united post-independence Sudanese state.[60] In a letter to the British Governor General of Sudan and the Sudanese Prime Minister, Benjamin Lwoki, leader of the Liberal Party, stated the two alternatives available to Sudan:

1. Either Autonomy in the South and Autonomy in the North under Federation, or if that is not acceptable to the Northerners.
2. A divided Sudan each ruling itself independent of each other … As the South went into Parliament on [its] own will so it can choose to walk out of [it] … We must determine to the future of the South in the way we think suits us or our aims.[61]

The Sudanese government's disregard for the southern Sudanese position was among the factors leading to the outbreak of the first north–south civil war

58 Charlton Doki, 'South Sudan drops case against four accused of plotting coup' *VOA* (24 April 2014), www.voanews.com/content/south-sudan-drops-case-against-four-political-detainees/1900499.html, accessed 10 March 2018.

59 Douglas H Johnson, 'Federalism in the history of South Sudanese political thought' *Rift Valley Institute Research Paper 1* (2014) 9.

60 The issue was publicly debated during the first ever pan-southern Sudanese conference and held in Juba in 1954, involving 250 delegates from all three provinces. The federal model was unanimously endorsed by a vote of 227:0 with seven abstentions by delegates of the northern National Union Party (NUP) in attendance, ibid.

61 Benjamin Lwoki to Foreign Secretary, et al, 15 November 1954, NA FO 371/108326, no 193, quoted in Johnson (n 59) 12.

in 1955. After seventeen years of fighting, with the signing of the Addis Ababa peace agreement in 1972, a federal arrangement was put in place for the first time with the establishment of a semi-autonomous regional government in southern Sudan.[62]

In the early 1980s, notions of federalism arose again, when the regime of President Jaafar Nimeri issued a decree dividing southern Sudan into three separate regions: Greater Bahr-el-Ghazal, Greater Equatoria and Greater Upper Nile. Though the decision carried federal overtones in that it created separate regions where there had previously been a single region, it is probably more appropriately conceived as decentralization, as it did not involve any devolution of additional power or resources to the regional level.[63] To the contrary, regionalization, as it was called, exacerbated inter-ethnic tensions in Southern Sudan and weakened the three southern regions relative to the national government. In Greater Equatoria (and to a lesser extent other regions), the decision was interpreted to mean that all southern Sudanese must live and work in their home regions, resulting in the expulsion of non-Equatorians from government and civil service positions in the regional capital of Juba and elsewhere. Shortly after the decree was issued, the second north–south civil war erupted in Southern Sudan.[64]

Federalism has again arisen in the contemporary context as a means of devolving power from a central government that was seen to be corrupt and ineffectual. The SPLM-IO placed federalism at the centre of its set of its political platform during the IGAD mediation that was seeking to resolve the December 2013 crisis. The SPLM-IO proposal used the old colonial districts as a model and proposed that the number of states be increased from ten to twenty-one.[65] While the notion of creating more states resonated with preferences for self-governance that

62 Addis Ababa Agreement (1972); Government of Sudan, Southern Provinces Regional Self-Government Act (1972).

63 Douglas H Johnson distinguishes federalism from decentralization with reference to the administrative system that South Sudan inherited at independence: 'In principle, southern Sudanese rejected Khartoum's version of federation when they voted for independence. In practice, they inherited Khartoum's division of the south into ten states, with Juba replacing Khartoum as the central power: in other words, they inherited "decentralization" rather than federation.' Johnson (n 59) 26.

64 For background on the political context of this time, see Abel Alier, *Southern Sudan: Too Many Agreements Dishonored* (Paul & Co. Publishing 1992); Francis M Deng, *War of Visions: Conflict of Identities in the Sudan* (Brookings Institution 1995).

65 'SPLM in Opposition Proposes 21 States with Ramciel as National Capital' *Gurtong Trust* (17 July 2014), www.gurtong.net/ECM/Editorial/tabid/124/ctl/ArticleView/mid/519/articleId/15464/SPLM-In-Opposition-Proposes-21-States-With-Ramciel-As-National-Capital.aspx, accessed 10 March 2018.The original ten states were formed in 1994 with the adoption of a federal constitution at the national level. As Johnson (n 59) 24, notes: 'The process of creating states in the south was also somewhat arbitrary in that originally nine states had been agreed until the southern governor of Bahr al-Ghazal Region insisted that his home area be made a state too; thus Warrap state was carved out of Northern Bahr el-Ghazal state for no other reason than that one of the government's most important southern allies wanted it that way.'

were present in many South Sudanese communities, the SPLM-IO plan did not provide detail on how power and resources would be redistributed to strengthen state governments.[66]

At the time, the government position was that any such change to the state structure would be more appropriately carried out through the constitution-making process and not through the peace agreement. Nonetheless, in October 2015, just weeks after the signing of the August 2015 ARCISS, President Salva Kiir issued a decree creating twenty-eight states drawn largely along ethnic lines. According to the President:

> Over the last ten years, the power which was given to you by the CPA has remained in the center. My administration in the center was busy with issues to do with your self-determination such that you become free and sovereign state. Now, indeed you are free, therefore, there is no reason for me to retain your constitutional right for self-governance, self-reliance, self-development and determine your [sic] through free, fair and democratic elections in three years to come.[67]

The decision prompted a firestorm of controversy. The SPLM-IO and other political parties declared it a violation of the peace agreement. Some communities hailed the decision for at long last recognizing people's right to self-governance. Others questioned the manner in which the state boundaries were drawn for giving their ancestral lands to other communities and putting them in states together with groups with whom they felt they did not belong.[68] Over the months that followed, several of these local disputes erupted into violent conflict.[69] Despite promises to suspend implementation of the decree at the insistence of IGAD and the international community, the government proceeded to appoint governors to the twenty-eight states in December 2015, which gave rise to a new axis of competition among actors at the local level.

The decision in many respects marks the culmination of the erosion of constitutionalism that South Sudan had been experiencing in the period following

66 At the time, Johnson noted: 'The SPLM-in-Opposition's recent proposal of making 21 states along the 1956 boundaries of the South's districts threatens to take the Ethiopian example [of ethnic federalism] to the extreme, creating weak states unable to challenge or restrain whoever holds power in the federal government.' Ibid 27.

67 'South Sudan president expands states to 28 as opposition accuses him of deal violation' *Sudan Tribune* (2 October 2015) www.sudantribune.com/spip.php?article56581, accessed 10 March 2018.

68 According to Radio Tamazuj, the 28 states decree would alter the ethnic power distribution by making Dinka groups the majority in 42 per cent of South Sudan's land area, up from just 25 per cent under the ten states arrangement. 'Map analysis: Ethnic balance to change if 28 states approved', *Radio Tamazuj* (22 November 2015), https://radiotamazuj.org/en/article/map-analysis-ethnic-balance-change-if-28-states-approved, accessed 10 March 2018.

69 The redrawing of state boundaries has been linked to violence in Upper Nile, Lol State and Mangala, among other areas.

independence. Changing state boundaries by executive decree is a clear violation of article 86 of the Transitional Constitution, which prohibits the President from issuing provisional orders:

> … on matters affecting the Bill of Rights, the decentralized system of government, general elections, annual allocation of resources and financial revenue, penal legislation or alteration of administrative boundaries of the states.[70]

Article 59 explicitly recognizes the competence of the Council of States to 'initiate legislation on the decentralized system of government and other issues of interest to the states and pass such legislation with two-thirds majority of all representatives', and to 'approve changes in state names, capital-towns and boundaries'.[71]

Indeed, the twenty-eight states decree shares many characteristics of the regionalization policy that the Sudanese government pursued in the 1980s, as well as its more recent efforts to change states' boundaries. Coming just weeks after the signing of the ARCISS, the twenty-eight states decree enabled the President to undermine an agreement that he did not want to sign in the first place while generating political currency in the form of additional state and local government positions that he could use to shore up support in advance of the transitional period.[72] However, the creation of twenty-eight states did not result in devolving power or resources to the local level.[73] As Douglas Johnson observes about earlier regionalization in Sudan:

> In the twenty year period between 1969 and 1989, the idea of federalism had been effectively replaced nationally by policies of 'decentralization' and 'regionalization', where the central government retained its power in part by devolving its responsibility for providing services to the regions who, nevertheless, were denied the resources to bear the burden of that responsibility.[74]

70 Transitional Constitution, Pt 5, Ch I, § 86(5).

71 § 59(a), (g) ibid.

72 South Sudan is no stranger to the use of principles such as federalism as political ploys. In the 1992 talks between the competing factions of the SPLM/A held in Abuja, William Nyuon Bany, the leader of the mainstream SPLM/A delegation said: 'In the Sudan serious words like "federalism", "participatory democracy", "grassroots democracy", "people's congresses" are thrown about here and there without any concrete content. They have become alibi for dictatorship. No system is federal merely because it claims to be federal. No system is federal merely because the word "democratic" has been tagged on to its name as one of its descriptive adjectives.' William Nyuon Bany, 'Opening address to the Abuja peace talks' (26 May 1992) (unpublished document collected by Yosa Wawa), quoted in Johnson (n 59) 23.

73 In at least one respect, the 28 states decree has resulted in the loss of powers at the state level. When the new state governments even began issuing car license plates with the new state names, the national government responded by declaring the issuing of license plates to be a competence of the national government, despite it clearly being a power afforded to state governments in the Transitional Constitution. Ibid Schedule B, Powers of the States, 37.

74 Johnson (n 59).

Even before the December 2013 crisis, 84 per cent of all revenue in South Sudan was budgeted to the central government in Juba, with just 16 per cent left to be divided among the ten states.[75] The creation of more states has not corrected this imbalance. Moreover, the government has exhausted all its resources on the war effort. Although the deals with foreign creditors are not well documented, the government is thought to have leveraged future oil revenue for many years to come.[76] Prior to the oil shutdown in 2012, when the government had a windfall of oil revenue, it was not able to adequately support ten state governments. It is unlikely that additional national resources will be allocated to the state level now that the government is virtually bankrupt and has twenty-two more states to support.[77]

Challenges to the decree also highlighted the judiciary's inability to uphold the constitution in the face of executive pressure. In October 2015, the other political parties under the leadership of Dr. Lam Akol, submitted another complaint to the Supreme Court to challenge the constitutionality of the twenty-eight states decree.[78] Chief Justice Chan Reec Madut had previously issued a public congratulatory message to the President on behalf of his community for the decree. The political parties argued that he should recuse himself from the case for his public position on the issue.[79] Nonetheless, the case went ahead under the Chief Justice. When Deputy Chief Justice Reuben Madhol expressed opposition to the way the Chief Justice was adjudicating the case, the President responded by removing the Deputy Chief Justice and appointing a new judge to his position.[80] If there was any doubts that constitutionalism in South Sudan was dying a slow death, they were put to rest.

75 'Only 16% of South Sudan's budget reaches state governments – report' *Sudan Tribune* (24 May 2012), www.sudantribune.com/spip.php?article42701, accessed 10 March 2018.

76 Denis Dumo, 'South Sudan seeks $300 million in external support for budget' *Reuters* (29 August 2016), www.reuters.com/article/us-southsudan-budget-idUSKCN1141CO, accessed 10 March 2018.

77 For more on South Sudan's economic crisis, see Enough Project, 'Addressing South Sudan's economic and fiscal crisis' (February 2016), www.enoughproject.org/files/SouthSudan_EconFiscalCrisis_022016.pdf, accessed 10 March 2018.

78 Waakhe Simon Wudu, 'South Sudan opposition politician files complaint over new states' *VOA* (15 October 2015), www.voanews.com/content/south-sudan-new-states-legal/3008884.html, accessed 10 March 2018.

79 'Supreme Court to meet Friday on chief justice bias case' *Radio Tamazuj* (24 February 2016), https://radiotamazuj.org/en/article/supreme-court-meet-friday-chief-justice-bias-case, accessed 10 March 2018.

80 Article 135(2) of the Transitional Constitution states: 'Justices and Judges may be removed by an order of the President for gross misconduct, incompetence and incapacity and upon the recommendation of the National Judicial Service Commission.' This provision would not empower the President to remove a judge simply for deciding in a manner contrary with the interests of the executive.

4 Conclusion

Within its seven years of existence, the Republic of South Sudan has in many ways relived the entire saga of post-independence rule in African states. The way the political leadership in the SPLM has changed the constitution at will, or even ignored it completely, has done harm to the legitimacy of the South Sudanese state. At the same time, the importance that the relevant actors place on making and unmaking decisions through legal and constitutional means demonstrates the significance that rule of law has for state legitimacy in a young nation such as South Sudan. The challenge is to provide more opportunities for these sorts of non-violent contests to take place by increasing the independence of the judicial and legislative branches while increasing the costs of blatant constitutional violations.

One way to empower the constitution and strengthen human rights protection is to involve people in the process and to ensure that their views and aspirations are reflected in the foundational document for the nation. Whatever strengths and weaknesses one might find in the ICSS and the Transitional Constitution, what is certain is that neither document was developed in a participatory manner. In both instances, the documents were developed by a small political elite at the heart of the SPLM and for a narrowly defined purpose, whether to structure governance during the interim period that followed the signing of the CPA or to provide a framework for South Sudan's transition to full nationhood. In both instances, the constitutional framework for change of power was hijacked in the interest of political expediency. This was evident in the unnecessary enactment of the Transitional Constitution and its consolidation of unitary power at independence and the extension of the government's mandate in 2015. Such wilful ignorance of the constitution would be more difficult to sustain if it were a document developed and owned by the people of South Sudan, and subject to democratic and judicial scrutiny.

Perhaps more importantly, South Sudanese should consider ways in which they can develop a constitution that reflects the myriad identities and rights of the peoples of South Sudan. Three-quarters of the population in South Sudan is illiterate; it is difficult enough to convince this population of the importance of a written constitution without reducing it to a copy-and-paste legal drafting exercise that tells us nothing of what it means to be South Sudanese. One of South Sudan's major assets is its rich cultural diversity, which is unique even amid the great diversity of other African states. If the constitution and the constitution-making process can find a way to capture traditional norms and practices of the peoples of South Sudan, it could help to provide a foundation for an authentic sense of nationhood.

Despite the immense tragedy of the conflict, it has provided a window of opportunity for South Sudanese to engage one another on fundamental questions of who they are as a nation. History has shown constitution-making processes in post-conflict states to unfold in a series of fits and starts, and we should not expect South Sudan to address all the many issues that it will need to address to secure long-term peace through a single constitution-making effort. Nonetheless, by reflecting on the history of constitutionalism and ensuring that certain principles are captured in the process, South Sudan can begin inculcating a more meaningful sense of the constitution as the highest authority in the land. This would in turn serve as a tool of human rights protection and conflict mitigation, by providing a credible and sorely needed forum for non-violent contests over power.

Part II

Constitutional protection of human rights

4 Human rights protection in Sudan's constitutions

A critique of Bills of Rights

Mohamed Abdelsalam Babiker

1 Introduction

This chapter provides a critique of constitutional Bills of Rights (BoR) as a mode of human rights protection in Sudan. It argues that such Bills have very limited impact in the absence of the rule of law, constitutionalism and in the context of a hybrid legal system (i.e. Islamic, customary, common law and continental law) in which international human rights norms clash with domestic norms. Hence, it examines what constitutional approaches can best address the structural factors that have resulted in human rights violations and maps out pivotal areas for reform based on a contextual analysis of Sudan's experiences.

The chapter briefly charts the history of BoR in Sudan's constitutions and argues that those contained in various constitutions from colonial to postcolonial Sudan primarily reflected the ideological orientation of the ruling regimes. It focuses particularly on the present 2005 BoR that was adopted after the signing of the Comprehensive Peace Agreement and largely incorporated in South Sudan's 2011 Transitional Constitution. Its examination entails close scrutiny of the rights protected, particularly their compatibility with international standards, and its article 27(3) which provides that binding international treaties form an integral part of the Bill. The chapter also examines the limited protection of economic, social and cultural rights (ESCR) in Sudan's 2005 Interim National Constitution (INC), arguing that it is reflective of Sudan's BoR, which have not envisaged or considered adopting a social model constitution that focuses on ESCR. Beyond the BoR, it addresses the lack of effective fundamental rights protection due to the absence of constitutionalism and rule of law institutions, separation of powers and the hegemony of the executive over the judiciary and the legislature. This includes an analysis of the role of the judiciary, the Constitutional Court's jurisprudence, the role of national human rights bodies and legislative and institutional reforms, or the lack thereof, in giving effect to the BoR. The chapter ends by critically interrogating the BoR model pursued, probing whether it should continue to guide constitutional approaches in Sudan, as advocated, for example, by many civil society organizations, or whether it needs fundamental changes to be effective in ensuring rights protection. In this respect, it considers models related to the primacy of international human rights norms over Sudan's national norms and to what extent a 'monist' or 'dualist' model is best suited for Sudan's context given its hybrid legal system.

The chapter concludes by arguing that Sudan's 2005 Bill of Rights has numerous substantive gaps. Several of the civil and political rights (CPR) and ESCR enshrined in the INC 2005 were not recognized or defined in conformity with international human rights standards. The various constitutional amendments of the INC 2005 between 2011 and 2017 have further undermined human rights protection instead of adequately addressing existing shortcomings, including the status of international human rights law and the modalities of its incorporation in Sudan's hybrid legal system. Constitutional human rights protection cannot be attained by virtue of mere textual recognition of substantive BoR provisions, which need to be complemented by legislative and effective institutional reforms, particularly security sector reform, judicial independence and parliamentary oversight. Constitutional protection of rights, the chapter concludes, will remainidle at 'the textual level' without a 'soul' and will not be worth the 'ink with which it was written' until constitutionalism, rule of law and effective human rights mechanisms are in place in Sudan.

2 Overview of the development of Bills of Rights in Sudan's constitutional history (1953–2005)

Various constitutions in Sudan have contained BoR, which generally reflected the ideological outlook or the nature of the regime in power. The Self-Government Statute of 1953 bears the heritage of narrow civil and political rights conceptions in a common law system, whereas BoR in the post-colonial era largely reflected the ideology of subsequent military regimes, whether of socialist or Islamic orientation. The BoR in Chapter II (Fundamental Rights) of the Self-Government Statute included the right to freedom and equality before the law and prohibition of discrimination in employment on the basis of disability. Notably, the latter provided for three distinct rights: the right to freedom and equality before the law and equality in employment for disabled persons, without distinguishing between CPR and ESCR. Similarly, its article 6 addressed freedom from arrest and confiscation of property – again dealing with two distinct rights in one article.

Besides stipulating the right to freedom of religion and freedom of association, or, to be more precise, freedom of expression and opinion in its article 7, the Statute also contained an important provision, article 8, 'The Rule of Law' according to which: 'All persons and associations of persons, official or otherwise, are subject to the law as administered by the Court of Justice, saving only the established privileges of parliament.'[1] The makers of any forthcoming Sudan constitution would do well to reflect on such a provision and its significance in

1 This provision on the rule of law was repeated verbatim in the 1956 and 1964 constitutional BoR.

ensuring good governance.[2] This generic 'rule of law' article was strengthened by article 9, which emphasized the independence of the judiciary and separation of powers, i.e. cornerstones of any constitution and constitutionalism. Yet, this provision was too ambitious at the time of colonial Sudan; the postcolonial State (as in the case of other postcolonial African States) fundamentally lacked any form of independent institutions and parliamentary Westminster model of liberal democracy. Transplanting such features of the English legal system was doomed to failure in a country emerging from colonialism that had itself been characterized by the lack of viable democratic processes and respect for the rule of law based on the separation of powers.

Under Article 10 (Right to Constitutional Remedy) 'any person may apply to the High Court for protection or enforcement of any of the rights conferred by this chapter and the High Court shall have power to make all such orders as may be necessary and appropriate to secure to the applicant the enjoyment of any of the said rights'. Ordinary courts were given constitutional powers to act as guarantors of human rights; again reflecting the common law traditions and bearing the features of English legal philosophy inherited by Sudan as a post-colonial State.

The fundamental rights provisions of the Statute were copied verbatim in the Interim Constitutions of 1956 and 1964. The Permanent Constitution of the Sudan of 1973 included a detailed BoR in Part III (Freedoms, Rights and Duties). It comprised provisions on CPR, on equality of all persons before courts of law, irrespective of origin, race, locality, sex, language or religion,[3] freedom of movement and residence,[4] the right not to be deported and to enter the country;[5] and inviolability of private life,[6] premises and prohibition of search without legal permission.[7] Other political rights included the right to participate in elections and referendums;[8] to participate in public life and be nominated for public office;[9] freedom of belief and religious practices;[10] freedom of opinion;[11] freedom of the press (within the limits of the law);[12] and the right to hold peaceful meetings and processions.[13]

2 Ali Suleiman Fadlalla, 'Constitution-Making in the Sudan: Past Experiences 1956–2005' (UNDP conference, The Republic of Sudan, Constitution Making Forum, Khartoum 24–25 May 2011) 72–9.
3 Art 38.
4 Art 41.
5 Art 40.
6 Art 42.
7 Art 43.
8 Art 45.
9 Art 46.
10 Art 47.
11 Art 48.
12 Art 49.
13 Art 50.

Some of the above CPR were not in conformity with universal notions of human rights as the BoR covered only Sudanese *citizens*. While non-nationals could not rely on the BoR, it contained a unique provision providing constitutional protection to political refugees against extradition.[14]

A close reading of the 1973 Constitution reveals the imprint of socialist ideology of the Nimeri regime then in power. The Constitution called for upholding 'the revolutionary achievements' as a sacred duty of every citizen.[15] Unlike other BoR in Sudan, this Bill reflected socialist values and conceptions of rights, and included a social model. This was evident in provisions stipulating the right to form trade unions, associations and societies;[16] the prohibition of forced labour;[17] and equality of opportunities and prohibition of any discrimination in work opportunities or conditions of pay on the grounds of origin, sex or geographical affiliations.[18] It also provided that the State shall endeavour to provide free education in all stages,[19] and free health care and medical treatment as a right of every citizen.[20] 'Mothers and children shall be accorded care and the State shall ensure adequate guarantees for mothers and the working women.'[21]

The Interim Constitution of 1985 was adopted after the popular uprising that ended the Nimeri regime on 6 April 1985. Its BoR bears similarities with the 1973 Constitution as far as CPR are concerned. However, ESCR had been removed, which reflected its liberal outlook. Nine years after the 1989 military coup, and a subsequent constitutional hiatus, having ruled on the basis of decrees, the National Islamic Front (National Congress) adopted the 1998 Constitution. Its BoR reflected the Islamic ideology of the then and current regime.[22] It echoes the aspirations of the draft 'Islamic constitution' of 1968 under which Islam was made the 'official religion of the State' and the propagation of communism or atheist ideas was made unlawful.[23] The 1998 Constitution

14 Art 44: 'Political refugees in the Democratic Republic of the Sudan shall not be extradited to another State, except within the limits permitted by the principles of International law and laws of the Sudan.' This prohibition is part of Sudan's international obligations under the Refugee Convention, 1951.

15 Art 57.

16 Art 51.

17 Art 52.

18 Art 56.

19 Art 53.

20 Art 54.

21 Art 55.

22 For such Islamic features of the constitution, see for example preamble and arts 3 (*Hakimiya)* (Governance), 7 (*Jihad*).

23 Art 33(1) of the draft constitution of 1968 embodied a chapter on fundamental rights and freedoms. Freedom of expression and the press was subject to the proviso that 'no person shall be allowed to propagate or seek to propagate communism or atheism or it overthrow or call to overthrow the system of the government by force or by coercion or by unlawful means'. Such powers raised concerns because they could easily be utilized by a party in power to curtail the freedom of action of its critics. Apart from the restrictions imposed on freedom of expression to make unlawful the propagation of communism or atheist ideas, the draft constitution sought to protect most of the usual CPR of citizens' subject to 'reasonable limitation' imposed by law.

sought to revisit the relationship of secularism, religion and the State, demonstrating a clear bias against liberal and secular forces. It contained various CPR, including freedom and sanctity of life; safety of the person; dignity; freedom from slavery; prohibition of forced labour, humiliation or torture (though not punishment);[24] equality before courts;[25] 'sanctity' of nationality;[26] freedom of movement and residence;[27]freedom of creed and worship;[28] freedom of thought and expression;[29] freedom of association;[30] 'sanctity' of cultural communities including preservation of their particular culture, language or religion;[31] 'sanctity' of earning and property;[32] and inviolability of communication and privacy.[33] The BoR also focused on administration of justice including pre-trial and post-trial guarantees and immunity against arbitrary detention,[34] right and sanctity in litigation,[35] without, however, providing for strong judicial protection of rights, and the right of innocence and right to defence.[36] Notably, it shares the lack of recognition of ESCR with most Sudanese BoR.

3 The Constitutional Bill of Rights, 2005 (amendments 2017): a critique of its substantive shortcomings

This part examines the current INC's BoR substantive and implementation gaps, including the constitutional amendments since 2011, particularly 2017, which have added another level of textual distortion.

3.1 Rights of non-discrimination and equality before the law

The importance of the concepts of equality and non-discrimination cannot be overstated. It has been suggested that 'equality and non-discrimination constitute the single dominant theme of the International Covenant on Civil and Political Rights (ICCPR).'[37] This emphasis is entirely appropriate; discrimination

24 Art 20.
25 Art 21.
26 Art 22.
27 Art 23.
28 Art 24.
29 Art 25.
30 Art 26.
31 Art 27.
32 Art 28.
33 Art 29.
34 Art 30.
35 Art 31.
36 Art 32.
37 Bertrand Ramcharan, 'Equality and Nondiscrimination', in Louis Henkin (ed.), *The International Bill of Rights: The Covenant on Civil and Political Rights* (Columbia University Press 1981) 246.

is at the root of virtually all human rights abuses,[38] an experience reflected in the Sudanese context. Article 31 of the 2005 INC provided for equal protection and equality before the law without discrimination: '[a]ll persons are equal before the law and are entitled without discrimination, as to race, colour, sex, language, religious creed, political opinion, or ethnic origin, to the equal protection of the law.' However, it omitted reference to 'national or social origin, property, birth, or other status'. The grounds of non-discrimination and equality before the law were therefore not as comprehensive as those found in articles 2(1) and 26 of the ICCPR. Article 31 also lacked detail. It neither used the language of 'obligations' nor specified that the State should take proactive measures to ensure realization of this right; it also did not include an *explicit duty* of the State to respect and ensure respect of the rights guaranteed therein to all persons without discrimination. A revised article 31 should therefore stipulate specifically that 'the law shall prohibit any discrimination and guarantee to all persons equal and effective protection against discrimination on any ground'. This is a critical issue given that Sudan's hybrid legal system derived from 'traditional' *Shari'a* law and customary laws, both of which may give rise to discrimination against certain individuals and groups, particularly women, and religious, ethnic and linguistic minorities.

One of the other limitations of article 31 is that it did not explicitly prohibit advocacy of various forms of national, racial or religious hatred which may amount to incitement to discrimination, hostility or violence.[39] Equally, the BoR did not prohibit the dissemination of ideas or theories of superiority of one race or groups of persons as provided for in article 4 of the International Convention on the Elimination of All Forms of Racial Discrimination (ICERD) to which Sudan is a party. This article requires States to enact criminal legislations to punish such acts. While ICERD is already part of the BoR by virtue of article 27(3), an express prohibition is essential to enhance awareness and strengthen protection. Sudan is ethnically and religiously diverse and afflicted with chronic armed conflicts and violence in which incitement and advocacy of hatred and 'ethnic criminalization' have been used as a ground for persecuting members of certain ethnic groups.[40]

Article 31 was repealed by the 2017 constitutional amendments.[41] Yet, the amendments did not address the substantive gaps discussed above.

38 Sarah Joseph, Jenny Schultz, and Melissa Castan, *The International Covenant on Civil and Political Rights: Cases, Materials and Commentary* (OUP 2005) 680.

39 National, racial, religious hatred is addressed as part of art 39 of the BoR, 'all media shall abide by media ethics and media shall not incite religious, racial, cultural hatred or call for violence or war'.

40 See *Report of the Special Rapporteur on the Situation of Human Rights in the Sudan, Sima Samar*, UN doc A/HRC/9/13 (2 September 2008) paras 20–33; Amin M Medani, 'A Legacy of Institutionalized Repression: Criminal Law and Justice in Sudan' in Lutz Oette (ed.), *Criminal Law Reform and Transitional Justice: Human Rights Perspectives for Sudan* (Ashgate 2011) 79–80.

41 See Arabic text of INC 2005 (amendments 2017), approved in two separate sessions by the National Legislature on 25 April 2017, and the Council of States, on 24 April 2017. It was signed by the President of the National Legislature, Ibrahim Ahmed Omer and approved by the President of the Republic, Omer Hassan Ahmed Al-Basheer on 3rd May 2017 (on file with author).

Instead, the new article 31(1) omits reference to 'political opinion' as one of the grounds of non-discrimination and replaced it with 'political allegiance' but the rest of the old text was kept. This formulation is peculiar; it has not been used in any human rights treaty as one of the prohibited grounds of discrimination. Most importantly, a new section was added to article 31 that distorts its text. Article 31(2) mixes non-discrimination with the principles of equality to 'hold election posts', equality to be 'appointed for public office', equality not to be discriminated against when parties are involved in disputes, or 'judicial transactions' or 'public humanitarian matters' unless such discrimination is justified on the ground of 'competence' or 'qualifications'.[42] The wording of this article is unclear in the Arabic text, and demonstrative of vague legal drafting. It evinces sheer ignorance on the part of the drafters who appear to lack basic knowledge and expertise of the substance and content of the BoR and relevant international human rights standards. This divergence is problematic in its own right, but also raises the question of how to square article 31 with the international standards that are an integral part of the Bill by virtue of its article 27(3).

Article 32(1) requires the State to guarantee equal rights of men and women in the enjoyment of all rights, including the right to equal pay for equal work and other related benefits. The State shall also promote the rights of women through affirmative action (article 32(2)). However, this article does not (as in the case of article 3 of the ICCPR) impose ***direct obligations*** on the State to take all necessary steps to enable women to enjoy those rights, including the removal of discriminatory laws (both direct and indirect) in various areas.[43] There are still laws which impose more severe penalties on women than on men for adultery and other offences that violate the requirement of equal treatment.[44] These criminal laws are applied through what is known as the public order regime[45] which has serious adverse impacts on the lives of women and girls, particularly the poor and other members of marginalized groups, including alcohol brewers and sellers as well as

42 Art 31(2) reads: 'All people are equal with regards to holding election posts, or holding public posts, or disputes, or judicial transactions or humanitarian public affairs or legal or national transactions without discrimination among them unless based on qualification and competence' (author's translation from Arabic).

43 See Human Rights Committee, *General Comment No 28: Equality of Rights between Men and Women (Article 3),* UN doc CCPR/C/21/Rev.1/Add.10 (29 March 2000) paras 3 and 18, 31.

44 See section XV of the Criminal Act 1991 which includes offences such as adultery, rape, sodomy, incest, gross indecency, indecent and immoral acts, practicing prostitution, seduction. On these offences see REDRESS and KCHRED, *Reforming Sudan's Legislation on Rape and Sexual Violence* (2008).

45 See SIHA, *Beyond Trousers, The Public Order Regime and the Human Rights of Women and Girls in Sudan* (A Discussion Paper, Submission to the 46th Ordinary Session of the African Commission on Human and Peoples' Rights, Banjul, the Gambia 12 November 2009) 5.

migrant women.[46] This legal regime is discriminatory and inherently incompatible with both the BoR and Sudan's obligations under international law.[47]

3.2 Administration of criminal justice

3.2.1 Freedom from arbitrary arrest and detention

This section examines the substantive provisions of the constitutional BoR of 2005 from a criminal justice perspective.[48] The prohibition of arbitrary arrest and detention stipulated in article 29 is one of the key provisions as it deals with the rights of accused persons which are constantly violated in Sudan. It provided that '[e]very person has the right to liberty and security of the person; no person shall be subjected to arrest, detention, deprivation or restriction of his/her liberty except for reasons and in accordance with the procedures prescribed by law'. However, a closer analysis shows that the article had certain substantive and procedural gaps. It did not include the word 'arbitrary' when referring to arrest, detention and deprivation of liberty. The lack of arbitrariness is central to the right to liberty and security under international law, and includes both lawfulness of the deprivation of liberty and the modalities of enforcement of the law.[49] Another serious gap was the lack of *procedural guarantees* that help ensure enjoyment of its substantive guarantees, particularly when compared to the procedural standards included in article 9(2) to (5) of the ICCPR. Requirements such as the right to be informed of a criminal charge; prompt presentation before a judicial officer or other person authorized by law; length of pre-trial detention; right to release pending investigation; right of *habeas corpus*; and the right to compensation were notably absent. These procedural guarantees are of utmost importance for defendants at the pre-trial stage. This applies in particular to judicial safeguards. Notably, article 29 (unlike article 9(3) of the ICCPR) did not require that any person arrested or detained on suspicion of having committed a criminal offence be brought promptly before a judge or other judicial officer authorized by law to exercise judicial power.

Article 29 was repealed and replaced with the same article in the constitutional amendments of 2017.[50] Instead of remedying its shortcomings, however, the

46 See, SIHA and REDRESS, *Criminalisation of Women in Sudan: A Need for Fundamental Reform* (2017); Liv Tønnessen, 'When Rape Becomes Politics: Negotiating Islamic law Reform in Sudan' *Wom Stud Int For* 44 (2014) 145–53.

47 See Asma Abdel Halim 'Gendered Justice: Women and the Application of Penal Laws in Sudan' in Oette (n 40).

48 See for a comprehensive review of key areas of Sudan's criminal laws repressive criminal legislation, arrest, detention and fair trial, accountability for international crimes and criminal law and gender-based violence the respective chapters by Medani, Adib, Babiker and Halim in Oette, ibid.

49 Joseph (n 38) 308–9. See also *Womah Mukong v Cameroon*, Comm 458/1991, UN doc CCPR/C/51/D/458/1991(1994).

50 See Arabic text of INC 2005 (amendments 2017) (n 41).

new article 29 has reduced substantive protection. Article 29(1) now provides that 'everyone has the right to freedom and the security of his endeavours'. This formulation is extremely vague and is not consistent with human rights treaties. Article 29(2) stipulates that 'no person should be arrested and kept in custody without having the right to liberty except under restrictions and regulations detailed under the law'. This amendment fails to ensure protection against arbitrary arrest and detention where provided for in statutory law; on the contrary, it gives constitutional legitimacy to these practices.

Sudanese criminal laws, security laws and anti-terrorism legislation are not sufficiently specific to allow individuals to foresee the consequences of their action. They also provide for wide grounds of arrest and detention, which have resulted in persistent concerns about violations of the right of suspects.[51] The National Intelligence and Security (NISS) Act 2010, in particular, allows security officers, who are evidently not judicial officers authorized by law, to arrest and detain individuals for a maximum period of four and a half months before a detained person must be brought before a judge.[52] The Criminal Procedure Act 1991 specifies a period of three days within which a person needs to be brought before a judge and provides for a number of safeguards.[53] However, pre-trial detention can be extended for a period of six months, after which any further extensions need to be approved by the Chief Justice.[54] The Act stipulates neither a time limit for pre-trial detention nor a timeframe for trials.[55] In practice, it is for the Chief Justice to decide on the time limit in any given case, which carries the risk of arbitrary decision-making without the possibility of judicial review.[56] This lacunae in Sudanese criminal laws needs to be addressed in any constitutional review process as pre-trial detention should be an exception and as short as possible as recognized in article 9(3) of the ICCPR.[57]

Neither the original nor the amended article 29 includes one of the most important guarantees, namely the right to *habeas corpus* which is enshrined in article 9(4) of the ICCPR. The right entitles any person who has been deprived of his or her liberty, for whatever reason, to challenge the lawfulness of his/her detention in a court without delay. This right, which constitutes a critical safeguard against both arbitrary detention and torture, is presently not provided for in the NISS Act 2010.[58] In the Act and beyond, Sudanese laws do not provide

51 See Adib, 'At the State's Mercy: Arrest, Detention and Trials under Sudanese Law' in Oette (n 40).

52 Art 50 (1)(f), (c), (g), (h) of the Act on powers of arrest and detention given to NISS members and Director under the Act.

53 The General Principles stipulated in art 4 of the Act provide some safeguards including the rights to be informed of the reason of arrest, to prompt access to a lawyer of one's choice, to access to a doctor and to communicate with a family member.

54 Art 79.

55 See Adib (n 51) 128–9.

56 Ibid.

57 See *General Comment 28* (n 43) para 3.

58 See arts 50 and 51 NISS Act 2010.

detainees with an effective remedy against arbitrary detention.[59] Again, it is essential that this right be included in a revised BoR, together with the right of access to a lawyer of one's choice. Access to lawyers is critical to *habeas corpus* and the Human Rights Committee has clearly linked access to legal representation with enjoyment of the right in article 9(4) of the ICCPR, particularly in instances of *incommunicado* detention.[60] The right for a lawyer to be present during the pre-trial stage is of particular importance in Sudan as criminal laws do not explicitly state that lawyers have the right to be present during the investigation stage or be able to review the legality of detention.

Finally, article 29, in contrast to article 9(5) of the ICCPR, does not provide for the right to compensation in case of unlawful deprivation of liberty. According to the Human Rights Committee, the right to enforceable compensation includes cases where detention is 'lawful' under domestic law but contrary to the Covenant.[61] Any revised BoR should explicitly provide for the right to enforceable compensation in the event of unlawful deprivation of liberty as provided for in the ICCPR's article 9(5) and other international human rights instruments. In Sudan, many victims have been arbitrarily detained for long periods pending trials and subsequently released without receiving any form of compensation or other forms of reparation.[62]

3.2.2 Fair trial guarantees

Fair trial guarantees are enshrined in international human rights instruments to which Sudan is a party, such as the ICCPR and the African Charter on Human and Peoples' Rights (ACHPR).[63] Article 34 of Sudan's BoR 2005 guarantees the right to a fair trial: 'In all civil and criminal proceedings, every person shall be entitled to a fair and public hearing by an ordinary competent court of law in accordance with procedures prescribed by law.' It also guarantees detainees' right to be immediately informed of the reasons of their arrest and of having charges promptly brought against them, and the right of accused persons to be tried in their presence on any criminal charges without delay, and their right to defend themselves through a lawyer of their choice.

One of the BoR's structural limitations is that articles 29 (personal liberty and security of person) and 34 (fair trial) were confused in terms of their logical

59 REDRESS and KCHRED, *Criminal Law and Human Rights in Sudan*, A Baseline Study (2008) 13.

60 In *Hammel v Madagascar* Comm 155/1983 (3 April 1987), incommunicado detention rendered habeas corpus action impossible.

61 Ibid para 11.

62 See Mohamed Abdelsalam Babiker, 'Victims Access to Justice in Sudan: At the Mercy of the State and Impotence of Global and African Justice Mechanisms', in Thomas Obel Hansen (ed.) *Victims and Post-Conflict Justice Mechanisms in Africa* (Kenya Human Rights Commission, LawAfrica 2017) 86–105.

63 Sudan's international obligation to provide an accused with a fair trial before Sudanese courts derives from art 14 of the ICCPR and art 7 of the ACHPR.

relationship. The rights of the accused person in both articles were not carefully drafted and do not take into consideration that criminal proceedings pass through various stages from arrest to post trial. For example, article 34(2) (fair trial) provides that 'every person who is ***arrested*** shall be informed, ***at the time of arrest***, of the reasons for his/her arrest and shall be promptly informed of any charges against him/her'. The requirement of prompt information, however, only applies once the individual has been formally charged with a criminal offence (article 14 (3)(a) of the ICCPR). It does not apply to those remanded in custody pending the result of police investigations, which is covered by article 9(2) of the ICCPR. The language of article 34 therefore systematically belongs to article 29. The use of the words 'arrest' and 'the time of arrest' indicates clearly the degree of confusion between articles 29 and 34; both articles guarantee human rights of suspects/the accused but these guarantees operate at different stages of criminal proceedings. It is important for this confusion to be addressed in any constitutional reform as fair trial guarantees are essentially linked to the preservation of other concomitant rights, including the right to life and the prohibition of torture. Practice indicates that many accused persons in Sudan have been compelled to confess guilt while in custody or detention. Several laws are not in harmony with international human rights treaties[64] and contradict the fair trial guarantees enshrined in article 34. For example, the Evidence Act 1993 does not outlaw evidence obtained through illegal means if such evidence is corroborated by other evidence.[65] In terms of judicial practice, verdicts have in some instances been based on confessions even though the defendants alleged that they had been obtained under torture.[66] Allegations raised by accused persons that they were forced to confess guilt have been routinely ignored.[67] Judges should have the authority – and duty – to consider at any stage of the case allegations made that the rights of the accused have been violated. It is therefore imperative that any constitutional review in Sudan results in the unequivocal prohibition of the use of confessions obtained by means of torture and enshrines the prohibition of self-incrimination.

BoR in Sudan do not address repressive laws which are repugnant or in conflict with constitutional fair trial guarantees.[68] The NISS Act 2010, the Criminal

64 E.g. art 14(3)(g) of the ICCPR provides that 'in the determination of any criminal charge against him', every person has the right 'not to be compelled to testify against himself or to confess guilt'.

65 Art 20 of the Evidence Act of 1993 appears to rule out the use of evidence extracted under torture. However, art 10 of the Act gives judges discretion to admit any evidence if they determine it to be acceptable, in particular where corroborated by other evidence.

66 See the submission in the case *of Mayor Hussein Ishaq Sayo and others v Director of North Darfur State Police and Others* lodged before the Sudanese Constitutional Court in 2007 (on file with author).

67 See in particular *Ishaq al-Sanousi and others v successors of deceased Mohamed Taha Mohamed Ahmed*, Case No MD/QD/121/2008, Constitutional Court Order (23 March 2009).

68 Art 27(4) of the INC provides that 'legislation shall regulate the rights and freedoms enshrined in this Bill and shall not detract from or derogate any of these rights'. This article demonstrates the INC's superiority over conflicting legislation.

Act 1991 (particularly crimes against the State), emergency and anti-terrorism legislation, and the Police Act 2008, all provide the authorities with broad powers. This includes the setting up of special courts,[69] public order courts, police courts and anti-terrorism courts. Sudan's practice illustrates that the systematic use of these laws has undermined the right to a fair trial and widened the scope of prosecutions.[70] These laws are overly broad and vague, provide grounds for arbitrary arrests and prolonged detention and violate the right to a fair trial. Again, a comprehensive review of the fair trial guarantees is required for any constitutional and law reform in Sudan, including those safeguards that need to be in place in situations of national emergency or armed conflict.[71]

3.2.3 The death penalty

Article 36 of the BoR prohibits the imposition of the death penalty on a person under the age of eighteen or a person who has attained the age of seventy, and delays its imposition on pregnant women or lactating women for two years after giving birth. However, it does not prohibit the death penalty outright, which runs counter to a growing trend towards its abolition worldwide. Capital punishment can be imposed in respect of a number of offences, including cases of retribution and some *Shari'a hudud* crimes.[72] The mandatory imposition of the death penalty envisaged for *hudud* offences is contrary to the right to life under international law.[73] The imposition of the death penalty also raises the question whether Islamic *hudud* crimes such as apostasy (*ridda*) and adultery (*zina*) can be considered as 'the most serious crimes'. Article 6(2) of the ICCCPR strictly limits the application of the death penalty, firstly, to States parties that have not abolished the death penalty, and secondly, to the most serious crimes.[74] Subsequent general comments adopted by the Human Rights Committee,[75] including its recent draft General Comment No. 36, confirm that article 6 'shall be applied only in the most exceptional cases, for the most serious crimes and under the strictest limits'.[76] The term 'the most serious crimes' must be read restrictively

69 The Emergency and Protection of Public Safety Act of 1997 (Act Number (1) 1998) also provides for the establishment of Special Courts without providing adequate fair trial.

70 See on similar practices, 'Repressive Criminal Legislation', in Oette (n 40) 59–65.

71 For such guarantees see *Aksoy v Turkey*, 23 EHRR 533 (1996) paras 67–87.

72 According to art 3 of Sudan's Criminal Act of 1991, '*hudud* offence' 'means the offences of drinking alcohol, apostasy (*ridda*), adultery (*zina*), defamation of unchastity *(quazf)* armed robbery (*hiraba*) and capital theft'.

73 *Weerawansa v Sri Lanka*, Comm 1406/2005 (14 May 2009) para 7.2.

74 See Human Rights Committee *General Comment No 36 on Article 6 of the ICCPR, on the Right to Life*, para 37. Revised draft prepared by the Rapporteur, adopted on First Reading during the 120th Session, www.ohchr.org/EN/HRBodies/CCPR/Pages/GC36 Article-6Righttolife.aspx, accessed 15 April 2018.

75 See *General Comment No 6* (16th session 1982) and 14 (23rd session 1984), respectively on art 6 of the ICCPR.

76 See *General Comment No 36* (n 74) para 37.

and appertain only to crimes of extreme gravity, involving intentional killing.[77] This entails that 'crimes not resulting directly and intentionally in death, such as drug offences, attempted murder, corruption and other economic [and political] crimes, armed robbery, piracy, abduction and sexual offences, although serious in nature, can never justify, within the framework of article 6, the imposition of the death penalty'.[78] In particular, it emphasizes: 'Under no circumstances can the death penalty ever be applied as a sanction against conduct whose very criminalization violates the Covenant, including adultery, homosexuality, apostasy [establishing political opposition groups,] or offending a head of State. States parties that retain the death penalty for such offences commit a violation of their obligations under article 6 read alone and in conjunction with article 2, paragraph 2 of the Covenant, as well as of other provisions of the Covenant.'[79] Such normative conflict between Article 6 and Islamic penalties in Sudan raises critical questions about the universality of human rights with regard to the compatibility of a liberal human rights perspective with orthodox Islamic perspectives.[80] One further problematic aspect is the imposition of the death penalty on minors. While seemingly permitted for *Shari'a* offences under the Criminal Act 1991, the Child Act 2010, which incorporated the Convention on the Rights of the Child, exempts children from the death penalty.[81] However, given the lack of clarity provided by article 36, Sudanese courts have struggled to settle the question of whether children are exempted from death penalty in cases of *hudud* crimes.[82]

3.3 The prohibition of torture and other cruel, inhuman or degrading treatment or punishment

Article 33 of the BoR (prohibition of torture) fails to prohibit cruel, inhuman or degrading punishment, such as corporal punishments, an omission that is incompatible with international standards binding on Sudan.[83] In addition, in line with

77 *Chisanga v Zambia*, Comm 1132/2002 (18 October 2005) para 7.4; ECOSOC Safeguards Guaranteeing Protection of the Rights of Those Facing the Death Penalty (25 May 1984) para 1.

78 See General Comment No 36 (n 74) para 39.

79 Ibid para 40 (footnotes omitted).

80 See Abdullahi An-Na'im, 'Universality of Human Rights: Mediating Paradox to Enhance Practice' in Miodrag Jovanovic & Ivana Krstic (eds), *Human Rights Today – 60 Years of the UniversalDeclaration* (Eleven International Publishing 2010) 29–50; Mashood A Baderin (ed.), *Islam and Human Rights* (Ashgate 2010).

81 Art 77(e) (Principles of passing sentences) provides that the Court, upon passing sentences, shall give due regard to the principle that 'death sentence is not inflicted on the Child'.

82 See Constitutional Court case, *Nagim Eldeen Gasm Elseed v (1) Government of Sudan and (2) blood heirs of Abdel Rahman Mohamed Ali*, Case no, MDG/GD/18/2005, (2008) 2 *Constitutional Court Journal*, 399.

83 See REDRESS and Sudanese Human Rights Monitor, *No more Cracking of the Whip: Time to End Corporal Punishment in Sudan* (2012).

recent constitutional practice in many countries,[84] the article pertaining to the right to be free from torture should stipulate a duty to criminalize torture and recognize a specific right to reparation for torture, both of which are absent in Sudan's law.[85] In terms of judicial practice there are serious concerns that when courts address the right to a fair trial, the right not to be subjected to torture/ill-treatment and prolonged detention without judicial oversight, Sudanese judges routinely do not order investigations into allegations of torture. In addition, evidence obtained through torture can possibly be accepted by Sudan's courts and contribute to proof of a defendant's guilt.[86] This indicates that Sudanese laws in terms of sources of law give prominence to Islamic laws and public order laws rather than applying international human rights standards prohibiting torture.

3.4 Religious rights and freedoms

Successive constitutions since Sudan's independence in 1956 have stressed respect for religious rights and freedoms irrespective of religious affiliation. Article 6 of the INC provides constitutional protection for religious rights and freedoms in the Guiding Principles which call for the right to respect religious rights to worship or assemble and to establish, possess, acquire and maintain places for worship and disseminate religious publications and teach religion or belief. Article 38 (Freedom of Creed and Worship) further guaranteed freedom of religious creed and worship, and the right to declare and manifest religion and religious practices. However, the 2017 constitutional amendments introduced a new text. The new article is entitled 'freedom of creed, religion and *mazhab*'.[87] It reads:

> Every human being has the right to believe, and to practice or manifest religion and nobody should be compelled to adopt a religion which he does not believe and has the right to express his religion and believe in accordance to regulations provided by law.

This amendment kept the right of belief (but omitted an explicit right to worship) and does not explicitly provide that the right can be restricted on the grounds of public order. Despite these constitutional guarantees, in actual practice Sudan does not take a neutral position towards all religious groups, including both Muslims and non-Muslims. Some members of minority religious groups are compelled to practice their religious rituals clandestinely, as they are systematically stigmatized

84 See e.g. art 22 of the Constitution of Morocco, 2011, and art 26 of the Interim Constitution of Nepal, 2007.

85 See REDRESS and SOAT, *National and International Remedies for Torture: A Handbook for Sudanese Lawyers* (2005) 32–7.

86 See (n 65–66) above on Sudan's Evidence Act of 1993 and relevant judicial practice.

87 *Mazhab* in Arabic means a religious school of thought which is different and unique in its way of thinking from other schools of thought regarding certain religious matters.

and accused of heresy, particularly by some *Salafi* figures.[88] The lack of equal protection runs counter to the State's role as supposedly neutral agent that has the duty to refrain from discriminating against individuals or groups based on their religion and belief (obligation to respect). The State is also required to prevent such discrimination, including from non-State actors (obligation to protect); and must take steps to ensure that every person within their jurisdiction enjoys all human rights without discrimination of any kind (obligation to fulfil).[89]

The right to manifestation of religion is restricted in Sudan, particularly with regard to some minority Muslim groups such as *Shii'a*, *Baha'i* and the Republican Brothers who adopt a liberal version of Islam despite the fact that religious groups have the freedom to manifest their religion or belief as enshrined in article 18 of the ICCPR.[90] The secession of South Sudan has adversely affected the freedom to worship or practice or manifest religion; after secession, there is a widespread perception that Sudan is a purely (Sunni) Muslim majoritarian State and hence non-Muslims have limited space to practice and manifest their religion.[91]

Although successive constitutions have guaranteed religious rights and freedoms, national laws contradict these constitutional norms. The emphasis on *Shari'a* as the main source of legislation enshrines limitations on the rights of non-Muslim communities, while criminal laws impose severe penalties for beliefs which are unpopular while other laws do not provide protection against religious hatred and incitement of violence against religious minority groups. For example, the inclusion of the crime of apostasy in the Criminal Act 1991 is a clear violation of the principles of freedom of belief and, though it has been used infrequently, creates an environment of fear in *particular* among Muslim minority religious groups.

3.5 Freedom of expression and media freedoms

Freedom of expression, the press and other media in a democratic society are protected by article 39(1) of the INC 2005, which provides that '[e]very citizen shall have an unrestricted right to the [sic] freedom of expression, reception and dissemination of information, publication, and access to the press without prejudice to order, safety or public morals as determined by law'. Yet, one of the major substantive gaps of article 39 (1) is that it does not provide for the right to access

88 See study on *Freedom of Religion and Belief in Sudan, Islam and Society in Sudan*, Islamic Research project (IRP) (Centre d'Études et de Documentation Économiques, Juridiques et Sociales-Khartoum branch February 2013).

89 See *The United Nations Declaration on the Rights of Persons Belonging to National or Ethnic Religious and Linguistic Minorities* (UN General Assembly 1992).

90 *General Comment No 22: The right to freedom of thought, conscience and religion (Art. 18),* Forty-eighth session (1993) para 3.

91 See Mohamed Abdelsalam Babiker, 'Freedom of Religion, Minority Rights and the 'Islamization' of Laws in Sudan: From Independence to Secession of South Sudan' (unpublished, on file with author).

and seek information and freedom of the media. It was amended in 2017,[92] and article 39(1) now reads:

> Every citizen has the free right to express and reflect his opinion to the public through media outlets and through public discourse, written and visual publications and through public demonstrations and in processions to advocate for his causes and in accordance with the law regulating and balancing the right of freedom of expression and the right of persons not to be defamed and the reassurance of the society of its morals and its activities of public demonstration.[93]

This amendment has various shortcomings. First, it unduly limits the scope of the right to freedom of expression, opinion and media to citizens, thereby excluding non-nationals. Secondly, it uses vague formulations such as everyone has 'the free right to reflect his opinion to the public through public demonstrations and in processions'. Such a formulation confuses the right to freedom of expression with freedom of assembly which are treated as separate rights in all human rights treaties and the INC (see article 40 for freedom of peaceful assembly). Finally, the new amendment tries to balance the right with 'the right of persons not to be defamed and the reassurance of the society of its morals and its activities of public demonstration', without, however, stressing the necessity and proportionality of any restrictions imposed in the exercise of such balancing.

Notwithstanding the constitutional rights, several laws violate international human rights standards regulating freedom of expression and media. The right to seek, impart and receive information is included in article 25(2) of the Press and Printed Materials Act 2009 (PPMA). However, the right of journalists to obtain information from official sources is *meaningless* in the absence of good freedom of information laws, in particular information related to national security, public health and other information which cannot be accessed by the public. This is because such laws do not provide substantive or procedurals guarantees to allow journalists to access information from government departments or official sources. Few regulations, including the restrictive Freedom of Information Act of 2015, provide for the right to access information under Sudan's national laws, as international norms were not properly domesticated or harmonized after Sudan's ratifications of international human rights

92 Art 39(2) was slightly amended. The original text reads: 'The State shall guarantee the freedom of the press and other media as shall be regulated by law in a democratic society.' In the new amendment 'democratic society' was removed from the text.

93 Author's translation. The Arabic text is unclear, vague and cannot be understood in plain Arabic. This is reflected in the above translated text. It is widely held that this text and the rest of the amended BoR was written by the late Dr. Hassan Al-Turabi who was known for using unclear and imprecise formulations, apparently to manipulate the interpretation of constitutional texts. The wording used in this Bill reflects his previous endeavours to Islamize Sudanese constitutions (i.e. the 1998 constitution).

treaties. National laws, including media laws, do not indicate the criteria to be used in determining whether or not information may be declared secret, or set forth clear and narrow categories of information that may be withheld with sufficient precision to enable persons to understand what information may be withheld and what should be disclosed.[94] Access to information laws should therefore be reviewed, and above all be an integral part of any forthcoming constitutional BoR. This is essential in a context like Sudan where the executive has wide discretion to restrict freedom of the media including the right to seek information.

Similarly, the press and publication laws, particularly the PPMA, impose restrictions that are incompatible with international standards on freedom of expression provided for in Article 19 of the ICCPR, and do not conform to the constitutional BoR. First, the Act provides for wide restrictions on freedom of expression justified on various grounds including national security, public order and morals, without specifying or defining the scope of these grounds. Although Article 19(3) of the ICCPR permits freedom of expression to be limited by measures 'provided by law', any restrictions shall be interpreted narrowly. The PPMA legitimizes the licensing, confiscation and closure of newspapers and media outlets, as well as detention of journalists or publishers. Under its article 24, editors in chief are criminalized for the newspaper's editorial performance and held accountable for 'whatever' is published in their newspaper. This, no doubt, restricts editors, creates an atmosphere of self-censorship and makes them vulnerable to being subjected to criminal sanctions. The excessive restriction under the PPMA tends to destroy the *essence* of the right. These restrictive legislative approaches render abstract, and systematically undermine, the constitutional protection of freedom of the media. At the institutional level, regulatory bodies are ill-equipped to guarantee rights and freedoms of media personnel. For example, the National Press Council (the regulatory body of journalists and the printed press) is not an independent, self-regulatory or autonomous body, as it is controlled by the Presidency and supervised by the executive represented by the Minster of Information. Eleven out of twenty-one of its members are appointed directly by the Presidency and are members of the political parties of the National Assembly.[95] The National Press Council does not enjoy financial independence as its budget and its financial auditing is controlled and supervised by the executive, which jeopardizes its operational independence. The council was granted – and has exercised – unprecedented powers, including imposing fines and revoking journalists' licenses, disciplinary measures against journalists, suspension of newspapers and imposing conditions

94 See Mohamed Abdelsalam Babiker, *International Human Rights Instruments on the Right to Access Information: their Domestication and Harmonization within Sudan's Legal Framework* (unpublished paper presented at Access to Information and Transparency workshop, Faculty of Law and Friedrich Ebert, University of Khartoum 2 August 2017).

95 Art 9 (constitution, composition, and term of the council).

of eligibility of journalists and chief editors.[96] Journalists are also subjected to both tort and criminal liability and the National Press Council is empowered to impose criminal sanctions for violations of the law.[97]

3.6 Bills of Rights and economic, social and cultural rights

Various BoR in Sudan have not envisaged or considered adopting a social model constitution. ESCR have been largely ignored, including by democratic regimes.[98] The 1973 Permanent Constitution remains the only constitution which focused on ESCR due to the socialist orientation of the military regime during the early 1970s.[99]

Several ESCR are absent from Sudanese constitutions, and the scope of recognized ESCR is deficient or ill-defined. Like most of the other key rights, the right to education, for example, was ignored until the adoption of the 1973 Permanent Constitution, which recognized education as a fundamental right in article 53 and included a considerable number of directive principles (articles 18–20 and 29). In contrast, the 1998 Constitution only recognizes the right to education as a directive principle.[100] The INC 2005 equally includes education as one of the directive principles of State policy in article 13 but also guarantees it as a fundamental right in article 44. The latter article provides for free and compulsory education at the primary level as 'a right of every citizen' and obliges the State 'to provide access to education without discrimination as to religion, race, ethnicity, gender or disability'. By virtue of these provisions, the INC 2005 covers the minimum standards as required by the International Covenant on Economic, Social and Cultural Rights (ICESCR) and the African Charter on Human and Peoples' Rights (ACHPR), albeit only for citizens as it does not apply to 'everyone'.[101]

It is evident that the right of everyone to the enjoyment of the highest attainable standard of physical and mental health has not constituted a priority for national governments (both democratic and totalitarian) since independence.[102] Again, with the exception of the 1973 Permanent Constitution, which emphasized that health care and medical treatment are a right of every citizen and that

96 Human Rights Committee, *Concluding Observations on the Fourth Periodic Report of the Sudan*, UN doc CCPR/C/SDN/CO/4 (19 August 2014) para 21.
97 Art 7 (functions of the Council), Article 8 (powers of the Council).
98 See Ahmed Abdelgadir, 'Economic, Social and Cultural Rights under the Constitutional Bill of Rights in the Sudan' in Mohamed Abdelsalam Babiker and Lutz Oette (eds), *The Constitutional Protection of Human Rights in Sudan: Challenges and Future Perspectives* (REDRESS, Faculty of Law University of Khartoum, Sudanese Human Rights Monitor 2014) 32–41.
99 See (n 16–21).
100 Art 12.
101 Abdelgadir (n 98).
102 Ibid.

the State shall endeavour to provide it for free (article 54), previous constitutions are silent on the right to health. However, article 19 of the INC 2005's guiding principles provides that the State 'shall promote public health and guarantee equal access and free primary health care to all citizens'. This recognition of the right to health care has been strengthened by article 46 of the INC 2005 to the effect that the State 'shall promote public health, establish, rehabilitate, develop basic medical and diagnostic institutions, and provide free primary health care and emergency services for all citizens'. While the international standard imposes upon the States parties an obligation to recognize the right of everyone to physical and mental health, the national obligation is confined to promoting public health for Sudanese citizens. The INC 2005 therefore does not recognize the right of everyone to the enjoyment of the highest attainable standard of health care as set out in the ICESCR and as provided for in the ACHPR, a gap that needs to be addressed in any future BoR.

States parties to the ICESCR including Sudan recognize, according to its article 11, the right of everyone to an adequate standard of living, including adequate food, clothing and housing. This right was not recognized as a fundamental human right in previous Sudanese constitutions though it was referred to in general terms as a directive principle in the 1973 Permanent Constitution[103] and in article 10 of the INC 2005 which calls for achieving a decent standard of living for all citizens. Similarly, Sudanese constitutions are silent on the right to social security, including social insurance, with the exception of the 1973 Permanent Constitution according to which the State shall provide a system for social security against disasters, sickness, orphanage, old age, unemployment and other causes of disability.[104]

In conclusion, it is obvious that various BoRs indicate that ESCR have been neglected if not altogether ignored by both civilian and military governments, as well as in legal debates and civil society advocacy. It is also apparent that social justice was not and still is not part of the political elites' discourse. ESCR are not regarded as 'justiciable' rights that can be invoked in courts despite the fact that article 27(3) of the INC 2005 incorporates the ICESCR and the ACHPR into the BoR. There is a lack of judicial recognition or interpretation by the Constitutional Court and a widespread disregard of these rights in administrative practice.[105] Courts in other jurisprudence have adopted creative approaches to realize ESCR.[106] In Sudan it is now imperative that recognition and adequate protection of ESCR, including for non-citizens, must be seen as one of the priorities for Sudan's future constitution.

103 See arts 30 and 31 of the Permanent Constitution of 1973.
104 Art 24.
105 Abdelgadir (n 98).
106 Jill Cottrell and Yash Ghai (eds), *The Role of the Courts in the Protection of Economic, Social & Cultural Rights* (Interights 2004).

4 The constitutional implementation of Bill of Rights: structural obstacles

4.1 The reception and 'domestication' of international human rights norms through the monism or 'dualism' theories of international law: a dilemma

One of the key concerns rarely raised in Sudan's constitutional debate is the reception of international human rights treaties within Sudan's legal system and the conflict between different legal norms or regimes, including international human rights treaties, constitutional BoR, Islamic or *Shari'a* laws and customary laws. The difficulties posed by the automatic transformation of international law into the national legal system raise the question whether article 27(3) needs to be maintained or whether a revised constitution is to opt for a dualist approach to international law or even a 'third way' in order to allow for its effective implementation. Experience has shown that there is no prospect of constitutional protection of human rights in Sudan as long as the uneasy and 'thorny' relationship between conflicting and competing legal norms is not adequately addressed.

The unclear reception and domestication of international human rights norms has contributed to the failure of successive BoR to provide adequate protection and ensure the effective implementation of CPR in Sudan. This can be attributed to the absence of concrete methodology, and legislative or judicial approaches towards incorporating international human rights law. In the context of Sudan's hybrid legal system, which gives rise to a competing environment in terms of the hierarchy of laws, article 27(3) is designed to transform all international human rights treaties ratified by Sudan into the BoR, and thereby national law. It reflects the 'monist doctrine', which advocates the superiority of international law over national legal systems without the need of their transformation into national law,[107] and can be invoked as a vehicle through which human rights can be protected at the national level.

The supposedly automatic transformation of international human rights law into Sudan's national legal system has raised serious difficulties in terms of the actual implementation of human rights law by officials and national courts. This has been particularly the case where a conflict arises between statutory laws and human rights norms. Furthermore, the incorporation of international human rights treaties into domestic law in Sudan has resulted in conflicting practices by courts. As a common law country, Sudan used to follow a dualist approach which means that international law and Sudanese laws have different spheres of application. Contrary to the monist approach expressed in article 27(3), judicial practice, which is still influenced by Sudan's common law heritage, i.e. a dualist approach, indicates that judges in ordinary courts rarely rely on the BoR and international

107 See further Antonio Cassesse, *International Law* (OUP 2008) 162–74.

human rights instruments. The Constitutional Court[108] has largely failed to protect constitutional human rights, including by relying on article 27(3) and international treaties in its interpretation of fundamental rights. Any constitutional design should therefore clearly stipulate that national courts must consider international human rights law and, when interpreting any legislation, must promote the spirit, purpose and objects of the BoR. Where there is a conflict between international human rights law and national law, the former law should prevail. There is no doubt that this question requires serious discussion and adoption of judicial guidelines or directives in order to inform judicial practices. Law-makers also have the responsibility to clarify the status of human rights law when applied by national courts, and above all, when constitutional human rights norms conflict with *Shari'a* law, particularly where the latter law is regarded as the source of legislation. However, neither the judiciary nor the Chief Justice has issued any guidelines, directives or policies (e.g. as in the case of judicial circulars) providing direction on the application of constitutional human rights *vis-à-vis* national legislation since the adoption of the BoR.

4.2 *Derogations from human rights treaties and emergency powers: Sudan's* de facto *Constitution*

The imposition of permanent or *de facto* derogations in Sudan is a real threat to the constitutional protection of human rights and the rule of law. Sudan is a country afflicted by armed conflicts and international crimes committed in multiple armed conflict zones. Human rights and humanitarian law guarantees have been constantly suspended during national emergencies.[109] Article 4 of the ICCPR (though not the ACHPR) allows States some latitude to determine the character of a public emergency and suspend the application of certain articles of human rights treaties as well as the suspension of derogable BoR provisions. This broad power of the State leaves human rights law in a precarious situation, particularly in the context of internal armed conflicts. Many abuses justified under these emergency powers have been amply documented by human rights organizations.[110] Successive governments have justified derogation from the ICCPR on various grounds. This includes the Nimeri regime (1969–85) and the transitional government represented in the Supreme Transitional Military Council and Transitional Cabinet of Ministers: (1985–1986). In January 2005, the state of emergency was lifted following the signing of the CPA. However, it remained in force in certain areas affected by the armed conflict such as Darfur, Blue Nile

108 Art 15(1) of the Constitution Court Act, 2005, confirms that the Court is the guardian of the constitution and one of its functions is the protection of rights and fundamental freedoms.

109 See Mohamed Abdelsalam Babiker, *Application of International Humanitarian Law and Human Rights Law to the Armed Conflicts of the Sudan: Complementary or Mutually Exclusive Regimes* (Intersentia 2007).

110 Ibid.

and South Kordofan. In sum, since the beginning of the armed conflicts in 1983, Sudan has enjoyed less than *two years* free of emergency rule. It has therefore virtually been subject to a permanent or *de facto* emergency. Under these circumstances, it makes sense to regard emergency powers as Sudan's *de facto* constitution.[111] Sudan's practice appears to support a position that gives States considerable latitude to derogate or suspend human rights, a view endorsed by national courts.[112]

In terms of constitutional powers to suspend human rights, the 1998 National Constitution gave the President of the Republic wide discretion to declare a state of emergency.[113] He could also declare war '*whenever he decides* that the country is subject to external aggression'.[114] The INC 2005 gives the President the same powers. The only exception is that the consent of the First Vice President is required before the President declares emergency or war.[115] These provisions provide inadequate safeguards against the imposition of emergency laws in Sudan, which have served as an enabling device to facilitate human rights violations.

5 Implementation mechanisms and constitutional guarantees of the Bill of Rights: a dichotomy between law and practice

While the current constitutional framework provides some human rights guarantees (despite the substantive gaps highlighted elsewhere in this chapter), in practical terms, the constitution has been hardly applied due to the absence of effective institutions and adequate judicial protection. The following subsections focus on the institutions and oversight mechanisms needed to enhance human rights protection in Sudan.

5.1 The judiciary and the Bill of Rights

National courts have been reluctant to challenge the executive branches of government and adopt purposive interpretations to give effect to constitutional rights. Judicial decisions rarely consider the application of international human rights law despite the fact that courts have an obligation under article 27(3) of

111 Adelsalam H Abdel Salam and Alex De Waal (eds), *The Phoenix State: Civil Society and the Future of Sudan* (The Red Sea Press 2002) 2.

112 See *Khalid Mohamed Khair v the Government of the Sudan*, in *J Jud. Dec.* (1987) 404, and *James Okolo v the Government of the Sudan*, in *J Jud Dec* (1987) 15.

113 Art 131(1) provides that the President 'may, upon the occurrence or *approach of any emergent danger*, whether it is war, invasion, blockade, disaster or epidemics, as may threaten the country, or any part thereof or the safety or economy of the same declare the state of emergency in the country, or in any part thereof, in accordance with the Constitution and the law' (emphasis added).

114 Art 135 (emphasis added).

115 See art 210 (Declaration of State of Emergency); art 211 (Powers of the President in the State of Emergency).

the INC to apply international human rights law. This judicial practice is not confined to the CPA era. Historically, courts only rarely issued decisions when interpreting the law to ensure that human rights are respected.[116] The practice since the adoption of the BoR shows that courts have failed (with few exceptions) to protect constitutional rights.[117] Examples abound.[118] Courts not only failed to address core human rights related to the administration of justice and freedom of expression but judges apparently lacked the expertise and skills when handling sensitive human rights cases.

Sudan's Constitutional Court has not effectively exercised its function of protecting constitutional rights. The INC provides the Constitutional Court with a clear mandate under articles 119–122 to protect human rights and fundamental freedoms[119] and the jurisdiction to 'adjudicate on the constitutionality of laws'.[120] However, the Constitutional Court has rarely considered international human rights law in its practice. When interpreting legislation it has not taken into account the BoR's spirit, objects and purpose, and best practices adopted in other countries.[121] The judiciary, as an institution, must guide judges to adopt purposive or golden interpretations (as in the common law system) in order to give effect to the BoR's words and spirit. The constitutional text should also dictate that judges should apply the spirit of the BoR. Any forthcoming constitution should put in place arrangements to ensure that rights guaranteed in the BoR shall not be subjected to unreasonable restrictions, particularly by means of applicable statutory law. To this end, any contradiction between the BoR and national laws shall be regarded as null and void, and the Constitutional Court be mandated to declare relevant provisions unconstitutional if they cannot be interpreted in conformity with fundamental rights.

The issue of constitutional interpretation leads to another related point, namely the need for judicial activism or judicial 'vitalization' in order to make the constitution a living document. This requires proactive, skilled and trained judges and a truly independent judiciary to assume its role. Constitutional developments in other jurisdictions testify to this reality. For example, Indian apex courts have redefined the relationship between fundamental rights and directive principles (which are not justiciable under the Constitution). The courts have approached

116 See Ali Suleiman Fadlalla, Fundamental Rights and Public Liberties in a Future (Sudanese) Constitution' (1990) Herouf J 69 (Arabic).

117 See REDRESS and Sudanese Human Rights Monitor, *Arrested Development: Sudan's Constitutional Court, Access to Justice and the Effective Protection of Human Rights* (2012).

118 *Kamal Mohammed Saboon v Government of Sudan*, Constitutional Court, 2009; *Faroug Mohamed Ibrahim Alnour v (1) Government of the Sudan; Legislative Body*, Final order by Justice Abdalla Aalamin Albashir President of the Constitutional Court (6 November 2008).

119 Art 122(1)(d) INC 2005.

120 Art 122n(1)(e) ibid.

121 See e.g. art 39(1) of the South African Constitution: 'When interpreting the Bill of Rights, a court, tribunal or forum (a) must promote the values that underlie an open and democratic society based on human dignity, equality and freedom; (b) must consider international law; and (c) may consider foreign law.'

the two categories in an integral manner, one result of which is to give some directive principles the status of fundamental rights.[122]

5.2 Institutional security sector reform

Article 151 of the INC 2005 envisaged that laws governing institutions such as the NISS (National Security Forces Act of 1999) be reformed. The goal was to bring the law in line with the CPA's vision that the National Security Force should only have a limited mandate to gather information and provide analysis and advice to appropriate authorities.[123] However, the 2010 NISS Act maintains the extensive powers of arrest and detention that were given to the NISS under the 1999 National Security Forces Act, contrary to article 151. It also maintains the immunity from prosecution that was granted to NISS members and fails to introduce the necessary guarantees to prevent arbitrary detentions, torture and other ill-treatment.[124] The constitutional amendments of 2017 repealed article 151 and replaced it with a new article, without, however, removing immunities of NISS. Furthermore, NISS was recognized as a security force, rather than purely an intelligence agency, vested with an array of new constitutionally sanctioned powers, including fighting terrorism, money laundering, and 'human trafficking and transnational crimes through regional and international cooperation',[125] thereby apparently sending a message to European countries that NISS can play an effective role in controlling migration through the Khartoum process.[126] Furthermore, the amended article 151 provided NISS with the constitutional right to establish NISS courts under a special Act to set out their powers, competences and jurisdiction to try their own forces.[127]

Any effective constitutional review process in Sudan should include (as a priority) what is commonly referred to as security sector reform (SSR) (i.e. police, security services, military). It is unfortunate, however, that the new constitutional amendments made NISS directly accountable to the President of the Republic; the latter is only required to provide reports and attend hearing before special parliamentary committees.[128] The amendments are silent on whether these committees have oversight powers over the President's or NISS's decisions on the

122 See *Olga Tellis v Bombay Municipal Corporation*, Supreme Court of India (July 1985) SCC3, 535 holding that the right to life under art 21 of the Indian Constitution includes the right to livelihood (art 37(a) of the Indian Constitution).

123 See for a thorough analysis, REDRESS and SORD, *Security for All-Reforming Sudan's National Security Service* (2009).

124 Amnesty International, *Agents of Fear: National Security Service in Sudan* (2010) Index: AFR 54/010/2010.

125 Art 151(3) INC 2005 (amendments 2017).

126 See Lutz Oette and Mohamed Abdelsalam Babiker, 'Migration Control à la Khartoum: EU External Engagement and Human Rights Protection in the Horn of Africa' (2017) 36 *RSQ* 64.

127 Art 151(7) INC 2005 (amendments 2017).

128 Art 151(4) ibid.

existing powers of arrest and detention, immunities of NISS forces, particularly by means of parliamentary and judicial oversight. Given the negative track record of constitutions, SSR remains at the heart of any constitutional reforms in Sudan.

5.3 Commissions and oversight bodies

The CPA and the INC established several commissions to function as oversight bodies mandated with the protection of human rights, envisaging such bodies to play an effective supervisory role, in particular the National Constitution Review Commission (NCRC),[129] the National Human Rights Commission (NHRC)[130] and the National Judicial Service Commission (NJSC).[131] The NCRC could have been an important actor with regard to law reform and harmonization of national laws with the constitution. In practice, however, it has largely failed to address the apparent dichotomy between constitutional human rights norms and existing legislation. During the CPA implementation (2005–11), the lack of a transparent process of law reform was evident and designated bodies such as the NCRC had limited powers and operational independence. Although the CPA identified specific laws that need to be reformed, and provided for the establishment of the NCRC to ensure compatibility with the CPA and the INC 2005, limited progress has been made.[132] One of the constitutional gaps is that it does not envisage establishing a Law Reform Commission, as in the case of other jurisdictions such as Uganda and South Africa which often have important roles in initiating or framing processes of law reform that are transparent and inclusive.[133]

Other commissions such as the NHRC could play an effective role in the protection and promotion of human rights. It was created by an Act of parliament in 2009 and its members were appointed in January 2012. Its establishment has the potential to strengthen the system of national human rights protection if properly constituted and resourced, and if commissioners act with independence from the executive branches of government. The Act vests the Commission with a mandate to monitor the application of the BoR rights and freedoms, as well as the powers to receive complaints of violations[134] and to ensure harmonization of laws

129 Art 140(1) ibid.
130 Art 142 ibid.
131 Art 129 ibid.
132 See REDRESS, *Promoting Law Reform in Sudan to Enhance Human Rights Protection, Strengthen the Rule of Law and Foster Democratic Processes* (15 October 2009), available at www.pclrs.org and www.redress.org/country_sudan.html, accessed 15 April 2018.
133 See Lutz Oette, 'Future Perspectives: Debating Criminal Law Reform and Human Rights in Sudan' in Oette (n 40) 297–301.
134 Art 9(2)(h) provides that the Commission is tasked to 'receive complaints from individuals and other bodies and to conduct investigations thereon and to take the necessary measures in accordance with the provisions of this Act or any other law and to recommend appropriate remedies to the relevant body'.

with the BoR.[135] However, there are a number of gaps in the Act that may hinder the Commission's ability to carry out its mandate effectively and independently, particularly in relation to the Commission's quasi-judicial competence to deal with complaints and investigate human rights violations *proprio motu*. Another area of concern is the selection and appointment process for the Commission's members, which is largely controlled by the executive.[136] For the past six years, it is obvious that many of the commissioners are government appointees who are not acting independently and with integrity. During this period the Commission has not published a single public report about the massive human rights and humanitarian law violations taking place in Sudan, including those in war zones.

Other commissions include the NJSC whose main purpose is to initiate the process of institutional reform of the judiciary.[137] The philosophy behind its establishment was to act as a supervisory body over the work of the judiciary. However, there are concerns that the body has not been able to perform its envisaged role and progressively achieve judicial reform and independence. The Commission was expected to focus on substantive issues including the promotion of the rule of law and judicial independence but instead has concentrated on procedural issues (i.e. removal and disciplinary of judges, conditions of service). As a result, its work did not lead to genuine and tangible changes in the actual performance of the judiciary in terms of public confidence and accessibility. It has not acted as a real supervisory body over the judiciary because the Chief Justice is the Head of the Commission and he is in a position to set its agenda and define its actual role. Further, the Commission has not addressed critical issues and adopted policies with regard to frequently raised concerns about judicial independence. This includes in particular judicial competence over judicial work and the interference of the Ministry of Justice in the work of the judiciary by staying or dismissing proceedings. Other issues include the role of the judiciary with regard to special courts, public order courts and immunities granted to law enforcement officials. The constitutional amendments of 2017 replaced the NJSC and established the High Judicial Council (HJC). Unlike the NJSC, the HJC was reinstated (a body operating before the CPA) and given a supervisory judicial role over the national judiciary under article 129 of the INC 2005 (amendments 2017). Its new powers include recommending to the President of the Republic the nomination of judges (including Constitutional Court judges), appointment of judges, promotion of judges, removal of judges, preparing the judiciary budget and providing input on

135 Art 9(2)(k) provides that the Commission shall 'endeavor to harmonize national legislations and practices with human rights standards'.

136 Art 6 provides that 'the Commission shall be composed of fifteen members appointed by the President of the Republic after consultations at the Presidency and obtainment of the approval of the First Vice President'.

137 Art 129 of the INC 2005 provides that the President of the Republic, after consultation within the Presidency, shall establish the National Judicial Service Commission to undertake the overall management of the National Judiciary.

the enactment of laws concerning the judiciary.[138] The new role of the HJC is distinct from the role of the NJSC. The HJC is now an integral part of the judicial authority while the NJSC was not part of the judicial authority but only used to have a supervisory role. One of the new aspects of this amendment is that the HJC (as the highest judicial authority) has full powers to nominate and recommend to the President of the Republic to appoint and remove judges. However, the article is silent in cases where the President refuses to endorse nominations or recommendations made to him by the HJC.

6 Conclusion

The INC 2005 constitutes a major achievement in Sudan's constitutional history. Yet, several of the CPR and ESCR enshrined in the INC 2005 were not recognized or defined in conformity with international human rights standards. Further, the various constitutional amendments of the INC 2005 between 2011 and 2017 have undermined human rights protection instead of adequately addressing existing shortcomings. These changes have taken place in the absence of any official debate on the status of international human rights law and the modalities of its incorporation in Sudan's hybrid legal system. The constitutional protection of human rights cannot be attained by virtue of mere textual recognition of substantive BoR provisions. Constitutional rights guarantees need to be complemented by legislative and institutional reforms, particularly security sector reform, judicial independence, parliamentary oversight and reform of CPA oversight bodies entrusted with the protection of human rights. The widespread human rights violations are due to the absence of effective institutional mechanisms that can subject such bodies to oversight and accountability. In turn, the effectiveness of these bodies requires a political system and modes of governance that take the separation of powers seriously. In order for human rights and rule of law to prevail in Sudan, constitutional protection of rights will remain at 'the textual level' and will not be worth the 'ink with which it was written' in the absence of constitutionalism and rule of law.

138 Art 129(3) INC 2005 (amendments 2017).

5 Citizenship, statelessness and human rights protection in Sudan's constitutions and post South Sudan secession challenges

Munzoul A. M. Assal

1 Introduction

What remained of Sudan after the secession/independence of South Sudan in July 2011 continues to be a deeply divided territory and a contested State[1] with an ever mounting crisis between the government and citizens. Contrary to the euphoria of some people in the North – that secession is for the good of Sudan – spaces for belonging have further contracted leading to shrinking spaces of citizenship in the country. The secession of South Sudan led to the loss of territory and resources, and also to new conflicts (in the Nuba Mountains and Blue Nile). The ruling party in Sudan has since toughened its political rhetoric, a development that threatens to further divide the country. It should, nonetheless, be made clear at the outset that the divided nature of Sudan and the crisis between successive governments and citizens are not a post-secession phenomenon. These are deep-rooted issues that are part of the wrap and woof of a troubled identity and unequal citizenship in the country.

Unequal citizenship has been at the heart of political instability in Sudan since 1956. It is the inequality in citizenship that led to the first civil war (1955–72), the second civil war (1983–2005), the Darfur conflict (2003–), current armed conflicts in South Kordofan and Blue Nile, and eventually to the secession of South Sudan in July 2011. Sudan is characterized by multiple diversities in religion and ethnicity. According to Madibbo,

> elitist debates confined the country's diverse identities to two dichotomous categorizations: Arabism, associated with Islam and Arabic descent and culture, and Africanism, linked to Christianity, indigenous beliefs and African culture. These polarized views, along with the dominant ideology of the imposition of Arabism and Islam as the basis of national identification, triggered a national identity crisis.[2]

1 Gunnar Sørbø and Abdel Ghaffar M Ahmed, *Sudan Divided: Continuing Conflict in a Contested State* (Palgrave Macmillan 2013).

2 Amal Madibbo, 'Conflict and conceptions of identities in Sudan' (2012) 60 *Curr Soc* 302.

The country has been torn between Arab and African belonging or blocs that largely reflect broader societal divides; its dominant elites want it to be appended to the Arab and Islamic worlds, while the less privileged want it to be part of an African world.[3] This tension between Arab/Islamic and African/Christian identities is at the heart of Sudan's citizenship problem. Sudan suffers multiple marginalities – something expressed in a mischievous popular Sudanese saying: 'instead of being the best of the Africans, we became the worst of the Arabs.' It is the failure to manage this diversity that led to a troubled and unequal citizenship, where some people are more 'equal' than others when it comes to enjoying citizenship rights. Even with the secession/independence of South Sudan, the ruling political elite, instead of drawing lessons from this problematic legacy, has since embraced and reinforced the same 'unity in conformity' perspective. It has done so by looking at what remained of old Sudan as a homogeneous entity, thus perpetuating and entrenching the same mistakes that led to the secession of South Sudan. As a matter of fact, the ruling National Congress Party (NCP) referred to the post-2011 Sudan as the 'second republic',[4] and deemed it an Islamic State (see the statement of President Omer Al-Bashir below).[5]

In essence, instead of expanding citizenship, post-secession Sudan is witnessing a shrinking of citizenship space. The main argument of this chapter is that enforcing unity through conformity disenfranchises people and compromises their citizenship rights. Furthermore, it argues that access to citizenship rights is highly stratified. Where one comes from determines how easy, or difficult, it is to obtain identity papers and to access rights. The chapter also contends that any notion of a homogenous Sudan following South Sudan's secession/independence is fallacious and problematic from a rights perspective. The secession of South Sudan created new challenges, particularly concerning the status of individuals with links to South Sudan, which is especially complex in respect of mixed marriages and children. It also brought to the fore long-standing, but neglected, problems of citizenship, particularly in the context of the armed conflicts that erupted in the Nuba Mountains and Blue Nile in June 2011 and September 2011 respectively.[6] The status of Abyei and its population also remains unresolved.[7]

3 Munzoul AM Assal, 'The Question of identity in Sudan: new dimensions for an old problem' (2009) 34 *Maghr Rev* 181; Sharif Harir, 'Recycling the past in the Sudan: an overview of political decay' in Sharif Harir and Terje Tvedt (eds), *Short-Cut to Decay: The Case of the Sudan* (Nordic Africa Institute 1994).

4 Einas Ahmed, 'The National Congress Party and the "Second Republic": internal dynamics and political hegemony', in Sørbø (n 1).

5 James Copnall, *A Poisonous Thorn in Our Hearts: Sudan and South Sudan's Bitter and Incomplete Divorce* (OUP 2014) 49.

6 Wendy James, 'Strategic movement: a key theme in Sudan anthropology' in Munzoul A.M. Assal and Musa Adam Abdul-Jalil (eds), *Past, Present, and Future: Fifty Years of Anthropology in Sudan* (Chr Michelsen Institute 2015).

7 Abdalbasit Saeed, *Challenges Facing Sudan after Referendum Day 2011: Persistent and Emerging Conflict in the North-South Borderline States* (Chr Michelsen Institute 2011).

2 Constitutional guarantees of nationality and citizenship rights

Successive Sudanese constitutions have accorded substantive protection to the right to nationality, including the constitutions of 1956, 1964, 1973, 1985 and 1998.[8] The 2005 Interim National Constitution (INC) of Sudan, currently in force, guarantees the right to nationality. Its article 7 stipulates that:

1 Citizenship shall be the basis for equal rights and duties for all Sudanese.
2 Every person born to a Sudanese mother or father shall have an inalienable right to enjoy Sudanese nationality and citizenship.
3 The law shall regulate citizenship and naturalization; no naturalized Sudanese shall be deprived of his/her acquired citizenship except in accordance with the law.
4 A Sudanese national may acquire the nationality of another country as shall be regulated by law.

Article 7(2) is a reiteration of article 22 of the repealed Constitution of the Republic of Sudan 1998, which had equally acknowledged the inalienable right of every person born to a Sudanese mother or father to obtain the Sudanese nationality.[9] Article 22 of the INC enshrines several notable principles and protections: citizenship is not based on race, religion or tribe; dual citizenship is permitted; and nationality may only be renounced according to the provisions of the law. The INC's Bill of Rights provides for other civil and political rights connected with the equal protection of citizenship rights on the basis of non-discrimination. Article 31 stipulates that '[a]ll persons are equal before the law and are entitled without discrimination, as to race, colour, sex, language, religious creed, political opinion, or ethnic origin, to the equal protection of the law'. These constitutional provisions are in conformity with international and regional human rights instruments related to nationality, albeit with the proviso that they do not explicitly include the protection required by the African Charter on the Rights and Welfare of the Child that a child born in Sudan shall acquire Sudanese nationality if he or she does not acquire any other nationality at birth.[10]

8 Art 22 of the 1998 Constitution states: 'Every person born to a Sudanese mother or father shall have a non-alienable right to enjoy the country's nationality and its rights and bear its obligations. Whoever is brought up or is resident in the Sudan for several years shall have the right to nationality as regulated by law.'

9 Although the 1998 Constitution is no longer in effect, it is, as per art 226(1) of the INC 2005, one of the sources of the INC. Republic of the Sudan Gazette, Special supplement No (1) 1419 A.H - 1998 A.D. Ministry of Justice, Republic of the Sudan.

10 Art 6(3) of the African Charter on the Rights and Welfare of the Child, CAB/LEG/153/Rev. 2 (adopted on 1 July 1990, entry into force 29 November 1999).

This international treaty to which Sudan is a party is an integral part of Sudan's legal system, as provided for under article 27(3) of the INC 2005.[11]

Sudanese constitutions, since 1973, have provided for nationality and citizenship rights that govern Sudan's nationality regime. However, limited attention has been paid to the question of citizenship (as in the case of other rights) in terms of public participation in Sudan's elitist constitution-making processes. These processes have lacked popular participation, both at the stage of deliberation and at the adoption stage. There is no instance where a constitution was put to a popular vote or referendum in Sudan. In reality, constitutions in Sudan have reflected the interests of the dominant or ruling political elite, more than being a genuine document that guarantees and protects citizenship rights. The only exception is the 2005 INC, which embodied the spirit of the moment although it reflects the views of the political and military powers who signed the CPA. While it is an elitist document, it is by far the best in the history of Sudanese constitutions in terms of guaranteeing rights. For example, article 27(1) of the INC is advanced with regard to citizenship rights, evoking, for the first time in any Sudanese constitution, the notion of a social contract between the governed and their government:

> The Bill of Rights is a covenant among the Sudanese people and between them and their governments at every level and a commitment to respect and promote human rights and fundamental freedoms enshrined in this Constitution; it is the cornerstone of social justice, equality and democracy in the Sudan.

The absence of popular participation in the process of constitution-making, and democratic processes and checks and balances more broadly, is reflected in the lack of respect for the constitution in legislation adopted after 2005. While articles 7 (citizenship and nationality) and 27 of the INC's Bill of Rights guarantee citizenship rights, there are a number of nationality laws that contradict them. The 1994 Nationality Act was amended in 2005 and in 2011. The latter amendment resulted in rendering thousands of South Sudanese stateless and arbitrarily losing their entitlement to nationality and citizenship rights. This shows that the legal framework in Sudan is flawed, providing limited, protection against a denial or abuse of citizenship rights in the absence of an accessible and rights-conscious Constitutional Court.[12] It is therefore unsurprising that at the dawn of South Sudan's secession, South Sudanese or those with origins from South Sudan were

11 Art 27(3) reads: 'All rights and freedoms enshrined in international human rights treaties, covenants and instruments ratified by the Republic of the Sudan shall be an integral part of this Bill.'

12 The fee to file a case before the constitutional court is high for ordinary people, hence it is not accessible to all. See further REDRESS and Sudanese Human Rights Monitor, *Arrested Development: Sudan's Constitutional Court, Access to Justice and the Effective Protection of Human Rights* (August 2012).

made stateless as shall be seen in the next section. This chapter addresses relevant legal issues, focusing on the constitutional and legal developments in Sudan and their impact on the question of citizenship rights, situating them within a sociological analysis of the shrinking spaces of citizenship in Sudan that builds on my earlier work on the struggle of citizenship in Sudan.[13]

3 Historical legacy and continuing flaws

Even before independence in 1956, the political elite in Sudan has consistently attempted to project an identity that is not consonant with what the facts tell about Sudan, namely that it is a multiethnic, multicultural and multi-religious country.[14] The Sudanese nationalist movement that preceded independence was actually the genesis of such projection.[15] Language and religion (Arabic and Islam) were, and continue to be, its pillars. While these were the language and religion of the majority, there are linguistic and religious minorities. These minorities include hundreds of tribes, unorthodox Muslim groups, Christians, and those adhering to their own traditional beliefs in the Nuba Mountains and Blue Nile.[16] The State should be an entity that represents and serves everybody who happens to be part of it and under its sovereignty, irrespective of whether they belong to the majority or a minority. The projection of an imagined identity[17] that conforms to something Arabic and Islamic presumes that Sudan is a nation-state. But Sudan never was.

There are many theoretical contributions that have addressed issues pertaining to nation, nationalism and citizenship. Eric Hobsbawm, Mahmood Mamdani, Toyin Falola and Ernest Gellner, among others, have placed nationalism and citizenship in broad perspective, looking at the role of history, culture, traditions and ethnicity in the formation of nations and the concept of nationalism.[18] Ethnic revival in many societies has turned the attention of both the public and

13 Munzoul AM Assal, 'Struggles of citizenship in Sudan' in Engin F Isin and Peter Nyers (eds), *Routledge Handbook of Global Citizenship Studies* (Routledge 2014).

14 Ali Mazrui, 'The multiple marginality of the Sudan' in Yusuf Fadl Hassan (ed.), *Sudan in Africa: Studies Presented to the First International Conference Sponsored by the Sudan Research Unit, 7–12 February 1968* (Khartoum University Press 1985); Paul Wani Gore, 'Contemporary issues in ethnic relations: problems of national integration in Sudan' in Sayed HA Hurreiz and Elfatih Abdullahi Abdelsalam (eds), *Ethnicity, Conflict and National Integration in the Sudan* (Institute of African and Asian Studies 1989).

15 Muddathir Abdel-Rahim, *Imperialism and Nationalism in the Sudan: A Study in Constitutional and Political Development* (Clarendon Press 1969).

16 James Gore, *The Ceremonial Animal: A New Portrait of Anthropology* (OUP 2004).

17 See further Benedict Anderson, *Imagined Communities: Reflections on the Origin and Spread of Nationalism* (Verso 2006).

18 Eric Hobsbawm, *Nations and Nationalism since 1780: Programme, Myth, Reality* (CUP 1990); Mahmood Mamdani, *Citizen and Subject: Contemporary Africa and the Legacy of Late Colonialism* (Princeton University Press 1996); Toyin Falola, *Nationalism and African Intellectuals* (University of Rochester Press 2004); Ernest Gellner, *Nations and Nationalism* (Blackwell 2006).

the academic community to the issues posed by ethnic nationalism. The war in the Balkans during the 1990s and other places in the world, and the ensuing divisions and re-divisions of States brought both new challenges and insights into nations and nationalism, and also to the question of citizenship. In the African context, States are facing mounting postcolonial challenges which include civil and ethnic wars that impinge on citizenship rights.[19] In response, the African Union (AU) is developing a new citizenship framework, which is contemplating an 'African Passport'.[20] It is thus breaking away from ethnic nationalism that was part and parcel of the struggle for independence. For countries such as Sudan, AU moves towards pan-African unity throw internal divisions and discrimination against minorities into stark relief.

Francis Fukuyama, Kenichi Ohmae, Montserrat Guibernau and Jean-François Bayart offer critical analyses of the concepts of State, nation and nation-state.[21] They deal with the challenges entailed in defining State borders, the effects of globalization on the nation-state and on citizenship, and the question of sovereignty. The concepts of nation and State are basic to any discussion of nationality and citizenship. On the one hand, a State is a self-governing political entity, with internationally recognized borders and a government that provides public services and police power. It enjoys sovereignty, meaning that no other State has authority over the country's territory, and, commonly, external recognition. A nation, on the other hand, is normally defined as a culturally homogeneous group of people, larger than a single community, which shares a common historical experience and set of institutions, generally including a common language and often a common religion. When a nation has a State or country of its own, it is called a nation-state. This definition of nation implies, however, that a nation can exist without a corresponding State. Large groups that overlap State boundaries, such as the Kurds who are scattered across Iraq, Syria, Iran and Turkey, may constitute such stateless nations.[22] In practice, the realities of States and nations are much more complex than can be captured by these formal definitions.[23] States may be defined precisely by international recognition, rather than by their correspondence to any nation. In addition, the definitions of nation and of 'nation-state' are subject to a wide range of understandings and views that may not be congruent.

19 Mamdani ibid; Bronwen Manby, *Struggles for Citizenship in Africa* (Zed Books 2009).

20 African Union, 'African Union passport launched during opening of 2nd AU Summit in Kigali' (16 July 2016).

21 Francis Fukuyama, *State-Building: Governance and World Order in the 21tst Century* (Cornell University Press 2004); Kenichi Ohmae, *The End of the Nation State: The Rise of Regional Economies* (Free Press 1993); Montserrat Guibernau, 'Nations without States: political communities in the global age' (2003) 25 *Mich JIL* 1251; Jean-François Bayart, *The State in Africa: The Politics of the Belly* (Longman 1993).

22 Guibernau ibid.

23 Liisa Malkki, 'National Geographic: the rooting of peoples and the territorialization of national identity among scholars and refugees' (1992) 7 *Cult Anth* 24; Malkki, *Purity and Exile: Violence, Memory and National Cosmology among Hutu Refugees in Tanzania* (University of Chicago Press 1995).

Sudan, with its pre-referendum and post-referendum boundaries, is a State, but it cannot be viewed as a nation-state, owing to the striking heterogeneity that characterizes it. It is on the basis of recognizing such heterogeneity that some scholars have called for the deconstruction of dominant conceptions of Sudanese identities. Instead, they have proposed multiculturalism as a model that could help to accommodate the country's diverse identities and foster stability.[24] However, the notion of multiculturalism as a liberal model has itself been criticized in recent scholarly literature as it is regarded as a tool through which minorities could be assimilated in the dominant or mainstream culture.[25]

Some of the flaws and challenges facing citizenship in Sudan today are historical and predicated in colonial legal frameworks and policies.[26] The British–Egyptian condominium (1899–1956) introduced a formal system based on English common law. Until the period of that condominium over the territory of Sudan, there was no Sudanese nationality as such. In 1948, the Definition of Sudanese Ordinance was the first formal document to describe who fell under the jurisdiction of the condominium. The ordinance defined a Sudanese as '[e]very person of no nationality who is domiciled in Sudan and has been so domiciled since 31 December 1897, or else whose ancestors in the direct male line since that date have all been so domiciled or who is the wife or widow of such a person'. The Ordinance therefore combined an automatic grant of nationality based on domicile, irrespective of place of birth (*jus soli*), with a male biased descent (*jus sanguinis*) rule.

It was not until after the independence of Sudan in 1956 that the first real nationality law was adopted.[27] The 1957 Act, amended several times, in 1963, 1970, 1972 and 1974, remained effective until 1994. Its article 5 provided that a person born before the Act came into effect was Sudanese if born in Sudan or if his (or her) father was born in Sudan, and he or his direct male ancestors had been domiciled in Sudan since December 1897 (prior to the defeat of the Mahdist forces).[28] A 1959 amendment gave the Minister of the Interior discretion to grant nationality to a person who and whose fathers were not born in Sudan, if the other conditions relating to domicile of male ancestors were fulfilled. A child born after the act came into force was Sudanese if his or her father was Sudanese at the time of birth (whether by descent or by naturalization).

24 Madibbo (n 2).

25 See further Will Kymlicka, *Multiculturalism: Success, Failure and the Future* (Transatlantic Council on Migration 2012). Others argue that multiculturalism may lead to integration but not assimilation. Vani K Borooah and John Mangan, 'Multiculturalism versus assimilation: attitudes towards immigrants in Western countries' (2009) 2 *Int J Ec Sc & App Res* 33.

26 Christopher Zambakari, 'Post-referendum Sudan: the nation-building project and its challenges' (2012) 9 *Rutgers JLPP* 505; Zambakari 'Sudan and South Sudan: identity, citizenship, and democracy in plural societies' (2015) 19 *Citiz Stud* 69.

27 For an outline of this history, see Bronwen Manby, *The Right to Nationality and Secession of South Sudan: A Commentary on the Impact of the New Laws* (Open Society Initiative for Eastern Africa 2012) 18. See also Nasredeen Abdulbari, 'Citizenship rules in Sudan and post-secession problems' (2011) 55 *JAL* 157.

28 This date was later amended to 1 January 1924.

However, children born before the naturalization of their father did not benefit from their father's naturalization, although the Minister could exercise his discretion to grant nationality to the child at the same time as to the father in favour of the child (article 8). A foreign woman married to a Sudanese man could apply for naturalization based on two years' residence in Sudan with her husband and renunciation of her previous nationality (article 9). Thus, the colonial authorities: 'and their Sudanese successors' had made descent as well as domicile in Sudan the basis of citizenship. However, colonial policies on citizenship were informed by some of the problematic anthropological writings of authors such as Harold MacMichael about genealogies of Sudanese tribes and particularly of Arabs, which continued to inform Sudanese law post-independence.[29]

The colonial nationality framework continued until the 1957 Nationality Act was replaced by the 1994 Sudanese Nationality Act.[30] The 1994 Act remains in force, as amended in 2005 (following the adoption of the INC) and again in 2011 (following the secession of South Sudan). Article 4 of the 1994 Nationality Act stipulated the following conditions for recognition of nationality at birth:

(1) With regard to persons born before the coming into force of this Act, a person shall be a Sudanese by birth:

  (a) If he has already acquired a certificate of Sudanese nationality by birth;
  (b) (i) If he was born in Sudan or his father was born in Sudan, or
    (ii) If he is resident in Sudan at the time of coming into force of this Act and he and his ancestors in the male line were resident in Sudan since 1 January 1956;
  (c) If neither the person nor his father were born in Sudan, he may, if he satisfies the requirements of para. (b)(ii), apply to the Minister to grant him Sudanese Nationality by birth.

(2) A person born after the coming into effect of this Act shall be a Sudanese by birth if at the time of his birth his father was a Sudanese citizen by birth;
(3) A person born to a parent who is Sudanese by naturalization shall be a Sudanese by birth if his or her parents acquired Sudanese nationality by naturalization before his birth.

The 1994 Act thus initially displayed a male bias, as it restricted transmission of nationality by descent through the male line, though shifting the date from which domicile should commence to 1956, the date of independence. The only exception was for abandoned children of unknown parents, who were presumed to be Sudanese by birth until the contrary was proved (article 5). A mother's nationality

29 Harold MacMichael, *History of the Arabs in the Sudan (Volume 1)* (CUP 1922).

30 Provisional Decree No 18 of 18 August 1993, amended and approved by Transitional National Resolution No 59 of 3 May 1994, and signed into law by the President on 17 May 1994.

was only considered when a child's father was unknown. The law did not include a provision providing for the acquisition of Sudanese nationality by a child born in the territory who could not acquire the nationality of one of his or her parents, thereby creating the risk that such child would be rendered stateless. In 2005 major changes occurred in Sudan's nationality laws as a result of the signing of the CPA and adoption of the INC. Article 7(2) of the 2005 INC (Nationality and Citizenship) recognizes that '[e]very person born to a Sudanese mother or father shall have an inalienable right to enjoy Sudanese nationality and citizenship'. Similarly, amendments to the Nationality Act adopted in 2005 inserted a new article 7(3) of the Nationality Act whereby '[a] person born of a Sudanese mother by birth is entitled to the Sudanese nationality by birth whenever he[31] submits an application for it'.[32] This law reform and constitutional amendments marked the first time that women were given the right to pass on their citizenship to their children, regardless of the citizenship of their spouse. Although this constitutional amendment is a progressive step, it remains gender discriminatory, in terms of procedure. A man's citizenship is passed to his children automatically, whereas a mother's citizenship can only be passed to her children after an application process.

The law thus provides for a predominantly descent-based (*jus sanguinis*) framework for nationality law.[33] This approach constitutes an important contributing factor for many postcolonial conflicts in Africa which revolve around the question of citizenship: who belongs and who does not belong. African countries did not reform colonial systems and Sudan is a good example of the failure of the African State to reform the colonial citizenship system and build an inclusive and equitable society. Along the same lines, Zambakari argued that the colonial system of indirect rule resulted in politicizing race and ethnicity in Sudan.[34] Tribes were given homelands, and tribal leaders were vested with the authority of tax collection and even judicial powers over their subjects.[35] In applying for nationality, a tribal subject had to secure the support or testimony of a tribal leader. The fact that other objective evidence was not sufficient to prove nationality fostered dependency and personalized nationality as an expression of loyalty to tribal leaders, with the colonial State lurking in their shadows. However, the system also had a pragmatic component. Tribal leaders were used in the process of proving the acquisition of nationality, which was largely due to the fact that they were community leaders and were able to recognize their own fellows as members of

31 Note that the legislation continued to use the male pronoun only.

32 See *Study on Nationality and Statelessness in Sudan Following the Secession of South Sudan*, compiled and edited by Mohamed Abdelsalam Babiker and Bronwen Manby (Faculty of Law, Khartoum University Press forthcoming) 22–3.

33 Babiker and Manby ibid.

34 Zambakari 2015 (n 26) 73–4.

35 Talal Asad, *The Kababish Arabs: Power, Authority and Consent in a Nomadic Tribe* (Hurst & Co 1970).

their own community. This was an essential part of the identification process in the absence of proper documentation.

Basing citizenship (nationality) on descent (*jus sanguinis*) allows ethnicity to become an instrument of abuse by various parties for political purposes. As already mentioned above, social stratification is entrenched where some groups consider themselves superior to others. Categories like *gharraba* (people from western Sudan), *gannobiyyin* (people from southern Sudan), *shimaliyyin* (people from northern Sudan) and *zurga* (blacks) are terms widely used in Sudan that have derogatory connotations.[36] Accordingly, some persons face difficulty in obtaining papers due to their ethnic background, while for others ethnic background is not an issue.[37] Tellingly, the former cases were from western Sudan (Darfur) while the latter were from central Sudan. Due to conflicts, individuals and communities are displaced from their original areas to other places where it takes them a long time to establish their lives. This is particularly the case in multiethnic States like Sudan and in countries with protracted conflicts that lead to population displacement.[38] Where people are forced to leave their traditional or habitual areas as a result of war or forced displacement, they often find it difficult to prove their citizenship. The challenge is how to devise a system that overcomes colonial shortcomings and takes into account the changing circumstances that resulted from wars and massive population displacement. The following section addresses some legal ambiguities surrounding nationality/citizenship rights in Sudan.

4 Nationality vs citizenship in Sudan: legal ambiguities

In Sudan, both law and common discourse focus on nationality (*jinsiya*) rather than on citizenship (*muwatana*). Yet these two terms are often used interchangeably even though, compared to nationality, citizenship has a precise legal meaning that provides access to specific rights.[39] In other words, citizenship is understood to relate to exercising rights, while nationality refers to belonging to a certain community or society. Sociologically speaking, citizenship is closely linked to the concept of rights as may be defined by national and international law, while nationality is a more ambiguous term which is closely associated with subjective understandings of community.[40] Nationality is often defined and used more broadly, with reference to origin and to membership in a culturally defined

36 Harir (n 3) 10–68.

37 Munzoul AM Assal, *Nationality and Citizenship Questions in Sudan after the Southern Sudan Referendum Vote* (Sudan Report Series No 1 Chr Michelsen Institute 2011).

38 See report of the Special Rapporteur on the human rights of internally displaced persons, Chaloka Beyani, *Addendum: Mission to Sudan*, UN doc A/HRC/23/44/Add.2 (25 June 2013).

39 Assal 2013 (n 13).

40 See for the notion of nationality and citizenship in international law, Alice Edwards and Laura van Waas (eds), *Nationality and Statelessness under International Law* (CUP 2014).

community,[41] and may refer to membership in an ethno-national group that need not be established as an independent State.[42] By failing to distinguish between these understandings of nationality and citizenship Sudanese law and discourse blur the distinction between cultural origin and rights given by the State. Both law and discourse place particular emphasis on ancestry as nationality is by descent. This model of *jus sanguinis* has been strongly endorsed in Sudan, to the extent that naturalized foreigners have fewer rights than those who belong to the country by blood.[43] In countries with multiethnic groups like Sudan, where ethnicity[44] provides the basis for stratification, the emphasis on ancestry has resulted in disenfranchising those who cannot establish that their ancestors belong to the country.

The question of deprivation of nationality of South Sudanese not only reflects the level of racism and sheer discrimination against them but also a violation of the right to nationality enshrined in article 7 of the Bill of Rights. Following the results of the 2011 referendum, Sudan's legislative framework fundamentally changed in July 2011. The Sudan National Assembly adopted amendments to the 1994 National Act (amendments 2011) in relation to the deprivation of nationality of southern Sudanese. Under its article 10(2) 'a person automatically loses his Sudanese nationality if he has acquired, de jure or de facto, the nationality of South Sudan'. It is quite obvious that article 10(2) arbitrarily deprives South Sudanese of their Sudanese nationality. In addition, it has made many persons stateless, because they cannot in fact acquire South Sudanese nationality.[45] Similarly, article 10(3) of the Act strips a minor of Sudanese nationality if his or her guardian acquires the nationality of South Sudan as prescribed in article 10(2). It is thus a recipe for the creation of statelessness of children, in particular those born after the secession of South Sudan.[46] This is in direct violation of the 'inalienable right' under the constitution of a child to Sudanese nationality if one parent is Sudanese, without qualification as to the nationality of the other parent.[47] The amendment also does not contain procedural safeguards to ensure that no individuals will lose their Sudanese nationality or be rendered stateless in the interim between the loss and acquisition of the nationality.[48] In practice, newspapers in Khartoum abound with reports of court cases concerning children, born to southern Sudanese fathers and Sudanese mothers, who are deprived of

41 Assal 2011 (n 37).
42 Rainer Bauböck, 'Citizenship and migration: concepts and controversies' in Rainer Bauböck (ed.) *Migration and Citizenship: Legal Status, Rights and Political Participation* (Amsterdam University Press 2006).
43 Assal 2011 (n 37) 3–4.
44 For a definition of ethnicity see Fredrik Barth, 'Ethnic groups and boundaries: introduction' in Barth (ed.), *Ethnic Groups and Boundaries: The Social Organization of Cultural Difference* (Universitetsforlaget 1969).
45 Babiker and Manby (n 32) 25–6.
46 Ibid.
47 Ibid.
48 Ibid.

citizenship.[49] Affected individuals have challenged the constitutionality of amendments of article 10(2) of the Nationality Act and its impact on denationalization of southern Sudanese before Sudan's Constitutional Court.[50] Following these challenges, on 25 February 2018, the Council of Ministers approved an amendment to the Sudanese Nationality Act to grant the nationality to any citizen born to a Sudanese mother and a South Sudanese father similar to the status of the sons of Sudanese mothers from foreign fathers of other nationals.[51]

In addition to the Nationality Act, other laws were employed to deprive South Sudanese of their inherent right to nationality. For example, prior to the introduction of the civil registration system under the Civil Registration Act of 2011, an elaborate and meticulous screening process and procedures were in place for the issuance of a nationality certificate.[52] Applying for a nationality certificate was often disenfranchising even though the immigration authorities had become more efficient in serving people especially with regard to issuing nationality certificates, personal identification cards and passports.[53] However, individuals faced difficulties when applying for nationality certificates, as they may not have had all the supporting documents needed for their applications. With the introduction of civil registration, the nationality certificate has been replaced with the 'National Number'. This number actually reduces peoples' identity to 'a number' as it tends to ignore certain categories who do not, and cannot, meet the requirements for obtaining nationality documents, such as women and children of mixed marriages and border tribes.

The new system of civil registration was introduced in 2011 and a nation-wide campaign was mounted, to encourage people to register immediately after the

49 See e.g. *Case of Seedona Peter v the Secretary General of the National Council for the Welfare of the Child*, No 2012/151, 18/11/2011, Administrative Appeals, Appellate Court, Khartoum (2012).

50 See e.g. the case of *Iman Hassan Benjamin v the Government of Sudan, Constitutional Court* (11 July 2012), unpublished (on file with author).

51 Najat Ahmed, 'Citizenship granted to persons from Sudanese mother and S. Sudanese Father', *Sudan Vision* (25 February 2018), www.svdaily.net/index.php/new-posts/local-news/13135-citizenship-granted-to-persons-from-sudanese-mother-and-s-sudanese-father, accessed 2 May 2018.

52 The steps needed in the application for nationality by birth include the following: (a) filing an application form that must be supported by the following documents: (1) nationality by birth certificate of either the father or the mother, brothers or close male relatives; (2) nationality certificates of both parents for those whose parents were naturalized Sudanese; (3) birth certificate; (4) consent of the guardian for a minor whose mother is Sudanese by birth and presenting marriage certificate; (5) documents showing mother custody of a child whose father is not Sudanese; (6) any other documents as maybe asked for by the immigration authorities; and (7) paying the prescribed fees. (b) Upon presenting the above documents, a thorough investigation is done with the applicant and his witnesses; (c) the immigration officer handling the case then recommends the award of nationality or rejection of the application; (d) the granting authority then takes the appropriate decision after reviewing the procedures and documents; and (e) the applicant is granted nationality certificate by birth upon exhausting the above procedures.

53 Abdulbari (n 27) 157.

secession of South Sudan. This system was apparently implemented to denationalize and initiate a new era of shrinking the space of citizenship in Sudan based on ethnic, identity-based stratification rather than citizenship rights. According to the new system, a Sudanese citizen shall be given a national registry certificate which includes a unique eleven-digit National Number, which replaces the old nationality certificate. Thus, if someone does not have a National Number, he or she will not be able to obtain a passport or be granted an exit visa, which is needed to leave the country.

The civil registry system makes it easy for individuals to obtain official documents. In addition, it establishes, for the first time, a system that puts emphasis on obtaining birth certificates for the new-born. Prior to the introduction of the civil registry system, little attention was paid to birth certificates, and most Sudanese have the so-called 'age assessment certificate' that sets the date of someone's birth as 1 January.

As good as the new system appears, there are concerns that it was meant first and foremost to screen, and thereby better control, people. For the sceptics, the system was introduced to deprive or denationalize southern Sudanese, and also to know who is who, in particular those who cannot prove their ethnic decent and belonging to any of the northern Sudanese tribes. As stated earlier in this chapter, this process of denationalization has effectively rendered many Sudanese of south Sudanese origin stateless.[54] Other concerns include the fact that the National Register contains data on every Sudanese. There is no guarantee that such data is protected by any data protection act, including the Freedom of Information Act 2015, and this violates civil liberties, not the least in the context of a repressive State. In any case, the introduction of the civil registration system is a significant shift in the laws and regulations surrounding citizenship in Sudan. Nonetheless, it is clear that the element of descent is still present even with the introduction of the new system. The challenges haunting citizenship in Sudan are more complex than can be resolved by the introduction of a new registration system. Ethnicity, social stratification and social exclusion are the factors that make the struggle for citizenship in Sudan similar to the experiences of other African countries, but also unique.

To conclude this chapter from a rights' perspective, following the evolution of Sudan Nationality Acts 1957, 1974, 1994 (amended 2005), and in spite of the otherwise difficult procedures and steps required in applications for a nationality certificate, it can be said that Sudan offers a generous citizenship law except for southern Sudanese or individuals of South Sudan origins. Reducing the period required for naturalization, allowing dual citizenship and granting women the right to bequeath citizenship to their children (though not automatic but upon submitting an application) are all positive changes in Sudan before the independence of South Sudan. Nonetheless, sometimes, bureaucratic red tape and other malpractices defeat these positive changes and may result in disenfranchising

54 See Babiker and Manby (n 32) 25–6.

some people, in particular women, Sudanese of south Sudanese origin and other African communities that have migrated to Sudan from West Africa and Eritrean refugees who settled for generations in Sudan. The intersection of ethnicity, tribalism and racism (in its Sudanese brand) also contribute to defeating the otherwise generous citizenship law. But will a policy of making accessible citizenship certificates to everybody in Sudan automatically enfranchise people? Will such a policy result in equal sharing of wealth and power in the country and hence balanced development? These are all questions to be kept in mind when analysing the struggles of citizenship in Sudan.

5 Practicing citizenship: challenges

In spite of the fact that Sudan's nationality law has changed many times, the law still predicates the basis of Sudanese citizenship on both ethnicity and birth or settlement in the territory. Citizenship continues to be based on claims to ancestral origin and blood, or *jus sanguinis*. Ethnicity is basically a political criterion.[55] While citizenship is also about boundary maintenance in so far as it defines membership in a given political community – a State – it is more objective as it defines rights and obligations of those included within its fold. Predicating citizenship on ethnicity and blood is problematic because it excludes or, at 'best', discriminates against those who cannot establish connections to Sudan as conditioned by the Sudan Nationality Act. Persons of West African ancestry represent an example of a category whose members struggle for citizenship. The following example illustrates the hassle through which some categories go.[56]

In November 2010 the dailies in Khartoum reported a case that illustrates how the system discriminates against certain segments of society. A young Sudanese woman, a housemaid in Khartoum, was arrested by the police in Omdurman while on her way to transfer money to her family. The police suspected that she was a foreign national living illegally in the country. The young woman, who was of West African descent, presented to the authorities all the necessary documents to show that she is Sudanese. But the police doubted the authenticity of the documents. The woman had to travel to where her family lives and obtain an affidavit from local authorities confirming her identity.[57]

Ironically, the family for whom the woman worked as a housemaid was of Asian origin, but its members were never suspected by the police or asked to show that they were residing legally in the country. The housemaid case suggests that discrimination is primarily based on class and colour. Poor and lower class people, especially those with darker skins, are more susceptible to random police checks. One can thus talk about some form of institutionalized racism in Sudan,

55 Barth (n 44); Richard Jenkins, *Rethinking Ethnicity: Arguments and Explorations* (Sage 1998).

56 Drawn from Assal 2013 (n 13) 201.

57 Ibid.

where State agents, not ordinary people, indulge in racist acts. In my fieldwork in Khartoum,[58] I found that some Sudanese migrants, while feeling disadvantaged by the system, do not appear resentful. During interviews, they did not remark on social–ethnic stratification or unequal treatment of different groups. They may have been afraid that criticizing the authorities as biased could lead to questions about their own ethnic identity as opposed to their national identity. As migrants to the national capital, they emphasized their Sudanese identity and downplayed their ethnic affiliation. They were clearly trying to adopt a neutral identity that will help them fit into their new social context. Many migrants idolize their original homelands or communities, preserving nostalgic memories even if they were forced to leave as a result of conflict or lack of opportunities. However, fondly recalling one's homeland does not necessarily mean that one wants to go back. To the extent that they have succeeded in Omdurman, they embrace a sense of belonging to this new place and try their best to avoid having their identity contested. But there are others who are openly critical about how disadvantaged they are.

Labels that are inscribed by society reflect some level of underlying racism in Sudan. While labels such as *shimaliyyin* (people from northern Sudan); *gharraba* (people from western Sudan); *jellaba* (people from the Nile Valley); *badawait* (eastern Sudan); *gannobiyyin* (people from southern Sudan), are not legally sanctioned or codified, they are socially inscribed in that members of the society condone their usage. The negative attitudes reflected in these labels influence law enforcement agencies and contribute to inequality in accessing social services provided by the State. For example, the case of the housemaid mentioned above shows that being of West African origin is disenfranchising. As a result of widespread stratification and social discrimination, nationality and citizenship issues are sensitive. In Sudan, when you ask someone about whether or not they possess an official document, the person may immediately fear that there must be a problem, feeling insecure and threatened. This is an indicator of the extent to which identity issues in Sudan are problematic, particularly against the background of arbitrary and discriminatory law enforcement.[59]

Arbitrary administrative decision-making regarding the granting or denial of citizenship is widespread. A look at the documentation needed when applying for the nationality number shows how difficult it can be for individuals to meet requirements and provide all the documents needed for supporting their applications. Immigration and administrative officials have actually exercised discretionary powers[60] in vital matters such as the right of women of mixed children, border

58 Assal 2011 (n 37) 7.

59 See SIHA and REDRESS, *Criminalisation of Women in Sudan: A Need for Fundamental Reform* (December 2017).

60 On this discretionary power of the immigration authorities, see Advocate General Official Legal Opinions No 2/2014 Re: Request for Legal Opinion on Nationality of South Sudanese Individuals with Long Residence in Sudan and Extent of Consistency with the Provisions of the Sudanese Nationality Act 1994 Amended in 2011, IS (30 March 2014).

tribes and some 'assimilated' groups of South Sudan origin. Various cases were adjudicated by courts, including the Constitutional Court,[61] in which claimants contest the denial of their rights to Sudanese nationality, in particular women whose children were denied the right to Sudanese nationality.[62] This means that the fate of individuals often depends on the whims of those in positions of decision-making, and therefore somebody whose belonging to the place is in doubt can be excluded from citizenship rights and its associated benefits, including the right to education and health.[63] Related to this is the inability of individuals to exercise effectively their rights as citizens. In Sudan, due to lengthy civil wars and political instability, and owing to the fact that post-independence governments were mostly authoritarian, the Sudanese people have been denied the effective exercise of citizenship rights due to the absence of rule of law in a democratic society where citizenry can be guaranteed. As in the case of citizenship rights, other civil and political rights such as the right to political participation in public affairs, freedom of expression, association, assembly and peaceful protest, are examples of rights that have been violated with impunity.[64] The legal and institutional framework for the protection of nationality and citizenship rights is also weak. The Constitutional Court, for example, has failed to effectively protect the constitutional rights of citizens in the majority of cases that have come before it.[65]

Marginalized groups bear the brunt of deprivations on the grounds of ethnic discrimination. According to Manby, 'marginalized groups can be excluded from *effective* exercise of citizenship rights even if their right to *legal* citizenship in itself is not contested'.[66] As indicated in the introduction of the chapter, nationality law reflects problems that are not strictly legal but are also, if not primarily challenges of nationalism and State building. Assal and El-Battahani discussed some of these larger problems and argued that inequality in citizenship rights is a reflection of, among other things, social stratification and propensity to make central Sudan culturally dominant.[67] Ahmed, in a similar vein, argued that the language and

61 *Case of Mazin Ali Deng and others v Sudan Ministry of Interior*, Ministry of Justice of Sudan, Constitutional Court, case No 2015 م / د م /د ق / 153 (23 August 2016).

62 On litigations at both administrative and constitutional courts, see the case of Benjamin (n 50). In this case the applicant has challenged the constitutionality of art 10(2).

63 Art 54(3)(4) of the Immigration and Nationality Act 1994 (amendments 2005) provides for the right of women to transfer nationality to their children provided that they make an application. This provision is discriminatory compared to men as it only gives women the right to transfer nationality but upon an application. This in turn has given the immigration authorities some discretion to deny women the right to transfer nationality to their children and has led to litigations at both administrative and constitutional courts.

64 See e.g. Human Rights Committee, 'Concluding observations on the fourth periodic report of the Sudan' UN doc CCPR/C/SDN/CO/4 (19 August 2014) paras 21–2.

65 On exceptional cases see above (n 50).

66 Manby 2009 (n 19) 21, emphasis in original.

67 Assal 2011 (n 37) and Atta El-Battahani, *Peace without Unity: The Dilemma of Reconciling Divergent Perspectives in Post-Conflict Sudan* (Sudan Working Paper No 4 Chr Michelsen Institute 2008).

dominant culture of those in power suppress regional cultures while neglecting other languages.[68]

6 Further shrinking: post-secession conditions

As South Sudan was heading towards the referendum vote in January 2011, President Al-Bashir outlined his vision for Sudan without the South in a grim manner. Addressing a rally in Gedarif town in eastern Sudan in December 2010, a few weeks before the referendum, the Sudanese President said:

> If South Sudan secedes, we will change the constitution and at that time there will be no time to speak of diversity of culture and ethnicity ... Sharia and Islam will be the main source for the constitution, Islam the official religion and Arabic the official language.[69]

Whether with the South or alone, Sudan is very diverse country. The above statement appears to encourage the formation of a more uniform, and, in light of Sudan's diversity and likely resistance to such a project, despotic state. As mentioned before, conflicts were already flaring even before the secession of South Sudan.

That secession marked the failure of the nation-building project pursued by all post-independence governments but notably by the incumbent Islamist government whose project and policies of *jihad* and Islamization significantly contributed to this development.[70] Waging wars against its opponents and against South Sudanese, the Islamist project turned into its anti-thesis: a destructive project that instead of building a strong nation ended up weakening Sudan. Needless to say, in the process, citizenship and human rights were often violated with impunity. An immediate implication of the secession of South Sudan for citizenship in Sudan is the loss of nationality for southern Sudanese. southern Sudanese who have been residing in Sudan (some for their entire lives) had their nationality revoked due to the amendment of article 10(2) of the Nationality Act 2005 (amendment 2011) outlined above. southern Sudanese who had very little or no connection at all with South Sudan had their nationality stripped even before acquiring the nationality of the new state of South Sudan. Following the results of the referendum of 9 July 2011 that overwhelmingly supported the secession of South Sudan, the Government of Sudan established a nine-month deadline for Southerners resident in Sudan to regularize their status by April 2012, but later the Ministry of Interior signed a Tripartite Memorandum of Understanding on 21 December 2011 with the Commission of Refugees (COR) and the United Nations High

68 Einas Ahmed, *Citizenship, Identity, Minorities and Sub-cultures in Sudan* (Unpublished paper, Department of Sociology and Social Anthropology, University of Khartoum 2012) (Arabic).

69 Quoted in Copnall (n 5) 49.

70 Ahmed (n 4).

Commissioner for Refugees (UNHCR). The purpose of this MOU is 'to register all South Sudanese in the territory of Sudan and to issue identity documentation in the forms of an ID card to each South Sudanese who is in Sudan'.[71] Political tensions between Sudan and South Sudan negatively affected citizens of the two countries who are living on the other side of the border. In March 2012, the two governments signed the 'Framework Agreement on the Status of Nationals of the other State and other Related Issues between the Republic of Sudan and the Republic of South Sudan', or what is called the 'Four Freedoms Agreement'.[72] It provides for principles and mechanisms for the treatment by each State of the nationals of the other State. In particular, the agreement emphasizes the following key rights in its preamble: freedom of residence and movement; freedom to acquire and dispose property; and freedom to undertake economic activities in the territory of each State. The Agreement calls in Part I for cooperation on the treatment of nationals in the territory of the other state. In this respect it provides for a formation of a High Level Joint Committee to oversee, supervise and approve all procedures and decisions with regard to the status and treatment of the nationals of each State in the territory of the other.[73] The agreement also calls for scaling up efforts to provide nationals of the other State with documentation, including residency and work permits.[74] This agreement has yet to be implemented as mutual mistrust and political tensions have thwarted its implementation. Later in the year, the two countries signed eight additional cooperation agreements, emphasizing the above four freedoms and economic cooperation between the two countries.[75] Resuming the pumping of oil, which is needed by both countries, was a key aspect in the framework agreement. Nonetheless, these different agreements have not been implemented because there are serious security and border problems that need to be resolved first.

Bronwen Manby and Mike Sanderson discussed in some detail the loss of nationality by southern Sudanese and the ensuing statelessness. Manby argues that,

> these people now have no recognized legal status in Sudan, exposing them to risk of arrest and detention on immigration charges, and the threat of expulsion to South Sudan. It is likely that some of those treated as South Sudanese nationals by the Sudanese authorities will in fact find themselves without the recognized nationality of either state, leaving them stateless.[76]

71 A Tripartite Memorandum of Understanding between the Directorate of Passport and Immigration of the Ministry of Interior (DPI) and the Commission of Refugees (COR) and the United Nations High Commissioner for Refugees (UNHCR) on the Registration of South Sudanese in Sudan (21 December 2014).

72 The agreement was ratified by both States in October 2012.

73 Art 1(1) of the Framework Agreement of 2012.

74 Art 2(1) ibid.

75 Copnall (n 5).

76 Manby 2012 (n 27) 1.

Along the same lines, Sanderson argues that a significant class of individuals habitually resident in Sudan, but with ethnic or familial connections with the South, will acquire the citizenship of South Sudan rather than their country of actual residence (i.e. Sudan).[77] This class is, in effect, 'displaced' by operation of the law as they are now outside their country of citizenship. Individuals left outside their country of nationality by operation of the new citizenship regime are left in a position of extreme vulnerability at risk of both *de jure* and *de facto* statelessness and arbitrary and/or mass expulsion.[78]

The civil war that broke out in South Sudan in December 2013 has further undermined possibilities for dealing with lingering issues between Sudan and South Sudan, which also requires cooperation between the two neighbouring States. Hundreds of thousands of South Sudanese have since returned to Sudan, effectively with undetermined status (i.e. refugees, foreigners, returnees, stateless persons), a country that used to be theirs less than a decade ago and in which they are now considered foreign nationals. At the beginning of the war, the Sudanese President declared that South Sudanese who were forced to come to Sudan due to the war in the South would not be considered refugees but brothers. However, he did not precisely define their status. Until early 2016, the status of South Sudanese in Sudan was ambiguous: they are neither refugees nor Sudanese, but were regarded as foreigners. This liminal condition deprives them of rights set out in the Refugee Convention of 1951 and to be provided by the State and, in practice, UNHCR. However, recently Sudan has acknowledged that South Sudanese are refugees.[79] Negative implications of secession on citizenship rights apply also in the case of Sudanese nationals living in South Sudan. These nationals include traders who have been living with their families in the South for decades, pastoralists, border tribes and farmers who used to live in the northern parts of Southern Sudan, and pastoral groups who traverse borders in search for water and pastures. These pastoralists cross the border to Southern Sudan during the dry season, represented by the Missiriya of Abyei and the Rezeigat of southern Darfur.[80] On both sides, however, there are many categories representing a 'population at risk';[81] these include: people of southern ethnicity resident in the North; people with one parent from Sudan and the other from South Sudan; people of mixed ancestry; members of cross-border ethnic groups; members of pastoralist communities; residents of Abyei (a contested area between Sudan and

77 Mike Sanderson, 'Statelessness and mass expulsion in Sudan: a reassessment of the international law' (2014) 12 *Northwest. JIHR* 74.

78 See Mohamed Abdelsalam Babiker, 'Nationality laws and statelessness in the context of state succession in Sudan: towards an objective, inclusive and non-discriminatory criteria' (2011) 1 *Disc* 50–71.

79 Idris Salim Elhassan, *South Sudan 'Arrivals' in the White Nile State (Sudan). Not Citizens, not IDPs, not Refugees: What Are They?* (Sudan Working Paper No 7 Chr Michelsen Institute 2016).

80 Saeed (n 7).

81 Manby 2012 (n 27) 6–10.

South Sudan); people separated from their families by the war; and members of historical migrant communities especially of West African stock (Mbororo and Fellata).[82]

7 Conclusions

The problem of citizenship in what remains of former Sudan is political and therefore the solution must also be political. As put by a recent report by the International Refugee Rights Initiative,

> while people talked about a strong racial dynamic as the basis for marginalization, it is also apparent that the logic of exclusion exercised by those in power extend beyond that to anyone who is not part of the elite power structures that controls the country … without the protection of the state – or even the legitimacy to be recognized as being in need of protection – Sudanese citizenship is shrinking.[83]

The experience of citizenship in both law and practice leaves a lot to be desired in spite of the progressive positive changes with regard to the efficiency of immigration authorities in paperwork and the introduction of the national registry. There is a need for a shift of focus from descent-based nationality to legally defined citizenship that recognizes the *ius soli* principle. A revised constitution needs to clearly set out a right to nationality (*jinsiyya*) and the rights of citizenship (*muwatana*) that flow from having Sudanese citizenship. This includes explicit protection of the right of children not to be rendered stateless, and the right of women not to be discriminated against in the field of nationality law, which would also remove one of the obstacles to becoming a party to the Convention on the Elimination of All Forms of Discrimination Against Women. It also comprises safeguards against deprivation of nationality, and discrimination in the field of, or on the basis of, nationality, which should be complemented with provisions that facilitate naturalization of certain categories of foreign nationals and stateless persons, such as refugees. Effectively implementing such changes entails the need to challenge the 'unity in conformity' framework that has structured the elite's political discourse since 1956. Without challenging this framework, it will be far-fetched to think that a regime change will end Sudan's deep-seated structural problems. A major step is to acknowledge the fact that Sudanese identities are multiple, fluid and changing and cannot succumb to such binaries as Arabism vs Africanism or Muslims vs Christians. Instead of clinging to the futile unity in conformity policy, there is a need to embrace a pluralistic model of identities that accepts both national and regional forms of belonging. This would make

82 See Babiker and Manby (n 32).

83 International Refugee Rights Initiative, *The Disappearance of Sudan? Life in Khartoum for Citizens Without Rights* (Working Paper No 9 2013) 19.

living together peacefully, with difference, possible. For some Sudanese scholars, multiculturalism is the ideal framework for countries like Sudan because it fosters spaces in which different groups of people grow and enrich each other, and at the same time creates a common culture since diversity is not perceived as incongruent with national interests.[84]

Challenging unitary conceptions of identity and embracing multiculturalism will not only settle citizenship problems but also tackle the identity problem, which is tearing the country apart. While multiculturalism as a model has in some contexts been criticized,[85] it certainly is one of the frameworks that can address challenges in societies with multiple forms of belonging. Perhaps the problem lies not so much in the model of multiculturalism as a framework, but in the term 'culture', whose definition is contentious. With or without multiculturalism, there is a need for a framework that respects diversity and includes minorities. Through ensuring the inclusion of minorities in the country's institutions and through fostering a shared civic (as opposed to ethnic) identity, peaceful coexistence is ensured and diversity can be celebrated; not feared. It goes without saying that for this to happen, there must be a democratic State or society, a State for the majority and minority alike. Lastly, the question of citizenship must be dealt with in the process of constitution-making through an awareness of the experiences of those who have suffered from failed approaches to citizenship, and by including and embracing the voices of ordinary Sudanese whose opinions have not been taken into consideration in previous constitutions not only with regard to the right to citizenship but also with regard to other rights. Creating a constitutional framework, and institutional protection, through relevant bodies and effective access to justice, that safeguards against a repeat of experiences of marginalization and deprivation of rights should therefore be paramount in the minds of the drafters of any forthcoming constitution in Sudan.

84 Madibbo (n 2).

85 Charles Taylor, *Multiculturalism: Examining the Politics of Recognition* (Princeton University Press 1994).

6 Constitutional dimensions of minority rights and the rights of peoples in the Sudans

Noha Ibrahim Abdelgabar, Mohamed Abdelsalam Babiker and Lutz Oette

1 Introduction

The status and debates surrounding the rights of minorities and peoples are issues of central importance for the protection of human rights and avoidance of conflict in Sudan. Multiple ethnic, religious, linguistic and cultural groups and practices account for the country's rich heritage and its diversity. Yet, this very diversity has been at the core of contrasting political visions for Sudan, from a rigidly imposed Islamic State to a multiethnic new Sudan, and the source of ongoing local, regional and national tensions and conflicts. South Sudan's secession has not at a stroke solved the underlying challenge of agreeing and implementing an adequate constitutional framework. Legacies of the North–South divide need to be addressed, as well as the rights of members of minorities and groups, as Sudan has not overnight become a mono-cultural, homogenous State. The same applies to South Sudan. As with Sudan, there are a great number of minorities and groups who have relatively recently, particularly during the colonial period, become part of a larger political unit, and whose place in the new State formation is still unsettled.

Against this background, the chapter provides an account of minorities and peoples in Sudan, including in relation to recent and ongoing conflicts, before examining the recognition, and protection, or lack thereof, of their rights in Sudan's constitutional history. It examines the degree to which the constitutional order and legislative and institutional frameworks have responded to apparent concerns and ensured the effective protection of rights in different contexts. This includes a review of peace agreements and other documents affecting minorities' rights, particularly in respect of South Sudan, Darfur, the Nuba Mountains and Blue Nile, including their relationship with the constitution. On the basis of an analysis of these core components, the chapter seeks to assess the coherence and effectiveness of approaches to the protection of minority rights and peoples' rights taken in Sudan to date.

The chapter focuses particularly on linguistic, cultural and religious minorities, non-discrimination, and equality before the law, with a primary focus on the constitutional framework, jurisprudence and national policies. It examines whether minority rights are historically included in the Bill of Rights of various constitutions, including the Interim National Constitution (INC) 2005, and whether minority groups have been accorded substantive protection. In particular, it charts the development of the rights of minorities and peoples since the Islamization of laws in Sudan in 1983. Its aim is to determine the extent to which 'the civilizational project' pursued by the current military regime after it assumed power in 1989 has affected minorities. These groups, particularly non-Muslim groups, have limited rights such as the right to political participation and to adopt a religion, to change their religion, to profess their religion and other such rights. The chapter outlines the conflicting norms between minority rights and Islamic laws and examines how such conflicts can be resolved or reconciled at the level of the constitutional Bill of Rights. In addition, it briefly analyses the right to self-determination in Sudan, with particular reference to South Sudan's referendum and secession in 2011. It does so by setting out the notion of minorities and peoples, their rights under international law, and the recognition and protection of these rights in Sudan's constitutions, legislative reforms, institutional mechanisms and actual practice.

2 Sudan's multiple diversities: a historical legacy

As aptly recalled by Munzoul A. M. Assal in his chapter in this collection:

> Even before independence in 1956, the political elite in Sudan has consistently attempted to project an identity that is not consonant with what the facts tell about Sudan, namely that it is a multiethnic, multicultural and multi-religious country. The Sudanese nationalist movement that preceded independence was actually the genesis of such projection. Language and religion (Arabic and Islam) were, and continue to be, its pillars. While these were the language and religion of the majority, there are linguistic and religious minorities. These minorities include hundreds of tribes, unorthodox Muslim groups, Christians, and those adhering to their own traditional beliefs in the Nuba Mountains and the Blue Nile. The State should be an entity that represents, and serves everybody who happens to be part of it and under its sovereignty, irrespective of whether they belong to the majority or minorities. The projection of an imagined identity that conforms to something Arabic and Islamic presumes that Sudan is a nation-state. But Sudan never was.[1]

The nation-state model can therefore only 'succeed' on the basis of a denial, and suppression, or forced assimilation of different identities. Alternatives would be modes of voluntary assimilation, various forms of integration, including multiculturalism, or high degrees of self-rule and autonomy. Yet, Sudan's history has been characterized by the lack of an open, democratic debate, and concomitant

1 See Assal, Chapter 5, 122, footnotes omitted.

constitutional processes, on what approach, or approaches, are considered most suitable, both by the groups concerned and society as a whole.

Many postcolonial conflicts in Africa revolve around the question of status and belonging. Sudan is a good example of the failure of African States to reform colonial systems and build up an inclusive and equitable society. Francis Deng succinctly captured the colonial legacy in this regard:

> The crisis of statehood and national identity in Sudan is rooted in the British attempt to bring together diverse peoples with a history of hostility into a framework of one state, while also keeping them apart and entrenching inequities by giving certain regions more access to state power, resources, services, and development opportunities than other regions.[2]

Sudan is most diverse in religious, cultural, ethnic and linguistic terms. Most of the Sudanese are adherents of the Sunni branch of Islam. Christians are a sizeable religious minority in Sudan, constituting more than a quarter of Sudan's population prior to the secession of South Sudan from Sudan.[3] Other important religious minorities are followers of traditional indigenous beliefs, Coptic Orthodox and Greek Orthodox.[4] Sudan is also extremely linguistically diverse. The Sudanese are divided among several ethnic groups and subgroups and speak more than 100 languages and dialects.[5]

Notwithstanding this diversity, successive Sudanese governments adopted strategies of governance based on colonial precedents by dividing the population on the basis of race, ethnicity or religion. The political history of Sudan has been characterized by the persistent marginalization of the citizens of the periphery. Policy-makers and Presidents of post-independence governments were drawn mainly from the Nile Valley, that is, predominantly of Arab origin and belonging to the Islamic faith, which resulted in undermining the influence of citizens from the peripheries.[6] Post-independence policies, laws and practices revolved around Islamization and Arabization of the State.[7] Successive post-independence governments pursued policies of discrimination against ethnic, racial or religious minorities, especially under President Abboud in the 1960s and President al-Bashir in the 1990s.[8] The question of freedom of religion in particular became a constant

2 Francis Deng, 'Sudan's Turbulent Road to Nationhood' in Ricardo René Laremont (ed.), *Borders, Nationalism, and the African State* (Lynne Rienner Publishers 2005) 41.

3 No reliable recent statistics are available.

4 Noha Ibrahim Abdelgabar, 'Rights of Religious Minorities in Sudan' in Rainer Grote & Tilmann J Röder (eds), *Constitutionalism, Human Rights, and Islam after the Arab Spring* (Oxford University Press 2016) 654.

5 John Ryle, 'Peoples & Cultures of Two Sudans' in John Ryle et al (eds), *The Sudan Handbook* (James Currey 2011).

6 See further Oette, Chapter 1.

7 See Mohamed Omer Beshir, *The Southern Sudan: From Conflict to Peace* (Hurst & Co 1975).

8 Ahmed T el-Gaili, 'Federalism and the Tyranny of Religious Majorities: Challenges to Islamic Federalism in Sudan' (2004) 45 *HILJ* 503.

source of conflict at the heart of struggles surrounding Sudan's identity. Sudan had been embroiled in a long civil war, the so-called North–South civil war, in which religious convictions, among other factors, played a crucial role.[9] The al-Bashir regime adopted a programme explicitly aimed at the Islamization and Arabization of the State, which further accentuated existing divides and aggravated, or prompted new, conflicts, such as in the Nuba Mountains and Darfur.[10]

3 Right to self-determination and rights of minorities: the international normative framework

By virtue of article 27(3) of the INC, the right to self-determination and the rights of minorities form an integral part of the Bill of Rights in respect of the relevant treaties to which Sudan has become a party. The right to self-determination is recognized in the respective article 1 of the International Covenant on Civil and Political Rights (ICCPR) and the International Covenant on Economic, Social and Cultural Rights (ICESCR). At the regional level, article 20(1) of the African Charter on Human and Peoples' Rights (ACHPR) defines it as the right of peoples to 'freely determine their political status and ... pursue their economic and social development according to the policy they have freely chosen'. The right to self-determination, which already features prominently in article 1(2) of the United Nations (UN) Charter, is foundational to international human rights law. However, its scope remains contested due to the inherent tensions between self-rule and collective freedom on the one hand, and territorial stability and international political order on the other. To begin with, the right holders, namely 'peoples', are not defined in international human rights law. The identity of 'peoples' proved largely unproblematic in respect of situations of decolonization, in which the right to self-determination is firmly recognized.[11] Beyond this context, the notion of 'peoples' requires a 'broad and inclusive' definition that comprises objective and subjective (self-definition) elements, and 'include[s] all those who are subject to "alien subjugation, domination and exploitation"'.[12] The right to self-determination has an internal and external dimension. Internal self-determination, namely 'a people's pursuit of its political, economic, social and cultural development within a framework of an existing state',[13] can take various forms, such as autonomy or federalism. External self-determination, such as

9 Douglas H Johnson, *The Root Causes of Sudan's Civil Wars: Peace or Truce* (Rev Edn, James Currey 2011).

10 Alex de Waal and AH Abdel Salam, 'Islamism, State Power and Jihad in Sudan' in Alex De Waal (ed.), *Islamism and its Enemies in the Horn of Africa* (Hurst & Co 2003).

11 Declaration on Independence for Colonial Countries and Peoples, GA Res 1514 (XV) (14 December 1960).

12 Robert McCorquodale, 'Group Rights' in Daniel Moeckli, Sangeeta Shah & Sandesh Sivakumaran (eds), *International Human Rights Law* (3rd edn, OUP 2018) 349, with reference to the Declaration, ibid.

13 *Reference Re Secession of Quebec* [1998] 2 SCR 217, para 126.

the right to secession, is viewed as an exception under international law, which is only applicable in cases of denial of internal self-determination, including serious human rights violations.[14] However, States are free to grant such a right in their national constitutions, such as in Ethiopia,[15] or in peace agreements by means of a referendum, as was the case in the Comprehensive Peace Agreement (CPA) of 2005 regarding the future status of South Sudan (see section 6 below). While the right to self-determination remains contested, there are a number of examples where 'peoples' have exercised their right to external self-determination, with varying outcomes.[16]

The right to self-determination has also been recognized in respect of indigenous peoples, particularly in the UN Declaration on the Rights of Indigenous Peoples of 2007. While article 3 of the Declaration provides that this right entitles indigenous peoples 'to freely determine their political status and freely pursue their political status and freely pursue their economic, social and cultural development', article 4 confines this right 'to autonomy or self-government'.[17]

The rights of minorities, whose development reaches back to the system operating under the League of Nations following World War I, are explicitly recognized in the ICCPR. Its article 27 states:

> [I]n those States in which *ethnic, religious or linguistic* minorities exist, persons belonging to such minorities shall not be denied the right, in community with the other members of their group, to enjoy their own culture, to profess and practise their own religion, or to use their own language.[18]

Minority rights have also been recognized in the UN Declaration on the Rights of Persons Belonging to National or Ethnic, Religious and Linguistic Minorities of 1992. In contrast to the essentially collective right to self-determination, the rights of minorities are conceived as individual rights of persons belonging to minorities.[19] These rights have a collective dimension, though, in as much as they depend on (and are aimed at preserving) the existence of the group. Parallel to the debate surrounding the meaning of the term 'peoples',

> [t]here is no internationally agreed definition as to which groups constitute minorities. It is often stressed that the existence of a minority is a question

14 Ibid, particularly paras 126 and 131ff. See also *Katangese Peoples' Congress v Zaire*, Comm 75/92 (ACHPR 1995).

15 Art 39(1) of the Constitution of the Federal Democratic Republic of Ethiopia of 1995.

16 See Jörg Fisch, *The Right of Self-Determination of Peoples: The Domestication of an Illusion* (CUP 2015); Jane A Hofbauer, *Sovereignty in the Exercise of the Right to Self-determination* (Brill Nijhoff 2016).

17 Critical, Karen Engle, 'On Fragile Architecture: The UN Declaration on the Rights of Indigenous Peoples in the Context of Human Rights' (2011) 22 *EJIL* 141.

18 Emphasis added.

19 Human Rights Committee, *CCPR General Comment No 23: Article 27 (Rights of Minorities)*, UN doc CCPR/C/21/Rev.1/Add.5 (8 April 1994) para 3.1.

> of fact and that any definition must include both objective factors (such as the existence of a shared ethnicity, language or religion) and subjective factors (including that individuals must identify themselves as members of a minority).[20]

Minorities are seen as groups that are in a non-dominant position in a society.[21] Members of minorities must not be nationals as long as they meet the relevant criteria.[22] Where they do, they enjoy the rights to their own culture, religion and language, as applicable. In addition to these specific rights with a group dimension, persons belonging to minorities enjoy the relevant individual rights, such as freedom of thought and religion, and the right to equality and non-discrimination. These rights are granted in the ICCPR and ACHPR, as well as in treaties that apply to particular groups of persons, such as the Convention on the Rights of the Child and the African Charter on the Rights and Welfare of the Child. Consequently, States must provide an adequate legal and institutional framework in which members of minorities can enjoy their own culture, religion and language, and are not subject to discrimination or other violations on account of their minority status.[23]

The ICCPR explicitly recognizes only certain minorities. There are a number of other persons belonging to groups that have shared identities, such as on the basis of disability or sexual orientation. While members of such groups do not fall within the scope of article 27 of the ICCPR, they have the right to equality and non-discrimination on account of other status, as well as the gamut of other civil, political, economic, social and cultural rights, including the positive right to be protected against violations of their rights.[24]

4 Sudan's constitutional framework on minorities and the rights of peoples

4.1 Constitutional framework in post-colonial Sudan

Since the colonial days, Sudan has had a legal system that reflects the diverse nature of Sudanese society. Formal and informal legal systems co-existed (Islamic Law, statutory law and customary law).[25] The Transitional Constitution of 1956, which was drafted after the independence of Sudan, and transitional constitutions that followed, recognized the country's religious plurality and the right to

20 Office of the High Commissioner for Human Rights, *Minority Rights: International Standards and Guidance for Implementation* (United Nations 2010) 2.
21 Ibid, citing UN doc E/CN.4/Sub.2/384/Rev.1, para 568.
22 *General Comment 23* (n 19) para 5.1 although certain political rights are confined to citizens.
23 See further OHCHR (n 20) 7ff.
24 Ibid 3.
25 See generally, Zaki Mustafa, *The Common Law in the Sudan: An Account of the Justice, Equity and Good Conscience* (Clarendon Press 1971); MI Khalil, 'The Legal System of the Sudan' (1971) 20 *ICLQ* 624, 627.

freedom of belief.[26] The post-independence constitutions have provided to varying degrees for the protection of religious, ethnic and cultural minorities, and guaranteed freedoms of thought, belief, religion and expression.[27] Nonetheless, minorities, especially in South Sudan, Darfur, the Nuba Mountains and Blue Nile, were deprived of their linguistic, cultural and religious rights, including the right to profess and manifest their religion.[28] President Abboud (1958–64) pursed a series of measures with a view to assimilating the South with the North through an overt policy of Islamization that led to the outbreak of open civil war a civil war between the South and the North of Sudan.[29] To put an end to the South–North Sudan civil war, the policy of discrimination against minorities had largely ceased when, under President Nimeri, the Permanent Constitution of 1973 was adopted, which accommodated the rights of South Sudan people (religious and political rights).[30] In particular, the 1973 Permanent Constitution was pluralistic on the issue of religion and granted South Sudan autonomous status.[31]

The pluralism provided for in the 1973 Permanent Constitution was changed with the introduction of *Shari'a* law in 1983 and the announcement that the Sudan would be an Islamic State. The governments that succeeded Nimeri kept *Shari'a* law intact. The present regime, when it came to power in 1989 through a *coup d'etat*, embarked on an Islamization project as a means of political change and as part of the civil war waged against South Sudan.[32] The Islamization project that was pursued through a prolonged period of religious conversion by the successive military governments (of Presidents Abboud, Nimeri and the present President al-Bashir) sought to impose an Islamist social and political system to the detriment of the different social, religious and political backgrounds that constitute Sudanese society. This development was also reflected or manifested 'ideologically' at the constitutional level as subsequent constitutions were marked by their Islamic ideological orientation to reflect or usher in a new era of Islamized constitutions. For example, the 1998 constitution provided for the protection of minorities as part of its directive principles but undermined the rights of

26 Akolda Tier, 'Freedom of Religion under the Sudan Constitution and Laws' (1982) 26 *JAL* 133.

27 See further Chapter 4 in this collection.

28 See 'Study on Islam and Society in Sudan', and 'Freedom of Religion and Belief in Sudan (Islamic Research project February 2013). The study was produced by Centre d'Études et de Documentation Économiques, Juridiques et Sociales –Khartoum branch (CEDEJ-Khartoum) as part of the research programme 'Strengthening Knowledge and Dialogue with the Islamic/Arab world'.

29 Emeric Rogier, *No More Hills Ahead? The Sudan's Tortuous Ascent to Heights of Peace* (Netherlands Institute of International Relations 2005) 10.

30 See further Abdelgabar (n 4).

31 See in particular arts 8 as well as 16 and 47 on the status of South Sudan and the status of, and rights relating to, religion respectively.

32 De Waal (n 10).

minorities, particularly religious minorities, by virtue of the priority accorded to *Shari'a* law.[33]

4.2 Constitutional framework on the rights of minorities under the INC 2005

The CPA, signed in 2005, brought the South–North conflict to an end. It was concluded to manage the diversity of Sudan and to serve as a vehicle for democratic reform in a country marked by both ethnic, linguistic, religious and cultural diversity, and economic disparity. Other peace agreements such as the Doha Document for Peace in Darfur (DDPD) have also touched on minority rights.[34] The CPA was translated into a constitution, the 2005 INC, to accommodate Sudan's diversity. The INC does not explicitly define the term minorities. Instead, it recognizes, and places emphasis on Sudan's diversity.[35] Article 1 of the INC defines the Sudanese State as 'a multi-cultural, multi-lingual, multi-racial, multi-ethnic and multi-religious country'. Article 1(2) goes on to portray the country as 'an all-embracing homeland where religions and cultures are sources of strength, harmony and inspiration'. Further, article 7 guarantees the right to nationality and citizenship rights to all Sudanese.[36] In addition, Chapter I and Chapter II recognize the cultural diversity of Sudanese society and all indigenous languages, and commit the State to develop strategies for social justice. The INC guiding principles for wealth-sharing are based on non-discrimination on the basis of gender, race, religion, ethnicity, language, region and political affiliation.[37]

33 Arts 11–15 of the 1998 Constitution of Sudan.

34 See Chapter (1), Art. 1: 'Promotion and Protection of Human Rights and Fundamental Freedoms', Darfur Peace Agreement. The Doha Document for Peace in Darfur (DDPD) does not include clauses identifying minorities groups. However, the absence of such clauses does not necessarily mean that these groups are disadvantaged. The DDPD contains a strong general non-discrimination article and a fundamental rights clause, and in the cases of affirmative action for people of Darfur, are likely to provide as much protection. Further, the General Principles of Power-Sharing, as provided for in DDPD, emphasize that the cultural and ethnic diversity of the Sudanese people is the foundation of national cohesion and shall therefore be promoted, developed and managed … to reflect both national unity and the diversity of the people of Sudan. Art. 20: 'Religion, beliefs, traditions and customs are sources of moral strength and inspiration for the Sudanese people. The cultural and ethnic diversity of the Sudanese people is the foundation of national cohesion and shall therefore be promoted, developed and managed according to national criteria that reflect both the national unity and the diversity of the Sudanese people. The Sudanese people share a common heritage and aspirations and accordingly agree to work together.'

35 See the Preamble of the INC.

36 See further Chapter 5 in this collection.

37 Arts 136, 185 of the INC.

4.3 Non-discrimination and the protection of minorities under the INC

The INC's Bill of Rights does not reflect in detail the rights of members of certain groups, such as minorities or other marginalized groups. However, it prohibits discrimination which is based on ethnic differentiation[38] and its article 47 entitled 'Ethnic and Cultural Communities' provides for the freedom of the members of ethnic and cultural communities to develop their particular cultures, to practice their belief, to use their languages and to observe their religion. Yet, minorities are not defined in Sudan's constitutional framework. This is not accidental. The question of definition proved particularly vexing during the negotiations of the CPA, with the question as to whether the State can and should define minorities prompting heated discussions.[39]

The concept of non-discrimination is integral to the INC. Its importance to minority rights protection cannot be overstated. This is because 'equality and non-discrimination' are a dominant theme at the heart of the ICCPR.[40] Discrimination is at the root of many human rights violations,[41] an experience reflected in the Sudanese context. Article 31 of the INC states: 'All persons are equal before the law and are entitled without discrimination, as to race, colour, sex, language, religious creed, political opinion, or ethnic origin, to the equal protection of the law.' However, the grounds of non-discrimination and equality before the law provided for under the INC lack reference to 'national or social origin, property, birth, or other status' contained in articles 1(1) and 26 of the ICCPR. Article 31 lacks detail and neither uses the language of 'obligations' nor specifies that the state should take proactive measures to ensure the realization of this right; the Bill of Rights also does not include an explicit duty of the State, similar to article 1(1) of the ICCPR, to respect and ensure respect of the rights guaranteed therein to all persons without discrimination.[42] This is particularly important in a country such as the Sudan where non-discrimination and equality before the law are linked to human rights violations related to religion, customs and equality between men and women. In this context, it is imperative that the State takes proactive measures to prohibit discrimination and, accordingly,

38 Arts 38, 39, 40, 44, and 46 ibid.

39 This paragraph draws on Abdelgabar (n 4) 660.

40 Bertrand Ramcharan, 'Equality and Nondiscrimination', in Louis Henkin (ed.) *The International Bill of Rights: The Covenant on Civil and Political Rights* (Columbia University Press 1981) 246.

41 Sarah Joseph, Jenny Schultz, and Melissa Castan, *The International Covenant on Civil and Political Rights: Cases, Materials and Commentary* (2nd edn, OUP 2005) 680.

42 See generally Mohamed Abdelsalam Babiker, 'Why Constitutional Bill of Rights Fail to Protect Civil and Political Rights in Sudan: Substantive Gaps, Conflicting Rights, and "Arrested" Reception of International Human Rights Law' in Mohamed Abdelsalam Babiker and Lutz Oette (eds), *The Constitutional Protection of Human Rights in Sudan: Challenges and Future Perspectives* (REDRESS, Faculty of Law, University of Khartoum and Sudanese Human Rights Monitor 2014) 16.

article 31 should stipulate specifically that 'the law shall prohibit any discrimination and guarantee to all persons equal and effective protection against discrimination on any ground'.[43] Such protection is important in Sudan's hybrid legal system derived from 'traditional' *Shari'a* law and customary laws, which may give rise to discrimination against certain individuals and groups, including women and religious, ethnic and linguistic minorities.[44]

One of the key limitations of article 31 of the Bill of Rights is that it does not explicitly prohibit advocacy, hostility or acts of violence or incitement of various forms of national, racial or religious hatred against linguistic, religious and cultural groups.[45] The lack of such prohibition is not in harmony with article 4 of the International Convention on the Elimination of All Forms of Racial Discrimination (ICERD) to which Sudan is a party and which requires States to enact criminal legislations to punish such acts.[46] It is striking also that the INC does not prohibit dissemination of the ideas of superiority of one race or group of persons.[47] The Committee on the Elimination of Racial Discrimination recommended that Sudan adopt and enforce legislation prohibiting the dissemination of ideas based on racial or ethnic superiority and expressions of racial hatred and incitement to racial discrimination and violence against any group of persons of another ethnic group.[48] Express prohibition of such acts under Sudan's constitutional and legislative framework is imperative in a country where violence, incitement and advocacy of hatred and 'ethnic criminalization' have been used as a ground for prosecuting members of certain ethnic groups.[49]

43 Ibid.

44 See on concerns over the lack of anti-discrimination legislation in Sudan, Committee on the Elimination of Racial Discrimination, *Concluding Observations on the Combined Twelfth to Sixteenth Periodic Reports of the Sudan*, UN doc CERD/C/SDN/CO/12-16 (12 June 2015) para 12.

45 National, racial, religious hatred is addressed as part of art 39 of the Bill of Rights but in the context of media ethics and obligations. The Article provides that 'all media shall abide by media ethics and media shall not incite religious, racial, cultural hatred or call for violence or war'.

46 Art 4(a) of the ICERD provides that states Parties 'shall declare an offence punishable by law all dissemination of ideas based on racial superiority or hatred, incitement to racial discrimination, as well as all acts against ant race or groups of persons of another colour or ethnic origin, and also the provision of assistance to racist activities, including the financing thereof'. See further CERD, General Recommendation 35: Combatting Racist Hate Speech, UN doc CERD/C/GC/35 (26 September 2013).

47 Babiker (n 42) 16.

48 CERD, Concluding observations (n 44), para 12(c).

49 For example, the attacks on the city of Omdurman by the Darfur rebel forces Justice and Equality Movement (JEM) led to the arrests and detention of thousands of suspected Darfurian citizens including women and children, simply on the basis of ethnic features, colour, accent or place of living. The separation of the country has also raised the spectre of enhanced discrimination of persons of southern Sudanese origin. The current armed conflicts in South Kordofan and Blue Nile states also raise similar concerns. See UN Special Rapporteur on the Situation of Human Rights in the Sudan, Sima Samar, UN doc A/HRC/9/13 (2 September 2008) paras 20–33, and Amin M Medani, 'A Legacy of Institutionalized Repression: Criminal Law and Justice in Sudan', in Lutz Oette (ed.), *Criminal Law Reform and Transitional Justice: Human Rights Perspectives for Sudan* (Ashgate 2011) 79–80.

4.4 Rights of religious minorities

Successive constitutions since the independence of the Sudan in 1956 have stressed respect for religious rights and freedoms irrespective of religious affiliation. Recently the CPA gave special recognition to the protection of religious rights. This commitment was subsequently translated in the INC which allows the sub-national level (the state), depending on the religion of its majority, to opt out of religiously inspired legislation and to legislate in accordance with the state's practices or customs.[50] The adoption of a dual legal system provides an answer to the question of mutual recognition of the religious diversity of Sudan to the extent that the laws are not based solely on *Shari'a* law.[51] The legal regime in Sudan thereby ostensibly allows for religious pluralism.

The current INC provides constitutional protection for religious rights and freedoms in its Guiding Principles which call for the right to respect religious rights to worship or assemble and to establish, posses, acquire and maintain places for worship and disseminate religious publications and teach religion or belief.[52] Article 38 of the Bill of Rights (Freedom of Creed and Worship) further guarantees freedom of religious creed and worship, and the right to declare and manifest religion and religious practices.[53]

Although successive constitutions since Sudan's independence in 1956 guarantee religious rights and freedoms, these guarantees are contradicted by national laws. Despite the constitutional provision that protected freedom of religion during the Abboud regime, Christian missionaries were expelled from South Sudan through the enactment of the so-called 1962 Missionary Societies Act.[54] During the Nimeri era, a series of *Shari'a*-based laws were issued, in contravention of the 1973 Constitution; the 1983 Penal Code in particular, which reflected the

50 See art 5(3) of the INC.

51 Art 5 ibid.

52 Art 6 provides: 'The State shall respect the religious rights to: (a) worship or assemble in connection with any religion or belief and to establish and maintain places for these purposes; (b) establish and maintain appropriate charitable or humanitarian institutions; (c) acquire and possess movable and immovable property and make, acquire and use the necessary articles and materials related to the rites or customs of a religion or belief; (d) write, issue and disseminate religious publications; (e) teach religion or belief in places suitable for these purposes; (f) solicit and receive voluntary financial and other contributions from individuals, private and public institutions; (g) train, appoint, elect or designate by succession appropriate religious leaders called for by the requirements and standards of any religion or belief; (h) observe days of rest, celebrate holidays and ceremonies in accordance with the precepts of religious beliefs; (i) communicate with individuals and communities in matters of religion and belief at national and international levels.'

53 Art 38 read: 'Every person shall have the right to the freedom of religious creed and worship, and to declare his/her religion or creed and manifest the same, by way of worship, education, practice or performance of rites or ceremonies, subject to requirements of law and public order; no person shall be coerced to adopt such faith, that he/she does not believe in, nor to practice rites or services to which he/she does not voluntarily consent'.

54 See general, Abdelgabar (n 4).

influence of the Islamists as a growing political force, was a harbinger of things to come post 1989.[55] The suppression of religious freedom has become particularly pronounced since 1989 under a regime that is based on an exclusive religious ideology. Under the current regime, religion has been used as a way of legitimating and supporting State power in Sudan. For example, the North–South conflict has long been perceived as an ethnic or religious conflict. The regime pursued an aggressive *Jihad* against South Sudan, and a vigorous campaign of Islamization with religion utilized as a pretext to wage a religious war.[56] During the conflict in South Sudan, the application of *Shari'a* law was critical to religious minorities. It formed part of a series of Southern grievances, and was a means of imposing a culturally alien, and repressive mode of governance on Southerners, particularly those living in the North of the country.[57]

The stress on *Shariʿa* as the main source of legislation enshrines limitations on the rights of non-Muslim communities; while some laws impose serious penalties for beliefs which are unpopular, such as apostasy, others do not provide protection against religious hatred and incitement of violence against religious minority groups. Article 126 of the 1991 Criminal Act, for example, which criminalizes apostasy, contradicts the provisions of the INC that recognize and accommodate the cultural, religious and linguistic diversity of Sudan. Notwithstanding the INC's Bill of Rights, article 126 was broadened in February 2015 to include blaspheming and insulting the Prophet, and other acts seen as adversely targeting the Qur'an, the Prophet's companions or A'isha.[58] The salience of the law on apostasy was illustrated by the case of Maryam Yaḥya Ibrahim who was sentenced to a hundred lashes for adultery and to death for apostasy. She was convicted on charges of apostasy for claiming to be Christian and because of her marriage to a Christian man from South Sudan was deemed invalid.[59] She was later released following a court of appeal ruling.[60] The case sparked a debate over apostasy in Sudan, and prompted disputes amongst Islamic scholars over the legality of imposing the death penalty for apostasy. UN mandate holders and human rights

55 See Aharon Layish and Gabriel Warburg, *The Reinstatement of Islamic Law in Sudan under Numayrī: An Evaluation of a Legal Experiment in the Light of Its Historical Context, Methodology, and Repercussions* (Brill 2002) and Olaf Köndgen, *The Codification of Islamic Criminal Law in the Sudan: Penal Codes and Supreme Court Case Law under Numayrī and al-Bashīr* (Brill 2018).

56 De Waal (n 10) and Human Rights Watch/Africa, *Behind the Red Line: Political Repression in Sudan* (1996).

57 Köndgen (n 55) 56, 64–5.

58 See for a brief analysis, ibid 301–2.

59 See e.g. Dallia M Abdelmoniem, 'Sudan: A Misconception of apostasy: Sudan's recent apostasy death sentence is a manifestation of the wrongful use of religion in politics' *Al-Jazeera* (17 May 2014), www.aljazeera.com/indepth/opinion/2014/05/sudan-woman-apostasy-2014517102213211469.html, accessed 5 June 2018.

60 Court of Appeal-Khartoum North and Sharg-el-Nil, Criminal Circuit (23 June 2014).

groups raised concern over the case and its incompatibility with Ibrahim's freedom of religion.[61]

The secession of South Sudan in 2011 has adversely affected the freedom to worship or practice or manifest religion; after secession there is a widespread perception that Sudan is a purely Sunni Muslim majoritarian state and hence non-(Sunni) Muslims have limited space to practice and manifest their religion.[62] The situation for Christians in Sudan has grown markedly worse in the aftermath of the secession of South Sudan in 2011. The President of Sudan announced prior to July 2011 that if South Sudan were to secede, Sudan would apply *Shari'a* law.[63] This means that if the current conservative interpretation of *Shari'a* persists, restrictions on the religious freedoms of Christians and other religious minorities can be expected to remain in place or worsen.[64] The Sudanese government has refused to issue any permits for the construction of new churches, arguing that the existing ones are sufficient to accommodate the country's Christian population.[65] Churches have been demolished and priests have faced harassment.[66] The nominal freedom of religion has therefore constantly been at risk of being undermined by administrative practices that have marginalized certain religious communities, and that have served as symbolic expression of unequal power relationships in a State that has paid scant respect for the rule of law.

The State has not taken a neutral position towards all religious groups and actors and treated them equally. This applies not only to non-Muslims but also to Muslim groups, particularly groups who adopt a liberal interpretation of Islam. *Shii'a*, *Baha'i* and the Republican Brothers as minority religious groups are restricted in their right to practice religion or to organize themselves freely without interference from the authorities despite the fact that the INC 2005 guarantees their rights.[67] They have been compelled to practice their religious rituals underground as they are stigmatized and accused of heresy, particularly by some

61 See *Report of the Independent Expert on the Situation of Human Rights in the Sudan, Mashood A Baderin*, UN doc A/HRC/27/69 (4 September 2014) paras 43–5.

62 See Mohamed Abdelsalam Babiker, 'Freedom of Religion, Minority Rights and the 'Islamization' of Laws in Sudan: From Independence to Secession of South Sudan' (unpublished article, on file with author).

63 'Sudanese President Asserts North Sudan's Arabic, Islamic Identity' *Sudan Tribune* (6 February 2011), http://sudantribune.com/Sudanese-president-asserts-North,37889, accessed 5 June 2018.

64 Suliman Baldo, *Radical Intolerance: Sudan's Religious Oppression and Embrace of Extremist Groups* (Enough Project 2017).

65 See for a Case Study: The Sudanese Church of Christ Seeking Land Registration in al-Bashir City, particularly the seemingly endless delays faced by the Church, Philippe Gout, 'Access to Land for Non-Muslims in Greater Khartoum: Disclosing Divergent Minority Models in International and Sudanese Laws' in Barbara Casciarri and Mohamed A Babiker (eds), *Anthropology of Law in Muslim Sudan: Land, Courts and the Plurality of Practices* (Brill 2018) 98ff.

66 See Baldo (n 64) and *Report of the Independent Expert on the Situation of Human Rights in the Sudan*, UN doc A/HRC/36/63 (27 July 2017) paras 30–1.

67 See Baldo (n 64) 8.

Salafi figures.[68] This violates religious groups' rights to manifest their religion or belief as enshrined in article 18 of the ICCPR.[69] It also violates Sudan's obligations under human rights law to respect and ensure respect for all individuals or groups within its jurisdiction not to be discriminated against.[70]

Persecution of religious minority groups is a phenomenon associated with many Muslim majority States[71] and raises critical questions about the status of minority religious groups in predominantly Muslim societies or States advocating an orthodox vision or interpretation of the relationship between religion and secularism in modern Islamic States.[72] In such contexts, discrimination against religious minorities also calls into question respect for, and the accommodation of minority rights in the context of constitution-making processes.[73]

4.5 The INC institutional mechanisms on the protection of minorities

The INC provides for positive measures, at least on paper, to respect the rights of minorities to enjoy and practice their rights and their ability to participate fully in economic, political and social life. Effective protection of the culture, languages, traditions and customs, and religious rights of minorities requires an effective institutional framework. For example, the rights of non-Muslims in the North generally and in the capital specifically have been one of the thorny issues during the negotiations leading to the signature of the CPA. This was due to the fact that the National Congress Party (NCP) rules the predominantly Muslim North by legislation based on *Shari'a* laws. In the end a formula was adopted that confirmed the rule of *Shari'a* in the North while excluding the South from

68 See 'Study on Islam and Society in Sudan' and 'Freedom of Religion and Belief in Sudan' (n 28).

69 UN Human Rights Committee, *General Comment No 22: The Right to Freedom of Thought, Conscience and Religion (Art. 18)*, Forty-eighth session (1993), para 3.

70 See the United Nations Declaration on the Rights of Persons Belonging to National or Ethnic Religious and Linguistic Minorities, adopted by the UN General Assembly (1992). The Declaration reaffirms the rights of persons belonging to minorities to enjoy all human rights and fundamental freedoms in accordance with the principles of non-discrimination and equality before the law.

71 See Mohammed S. M. Eltayeb, 'A Human Rights Framework for Defining and Understanding Intra-Religious Persecution in Muslim Countries', in Nazila Ghanea (ed.), *The Challenge of Religious Discrimination at the Dawn of the New Millennium* (Martinus Nijhoff 2004).

72 See Abdullahi Ahmed An-Na'im, *Islam and the Secular State, Negotiating the Future of Shari`a* (Harvard University Press 2010). An-Na'im argues that the coercive enforcement of *Shari'a* by the state betrays the voluntary acceptance and reception of Islam. Just as the state should be secure from the misuse of religious authority, *Shari'a* should be freed from the control of the state. State policies or legislation must be based on civic reasons accessible to citizens of all religions.

73 See Abdullahi Ahmed An-Na'im, 'The Legitimacy of Constitution-Making Processes in the Arab World: An Islamic Perspective' in Grote (n 4); Abdullahi Ahmed An-Na'im, 'Religious Minorities under Islamic Law and the Limits of Cultural Relativism' (1987) 9 *HRQ* 1.

it, while the national capital was offered a special status, where the non-Muslims are protected from the application of *Shari'a* laws.[74] Accordingly, the CPA grants non-Muslims full citizenship rights, including the provision that 'eligibility for office, including the presidency, public service and the enjoyment of all rights and duties shall be based on citizenship and not on religion, beliefs or customs'.[75]

The INC provides for institutional mechanisms with a view to recognizing claims of national, religious and ethnic minorities. It sets out institutional arrangements to protect the rights of religious minorities, and accommodate the cultural and social diversity of Sudan, particularly by providing for the establishment of the Commission for the Protection of Non-Muslims in the Capital. The Commission has jurisdiction to promote social diversity and religious co-existence between the different cultures in Sudan.[76] The INC also mandates the establishment of special courts and prosecutors to ensure that all religious practices and beliefs are protected and enforced in the capital Khartoum by the law enforcement agencies which will be trained and made sensitive to the cultural, religious and cultural diversity in Khartoum.[77] The INC instructs law-enforcing agencies to be guided by tolerance towards Sudanese people of different cultures, religions and traditions while dispensing justice in the capital;[78] it also decrees that law-enforcing agencies should recognize that 'behavior based on cultural practices and traditions' within the prescribed limits 'shall be deemed in the eyes of the law as an exercise of personal freedoms'.[79] The courts are instructed to observe the 'long-established *Shari'a* principle that non-Muslims are not subject to prescribed penalties and therefore remitted penalties shall apply according to law'.[80] Other mechanisms for guaranteeing minority rights are envisaged in article 156 of the INC (Dispensing Justice in the National Capital), which includes judicial circulars, establishment of specialized courts and establishment of specialized public attorneys.[81] These systems are supposed to guarantee respect for the rights of non-Muslims in the capital according to the principles enshrined in the INC.

The Commission for the Protection of the Rights of Non-Muslims in the National Capital was established[82] to ensure that the rights of non-Muslims are protected and respected in accordance with the CPA and the INC, and particularly non-Muslims are in fact exempted from the *Shari'a* laws in Khartoum.[83] However, the effectiveness of the Commission proved to be

74 Art 5 of the INC.
75 Principle 6.3. of the Machakos Protocol of 2002.
76 See arts 154, 155, 157 of the INC.
77 Ibid.
78 Art 156 (a) ibid.
79 Art 156 (b) ibid.
80 Art 156 (d) ibid.
81 Art 158 ibid.
82 Republican Decree no 24 of October 2006.
83 The Commission consists of twenty-eight members including five Muslim's scholars and five Christian scholars, ten from the community leaders and two specialists in customs and traditions and one representative for Khartoum state, judiciary body, ministry of justice and police and national security.

questionable during the implementation of the CPA. It was dismantled after the secession of South Sudan against the desire of non-Muslim minorities that requested the authorities to retain the Commission so as to ensure that non-Muslims are not discriminated against after the session of South Sudan.[84]

5 The rights of peoples in the two Sudans

5.1 The right to self-determination in Sudan and South Sudan

The CPA constitutes an important example of State practice guaranteeing the right to self-determination. The agreement, which ended the long-standing civil war, was based on power- and wealth-sharing. The Machakos Protocol of 2002 stipulated that 'the people of South Sudan have the right to control and govern affairs in their region and participate equitably in the National Government'.[85] This arrangement lasted for the CPA interim period from 2005–11. The Protocol also explicitly recognized the right to external self-determination, which was subsequently, with a slight modification, enshrined in the INC: 'The people of South Sudan have the right to self-determination through a referendum to determine their future status.'[86] As envisaged in the Protocol and the INC, an internationally monitored referendum was held at the end of the six-year interim period in 2011, for the people of South Sudan to '(a) confirm unity of the Sudan by voting to sustain the system of government established under the Comprehensive Peace Agreement and this Constitution, or (b) vote for secession'.[87] After the death of John Garang, leader of the Sudan People's Liberation Movement/Army (SPLM/SPLA) who had advocated a new Sudan that would have transformed the country as a whole, in 2005 the party's position shifted towards seeking South Sudan's independence.[88] Consequently, largely given the National Congress Party's (the main partner to the CPA) limited efforts to 'make the unity of the Sudan an attractive option'[89] and the SPLM/SPLA's dominance in South Sudan's politics, the referendum's outcome was a foregone conclusion, resulting in a 98.83 per cent vote in favour of independence.[90]

The referendum represented an important, consensual exercise of the right to external self-determination. However, the CPA had various flaws in terms of

84 This paragraph draws on Abdelgabar (n 4) 668–9. Non-Muslim communities protested, including the members of the Commission (Interview with members of the Commission for the Rights of non-Muslims in Khartoum, 2012, on file with author).

85 Principle 1.2.

86 Art 119 of the INC.

87 Art 222(2) ibid.

88 Douglas H Johnson, *South Sudan: A New History for a New Nation* (Ohio University Press 2016) 151ff.

89 Principle 1.5.5. of the Makakos Protocol of 2002.

90 See final certified results from the Southern Sudan Referendum Commission, available at https://southernsudan2011.com, accessed 5 June 2018.

its substantive provisions and modalities of implementation. It paved the way for self-determination of South Sudan by not addressing the critical question of how attractive unity could be realized through a genuine democratic transformation.[91] This question applied equally to the South, and included South–South minority rights and human rights violations committed by southern factions during the internal civil war. The two parties who shared wealth and power adopted 'undeclared' policies and actions, with the tacit support of international actors, which led to the secession of South Sudan with no democratic transformation in place. This constituted the outcome of a liberal peace-making model which brought the parties to enter a peace agreement even where it is well known that they have poor human rights records, including disregard for minority rights, and are not genuinely committed to transform Sudan, or South Sudan for that matter.[92]

South Sudan has faced an armed conflict since 2013, which is characterized by a mixture of political rivalries and tribal, ethnic and regional features. Notwithstanding South Sudan's diversity, neither the 2011 Transitional Constitution nor the 2015 Agreement on the Resolution of the Conflict in the Republic of South Sudan recognize the right to self-determination. Instead, the 2015 Agreement is based on a combination of power- and wealth-sharing and federalism. At the time of writing, almost three years later, the agreement has largely remained a dead letter. Again, the flawed liberal peace-making model of the CPA is replicated in South Sudan. This flawed process has been acknowledged by the AU Commission of Inquiry on South Sudan (AUCISS) in its report. It takes the view that the current conflict can be attributed, in part, to the flaws of the CPA (in terms of process and outcomes) as well as its implementation modalities. It adopted the dominant paradigm of 'liberal peace-building', which in practice tends to privilege 'negative peace', with its preoccupation with ending violence but without a vision of building sustainable peace and viable institutions.[93] The AUCISS concluded:

> The crisis is beyond anything we have seen in scale, magnitude and depth. A quick fix power-sharing agreement will not work – problems of the country and leadership are too deep. ... We need to re-boot South Sudan – no quick fix, no deal, will do it.[94]

91 Mohamed Abdelsalam Babiker, 'South Sudan's Hybrid Court: The Challenge of Redressing Victims of International Crimes', in Steven C. Roach and Derrick K. Hudson (ed.), *The Challenge of Governance in South Sudan: Corruption, Peacebuilding and Foreign Intervention* (Routledge 2018) 157.

92 Ibid.

93 *Final Report of the African Union Commission of Inquiry on South Sudan* (15 October 2014) para 45.

94 Ibid para 165.

5.2 Popular consultations and regional autonomy for Blue Nile, the Nuba Mountains and Darfur: are they people or minorities?

The CPA was partially flawed, as the situation in South Kordofan, Blue Nile and Abyei were not subject to a referendum, even though a claim can be made that many of these areas' inhabitants are either South Sudanese (or want to belong to South Sudan) or constitute a people in their own right, such as in the Nuba Mountains. The fact that there was no general right to self-determination also reflects on the unequal treatment of other peoples in Sudan, such as the Darfuris, whose status has been subject to a separate peace agreement. The Darfur Peace Agreement provided that '[t]he permanent status of Darfur shall be determined through a referendum held simultaneously in the three states of Darfur'.[95] However, it equally made clear that the options for such a permanent status were confined to the creation of a Darfur Region composed of the three states or retention of the status quo,[96] which addressed the administrative status rather than the right to self-rule of the region. The Doha Document for Peace in Darfur of 2011 largely replicated this approach.[97]

5.3 Abyei and the two Sudans

As indicated above, the CPA accorded southern Sudanese the right of self-determination. However, Abyei is still contested by the Messiriya Humur and Dinka Ngok tribal communities and remains a challenging case for both the governments in Sudan and South Sudan. The CPA accorded Abyei a special status and dealt with it in a separate Protocol, but the Protocol is vague when it comes to rights and claims of the two groups.[98] The Abyei Protocol stipulates that (1) Abyei is a bridge between the North and the South; linking the people of Sudan; (2) the territory is defined as the area of the Ngok Dinka chiefdoms transferred to Kordofan in 1905; and (3) the Messiriya and other nomadic peoples retain their rights to graze cattle and move across the territory of Abyei. However, both the Ngok Dinka and the Messiriya claim Abyei. Succumbing to the pressure of the Messiriya and the Ngok Dinka, the NCP and SPLM took the case to the International Court of Arbitration, but people at the local level (the Messiriya) were not happy with the court's ruling.[99] The Ngok Dinka were also unhappy about it, and at various points in time there was a genuine possibility of the outbreak of armed conflict. The fact that both the NCP and the SPLA resorted to the International Court of Arbitration is not only indicative of the

95 Darfur Peace Agreement of 2006, 55.

96 Ibid 57.

97 See Doha Document for Peace in Darfur (DDPD), UN doc A/65/914, S/2011/449 (2011) Enclosure 2.

98 Protocol between the Government of Sudan (GoS) and the Sudan People's Liberation Movement/Army (SPLM/A) on Resolution of Abyei Conflict (26 May 2004).

99 See further Gary B Born and Adam Raviv, 'The Abyei Arbitration and the Rule of Law' (2017) 58 *HILJ* 177.

various costly mistakes of the CPA in terms of its Protocols but also the failure of the referendum laws to adopt substantive provisions which could rectify or mitigate the 'legal blunders' committed in the peace process.

Furthermore, Abyei as a unique case is an 'anomaly' in the recent practice of international law. The Abyei case and the South Sudan secession/independence are unique in the sense that they create new precedents in the African context; both cases justified the redrawing of the African map or boundaries on an ethnic basis rather than the preservation of the status quo of the colonial State based on traditional international law (*uti possidetis*).[100] Redrawing a new map on an ethnic basis risks opening the door for endless communal conflicts, disputes and historical claims of ancestral lands. It also raises issues of minority rights protection and rights of minorities to their indigenous ancestral land. There is no doubt the CPA has created a dilemma for the two Sudans which reflects confusion and socio-legal conundrums, in particular the uneasy relationship between States and minorities in post-colonial Africa.

Unlike South Sudan, the Abyei case is different from southern Sudan; here a distinction needs to be made between southern Sudanese as a people and 'other' Sudanese ethnic groups such as the Messiriya and the Ngok Dinka. It raises human rights questions that are best resolved within the minority human rights regime and its developed jurisprudence. The question in relation to rights of these ethnic groups is the status of non-ethnically southern Sudanese in Abyei after separation should the Ngok Dinka and the other residents of Abyei decide to be part of Southern Sudan. What are the measures that could be taken to avert minority rights violations in such situations? The same applies to Ngok Dinka. What about the groups that are not considered indigenous in the rest of Southern Sudan? These pertinent questions on the Abyei case can be addressed within the framework of international human rights law on minority rights. This framework includes the rights of national and ethnic minorities and the fundamental principle of non-discrimination stipulated in the international human rights regime. Particular reference shall be made here to article 27 of the ICCPR providing for the rights of ethnic, religious or linguistic minority. It also guarantees indigenous land rights claims and protection of individual and communal rights. Other instruments and treaties can also be invoked here to protect traditional rights of communities such as the UN Declaration on the Rights of Indigenous Peoples of 2007, the ILO Convention Concerning Indigenous and Tribal Peoples in Independent Countries (No 169), and ICERD.[101] The jurisprudence on traditional land rights can provide guidance as to the protection of indigenous and minority rights in the post-referendum context.[102] Thus, a human rights approach related to the rights of the ethnic minorities in Abyei area can be

100 Dirdeiry M Ahmed, *Boundaries and Secession in Africa and International Law: Challenging Uti Possidetis* (CUP 2015).

101 See CERD, General Recommendation 23: Indigenous Peoples (18 August 1997).

102 See further Casciarri and Babiker (n 65).

guided by international human rights treaties and developed jurisprudence in this particular area.[103]

6 Critical appraisal of minority and peoples rights protection in Sudan

The INC, based on the CPA, set out a far-reaching constitutional framework that combined a symbolic commitment to Sudan's diversity with non-discrimination, specific rights for religious communities, inclusive citizenship and nationality and respect for indigenous languages (article 8). The rights of Non-Muslims were specifically protected by a special commission and mechanism for guarantees. This framework, which also included the integration of international treaties binding on Sudan as part of the Bill of Rights, has failed in practice, as evident by persistent concerns over the rights of minorities, particularly religious minorities. This is unsurprising given that the power structures and ideologies, which have privileged an exclusionary, narrow Islamic vision of the country, have remained intact. Respect for the rule of law has equally remained weak, which means that the framework for institutional protection, however well-conceived, has provided inadequate protection. Instead of promoting genuine equality, the INC's institutional set-up enshrined marginalization. One of the key lessons learned about minority rights protection in both Sudan and South Sudan is that national minority guarantees were not adequately taken into considerations within the CPA and the INC framework, particularly in respect of more than two million Southerners living in the North, a great many of whom are internally displaced persons (IDPs) who fled the war. In addition, there are both southerners and northerners who live and work in the other States (Sudan and South Sudan respectively). Furthermore, and as outlined above, the constitutional framework is flawed in the sense that some regions in Sudan were accorded the right to self-determination while other regions or areas were given limited rights. Recognition and protection of minority rights requires a fundamental transformation in Sudan's system. The power- and wealth-sharing formulas and formulas aimed at bringing about democracy reflect the awareness of key actors of the need for change. However, instead of a democratic transformation and strengthening of rule of law institutions, the country divided, entrenching existing power structures, and fuelling further conflicts. The main exception, namely the vindication of the right to self-determination in the form of South Sudan's referendum leading to its independence, has ironically aggravated the situation, rather than enhanced respect for minority rights and peoples in either Sudan. The peace agreement approach, while allowing tailored responses, has been captured and manipulated by political actors,

103 In particular in respect of cases such as *Jonassen et al v Norway*, Comm 942/00 (25 October 2002), a communication to the Human Rights Committee concerning a State party's alleged failure to recognize and protect the author's traditional grazing rights. See further Ben Saul, *Indigenous Peoples and Human Rights: International and Regional Jurisprudence* (Hart Publishing 2016).

and has done little to open up broader democratic processes. Its main advantage has been temporary ceasefires, with the proliferation of peace processes highlighting, if anything, the many conflicts, and unaddressed causes thereof. A truly participatory constitution-making process therefore needs to ensure the rights of minorities to both adequate protection and democratic representation, which itself presupposes democratization. As such, the rights of minorities and peoples' to self-determination in the Sudans cannot be disassociated from broader structural changes and democratization processes.

7 Women's rights in Sudan

Constitutional recognition and lived experiences

Ebtisam Sanhouri Elrayh

1 Introduction

Women's role in shaping Sudan's history through their dynamic political participation and substantial contribution in forming the State is evident but insufficiently recognized. Women were on the frontlines demonstrating against the colonial authority as early as 1916 and their role continued throughout the independence phase to the present. Official statistics confirm women's valuable contribution to Sudan's economy, in all sectors, including agriculture, manufacturing and civil services. Except for a few academic disciplines where women's enrolment is barred by law, the number of female students at institutions of higher education significantly exceeds that of their male counterparts. Women form nearly half of the population of Sudan and care for the other half, yet they live in a minority-like situation, representing the largest group whose vital social, economic and political worth remains undervalued and barely considered.

With Sudan entering a new phase in its history, following South Sudan's secession in 2011, there is a general consensus on the need for a new constitution. To acquire legitimacy and foster durability, the forthcoming constitution has to respond to the major outstanding issues and challenges. This includes the nature of the State, the type and structure of governance, institutional safeguards, allocation of power and resources, human rights and fundamental freedoms, diversity, ethnic and religious minorities, and, finally *women*: their status, role and constitutional and legislative rights.

The question of women and their rights in the future constitution has generated considerable debate. A radical position, invoking religious and social values, believes that some of the established constitutional and legal rights of women in Sudan need to be curtailed. Others consider the question of women's rights as trivial, time-consuming and of little importance, diverting time from focusing on more pressing issues. A third view considers women's rights as inseparable from the problems that impact the whole population and can only be resolved through a holistic reform of State institutions. Supremacy of the rule of law and ensuring human rights for all would be sufficient to address women's position in society and guarantee the protection of their rights. Therefore, women's rights should be addressed as a cross-cutting issue, rather than as an isolated concern.

Another group sees the issue as one of discrimination in the provision and enjoyment of the rights recognized under the constitution; women are given less rights compared to their male counterparts. Aware of this fact, several initiatives were launched across the country to consider women's role and rights concerning the substance and process of constitution-making.[1] Their main objective is to engender the process of constitution-making and integrate gender equality, with a view to securing full and equal citizenship, protecting women's inalienable rights and eradicating all forms of discrimination in what has often been a hostile environment based on cultural conservatism and religious tenets.

This chapter examines the gender dimensions of Sudan's constitution, locating them in broader regional and international debates and developments. It takes a holistic approach that analyses the extent to which constitutions, beyond any bill of rights, are conducive to the basic right to equality and non-discrimination, and the realization of women's rights. This includes consideration of structural factors, such as political participation, institutions, particularly commissions mandated to consider questions of women's rights, and procedures for legislative and institutional reforms needed to ensure the rights of women. The chapter reviews the Bill of Rights and women's position across Sudan's constitutions in light of international standards as well as the legislative and institutional frameworks, practice and the experience of women, so as to identify the gaps and issues that need to be addressed to ensure the effective recognition of women's rights.

2 Status, role and rights of women in society and State

Sudanese women face multiple dilemmas regarding their status, prescribed roles, rights and duties, and position in State and society. Despite their number and indispensable contribution in the private and public sphere, they suffer from discrimination, marginalization and exclusion for most of their lives. Throughout the history of governance of Sudan, women have not been given a fair share in the decision-making processes in major political, social and economic affairs, even though they were, and continue to be, the primary casualties thereof. Women experience different forms of victimization as the result of the political decisions (choices) made by male-dominated governments regarding warfare and peace. They have been used as weapons in those wars, experiencing rape, displacement and loss of life. Nevertheless, they have played no or an insignificant role in peace

1 Namely, Development Studies and Research Institute at the University of Khartoum; Regional Institute for Studies of Gender, Women and Human Rights at Ahfad University; Alayaam Centre for Cultural Studies and Development, Gender Centre for Research and Studies; NEWAIDA, Faculty of Law at University of Khartoum; Sudanese Initiative for Constitution Making; Ministry of Welfare and Social Security through its Directorate of Women and Family Affairs and Women's Human Rights Centre; Human Rights Advisory Council at the Ministry of Justice; Sudanese Woman Union and Women's Parliamentarians Caucus.

negotiations.[2] Women belonging to marginalized groups experience multiple discrimination based on ethnicity, religion, displacement and disability among other status.[3] Sixty-two years since Sudan's independence, women's role and rights are not a done deal; they are still subject for discussion and generate huge controversy at the State and society level.

2.1 Fluidity and instability of women's position and entitlements

The struggle women face in Sudan is not unique. It confronts similar political, social, cultural and religious obstacles that constrain women's advancement and entitlement to basic rights and freedoms elsewhere. Nonetheless, some specific characteristics need highlighting. Women's position and rights in Sudan have shifted constantly, moving forward and backward, following the change of regime that seizes power, its ideological premise, and the laws and policies it adopts. The range of rights women enjoy depends largely on the societal attitude, which shuffles between modernization and conservative, if not reactionary, attitudes. In addition, the economic volatility caused by the ongoing conversion from the socialist to liberal economy and later on the Islamic model, produced sudden, massive economic growth and soon after a sharp downfall.[4] These and other factors have left women's position and rights in Sudan wide open to socio-religious debates influenced by economic uncertainty and political manipulation.

Sudan's women's movement is by many considered to be the most vibrant in Africa and the Middle East,[5] having survived three periods of repression. The first setback occurred when the right to stand for election, gained by women in 1964, was lost in 1968 due to the abolition of the Graduate College constituencies, the single platform for women candidacy. In the 1970s, women gathered forces again, continued their struggle and succeeded in achieving their right to full political participation, among other rights.[6] A decade later, the second drawback occurred when the May Regime (the second military rule, 1969–85) abandoned its socialist, leftist ideology and took a sharp turn to introduce the Islamic laws of

2 Anne Itto, *Guests at the Table? The Role of Women in Peace Processes* (Conciliation Resources 2016).

3 Equal Rights Trust, in partnership with SORD, *In Search of Confluence: Addressing Discrimination and Inequality in Sudan* (2014).

4 Siddig Umbadda, *Towards Institutional Reform and Economic Policies Supporting Stability (After Political Reconciliation)* (Sudan Democracy First Group, Institutional Reform Series, Paper No 3 2014).

5 Sondra Hale, *Gender Politics in Sudan: Islamism, Socialism and the State* (Westview Press 1996). Also Balghis Badri, 'Feminist Perspectives in the Sudan: An Analytical Overview', in *Gender Politik Online* (2006), www.fu-berlin.de/sites/gpo/tagungen/index.htm, accessed 23 March 2018.

6 Ebtisam Sanhouri Elrayh, *The Political Participation of Women in Sudan: The Formal and Political Parties Framework of Empowerment* (DSRI and ECCO project, March 2017).

1983 (often referred to as the 'September Laws').[7] These laws curtailed most of the rights and freedoms protected under the 1973 Constitution, including, but not limited to, the right to privacy, the prohibition of inhuman treatment and punishment, and freedom of religion. The September Laws struck at the basic principle of equality and non-discrimination, imposing numerous constraints on women. Further regulations were enacted to control women in public and private life in contravention of their constitutional entitlements. These measures included enforcing a special dress code on women, setting specific working hours for them, and introducing the next-of-kin companionship policy in respect of their movement and travel.

The third wave of critical change in women's position was brought about with the capture of power by the *Inqaz* Regime (the third *coup d'état* of 1989). The military council ruled the country up to 1998 through constitutional decrees following the suspension of the constitution and the dissolution of all political parties. It imposed a radical Islamic approach, whereby rights and freedoms were subject to religious rules. Detention, torture and oppression of political opponents were widespread.[8] A severe dress code imposed on women, along with series of measures restricting their movement inside and outside the house and the country, gradually ushered women into seclusion and confinement. Among the first measures taken by the regime was the large-scale dismissal of women from different sectors of government, and their deliberate exclusion from certain fields of study and work. Prior to 2005, no woman was allowed to enter the judiciary and very few were left working in the field of foreign affairs. Women and girls became targets of police harassment and intimidation and the main subjects of prosecution under the penal laws and public order regime.[9]

Following a decade of suffering and fierce resistance, women were able to recover some basic rights and maintain limited presence in the political scene from 1998 to 2005. Nevertheless, the fear of a fourth wave of restrictions is present, manifested by the conflicting viewpoints of the groups working in the constitution-making process and the broader socio-political context. Hence, it is of great importance that women articulate their vision and join forces to defend their rights and tackle any possible regression concerning their role in society and State. Holding a national unified stand regarding women's status, role and rights in the constitution-making may assist in ending the fluidity and precariousness that has characterized their position and rights in the history of Sudan.

7 E.g. Amin M Medani, 'A Legacy of Institutionalized Repression: Criminal Law and Justice in Sudan' in Lutz Oette (ed.), *Criminal Law Reform and Transitional Justice: Human Rights Perspectives for Sudan* (Ashgate 2011) .

8 See Human Rights Watch/Africa, *Behind the Red Line: Political Repression in Sudan* (1996); Amin M Medani, *Crimes against International Humanitarian Law in Sudan: 1989-2000* (Dar El Mostaqbal El Arabi 2001).

9 Asma Hadel Halim, 'Gendered Justice: Women and the Application of Penal Laws in the Sudan', in Oette (n 7).

2.2 *Structural factors: the socio-economic position and gender inequality*

Women live under difficult conditions in Sudan, notwithstanding constitutional provisions on social justice, equal distribution of wealth and power, and women's right to equal participation in public life. Due to the State's persistent failure to adopt suitable economic plans, the ratio of women living below the poverty line continues to surpass that of men.[10] The deficiency of healthcare polices and plans and the failure to make good quality care available and accessible to all women continue to contribute to high pre- and post-natal mortality in Sudan, which has one of the highest maternal mortality rates worldwide.[11] Economic and social development plans remain insensitive to gender issues and women's needs, and barely recognize or consider women's vital contribution to the economy and development, leaving the majority of female workers outside the formal sector without social benefits, healthcare coverage and official recognition. Women also face harassment from the public order police while selling food and drinks on public places, alongside the recently imposed excessive fines of the local authorities.[12]

Inclusion of 'positive discrimination' and 'affirmative action' clauses in the current constitution were received with great hopes to enhance women's participation in the public and political arena.[13] However, the failure to effectively implement these provisions perpetuated women's lower status in the workforce. The estimated percentage of women graduates in higher education is 58.2 per cent compared to men. However, only 26 per cent of them find their way into the formal employment sector; 77 per cent of them perform administrative work, 87.8 per cent work in farming and 4.8 per cent in industry.[14] The majority of women have no social security cover. Statistics also confirm that of the 90 per cent of Sudanese who live below the poverty line, 65 per cent are women.[15] The right to education has been stipulated in Sudan's recent constitutions, including the current one.[16] While it is considered a key instrument in women's advancement, its lack of adequate implementation has left 50.6 per cent of women illiterate.[17] Further, the deteriorating economic situation of families has left its mark

10 See Gender and Development Unit, the Institute of Developmental Studies and Research (IDSR), University of Khartoum in collaboration with UN-Women (Sudan) 'Women's Problems under Interim Constitution 2005', in their series *Sudanese Women and the Upcoming Constitution, 1, 2 and 3* (August 2011) (Arabic).

11 Sudan ranks 165th out of 179 in the Gender Inequality Index, UNDP, *Human Development Report* (2016) 216.

12 REDRESS and SIHA, *Criminalisation of Women in Sudan: A Need for Fundamental Reform* (2017).

13 See in particular art 32(2) of the Interim National Constitution (INC) of 2005.

14 Suad Ibrahim Issa, *Women's Rights between Legal Admittance and Curtailment in Practice* (2010) (Arabic), 113, 140 and 146.

15 Ibid.

16 Art 44 INC.

17 See IDSR (10), Publication No (1), and Sudanese Women Union, *Sudanese Women: Facts and Figures* (no date) (Arabic).

on women's and girls' right to education, as males are preferred due to religious and customary beliefs on gender roles.

Any future constitutional arrangement must adequately address these structural factors. While the focus on equality and civil and political rights in the Bill of Rights is important, it is on its own insufficient to change deep-seated societal and economic inequalities.

2.3 Disparity between constitutional principles and legal rules

The discussion surrounding women's rights plays out against the background of the disparity between the *de jure* and *de facto* position of women. Besides differences and inconsistencies among the diverse constitutions regarding women's position, women's enjoyment of the prescribed rights and freedoms are often compromised in practice. This is either because no laws have been enacted to facilitate the enjoyment or the laws in force are not repealed or amended to comply with the constitution. This lack of alignment is a general problem; however, its impact is particularly pronounced concerning women's issues.

The State has failed to secure women's rights, notwithstanding Sudan's Interim National Constitution (INC) of 2005. Eight years after its adoption, there are over twenty-six laws that are not in line with the constitution.[18] A series of laws, including but not limited to the Muslim Personal Status Act of 1991, the Criminal Act of 1991 and the Evidence Act of 1994, violate women's rights and some of them openly discriminate against women.[19] Several regulations and orders issued by the state and local authorities, such as the Public Order Act of Khartoum State of 1998, are directed towards women in particular, imposing various restrictions on their movement inside and outside the country, and adversely impact the work of marginalized women.[20] Notwithstanding the constitutional protection of individual integrity and the prohibition of torture, legislation fails to adequately protect women and girls from violence, which perpetuates a climate of fear and facilitates the commission of crimes, both inside and outside conflict zones.[21]

Any forthcoming constitution must address the problem of conflicting statutory law through avoiding the use of open-ended phrases when subjecting the enjoyment of rights and freedoms to clauses such as 'as prescribed by the law', 'subject to the provisions of the law'. There is also an urgent need to remove contradicting or

18 Women Centre for Human Rights, Ministry of Welfare and Social Security, *Report on the Project: Review and Reform of Women Position in Legislation*, presented at the 'First workshop for the Reform of Women Position in Criminal and Personal Status Act' (2–3 March 2013) (Arabic).

19 *Report of the Human Rights Council on Sudan*, UN doc A/HRC/WG.6/11/SDN/2 (2011) 1–3.

20 Nabil Adib, 'The State Government and Women Tea Sellers' *Al-Sudani Newspaper* (May 2010) (Arabic).

21 Halim (n 9) 227.

conflicting principles that generate confusion and uncertainty in practice, including when adjudicated in courts. This applies particularly to referring to *Shari'a* as the main source of law, and at the same time upholding international human rights instruments and treaties ratified by Sudan as an integral part of the Bill of Rights.[22] In addition, the composition of the judiciary and attitude of (largely male) judges, who give primacy to religious sources and laws derived from them and thereby seriously compromise women's and girls' rights,[23] requires fundamental change.

2.4 The restrictive religious and cultural milieu

The most important factor that undermines women's position in Sudan and Muslim communities in general remains the dialectical cultural and religious contest over women's status, role and rights. In Sudan, religion and cultural beliefs and practices still generate male supremacy and dominance, turning equality and non-discrimination constitutional clauses into mere lip service. There is a common, deeply rooted conviction, even among some women, that women are not able to hold equal roles, shoulder similar responsibilities and enjoy the same rights as men in all spheres. This belief is partially attributed to the limited understanding of religion and erroneous application of certain Islamic principles.[24] The outdated customs and traditions, which propagate women's inferiority, play a significant role as well. This includes the failure to develop a new understanding and interpretation of *Shari'a* law that is able to accommodate contemporary challenges and meet current needs, including those of women.

The debate on women's status and rights is critical in light of the rise of cultural and religious conservatism around the world, and particularly in Arab States where the beliefs and practices are more radical than in non-Arab countries.[25] The inability to create a solid base for women's rights in these communities is partially attributed to a lack of belief in these rights and will and commitment to enforce them. Debating the rights of women as a fundamental issue in the process of constitution-making, a comprehensive national dialogue and legal and institutional reforms is the best way to address the inconsistency of religion and cultural norms *vis-à-vis* human and women's rights treaties and declarations.[26]

22 Arts 5(1) and 27(3) of the INC 2005.

23 An example is the conviction for murder of the 19-year-old Noura Hussein, for having killed her husband in self-defence, when he tried to rape her following a forced marriage. See SIHA, *Trapped in between Misogyny and Dogma: Nour's Case and the Dilemma of Sudan's Legal System* (14 May 2018).

24 Fatima Mernissi, *Le Harem Politique: le Prophète et les femmes* (Albin Michel 1987).

25 See USAID & Kemitraan, *Patriarchal Barriers to Women's Political Participation in South-East Asia: Lessons from the Philippines, Cambodia, Malaysia, Indonesia, and Timor-Leste on Patriarchy and the Rise of Women's Participation in State Politics* (August 2014).

26 Ebtisam Sanhouri Elrayh, 'Women's Rights in the Constitutional Bill of Rights: Issues of Status, Equality and Non-Discrimination', in Mohamed Abdelsalam Babiker and Lutz Oette (eds), *The Constitutional Protection of Human Rights in Sudan: Challenges and Future Perspectives* (REDRESS, Faculty of Law University of Khartoum, Sudanese Human Rights Monitor 2014) 24.

In Sudan, the gulf between the current draft constitutions presented by pro-women's initiatives and radical groups demonstrates the acute necessity to develop a joint women's agenda. To illustrate, the pro-women's rights group, the Engendering the Constitution Forum, stresses the need to involve women throughout the process of constitution-making and insists that the constitution shall incorporate a gender dimension and be responsive to women's needs and concerns. In their proposal, the constitution ensures women's equal status based on citizenship and full entitlement to equal civil, political, economic, social and cultural rights. It calls for women's right to equal representation within all government organs – legislative, executive and judicial – by not less than 30 per cent, to be gradually increased to reach 50 per cent. To achieve the required proportion, the constitution shall sanction the use of special measures, such as positive discrimination. International and regional treaties shall be the source of women's rights, particularly the equality and non-discrimination clauses.[27]

The conservative radical group Islamic Constitution Front calls for the establishment of a unitary sovereign State and for Islam to be named as the religion and law of the State.[28] Its draft constitution assigns the State to be the guardian of rights and duties as regulated by the provisions of *Shari'a*, which is built on the 'principle of justice, not absolute equality'. It stipulates that the candidate for the positions of President and governor must be a 'Muslim' and 'male', who has the 'physical strength' to protect the people and fight the enemy, and possesses all senses and body parts. Judges shall be selected from the most qualified 'men'. The draft constitution clearly classifies citizens into different categories and draws a marked distinction between Muslim men on the one hand and Muslim women, non-Muslims and persons with disabilities on the other. The draft makes most of the rights subject to the provisions of the law, which further undermines their limited constitutional protection.

There is no way for Sudan to survive, develop and prosper with half of its population undervalued, marginalized and neglected. To change the status quo, people must renounce outdated beliefs and practices and adopt perspectives that adequately respond to lived realities. The forthcoming constitution should outline these perspectives and guarantee their realization.

3 Rights of women in Sudan's past and present constitutions: human rights and gender perspectives

Studies of Sudan's history have documented the power dynamics in the country and their impact on the political and legal system and the socio-economic status

27 See the Series (n 10).

28 The 'Draft Constitution of the State of Sudan', issued by Islamic Constitution Front, Ramadan 1432 H (August 2011), arts 1, 2, 26, 27, 44(1)(b), 4, 5, 113(b), 174(b), 35(m) and 26 to 38 in the Rights Section (Arabic).

of men and women.[29] The analysis in this part focuses on women's status and rights in the era immediately preceding the country's independence until the present. It examines the rights and level of constitutional protection conferred upon women under Sudan's successive constitutions in view of relevant international and regional treaties.

3.1 Women's constitutional rights (1953–2005)

3.1.1 From pre-independence to unstable statehood: 1953–73

In its recent history, Sudan has adopted seven constitutional documents and a draft Islamic constitution (1968). The Self-Government Statute 1953 and the Interim Constitution 1956 took minimal account of human rights and fundamental freedoms, both in general and in relation to women. They included a section on fundamental rights comprised of six articles, three of which related to the rule of law, independence of the judiciary and constitutional protection of rights. One of the provisions affirmed the right to 'equality before the law' and the prohibition of 'disability by reasons of birth, religion, race or sex in regard to employment, occupation, trade, business or profession'.[30] The other two articles singled out freedom of religion, freedom of expression, prohibition of arrest, imprisonment, as well as detention and confiscation of property except by due process of law.[31] Both constitutions failed to live up to the broad principles of equality, inherent dignity, non-discrimination, gender equality and the firm 'belief in human rights, dignity and worth of human being, and equal rights of men and women' recognized in the Universal Declaration of Human Rights 1948 (UDHR).[32]

Neither the 1953 Self-Government Statute nor the 1956 constitution embraced the rights referred to in the UN Convention on the Political Rights of Women (1952),[33] namely, the right to vote, run for election, hold public offices and exercise all public functions on an equal footing to men and without discrimination of any kind. However, the period witnessed the birth of the first women's union in the country, formed by a group of activists who faced the resistance of traditional and religious forces.[34] One of the union's important goals was to raise women's awareness and campaign for women's basic human rights and freedoms, especially civil and political ones. Leading numerous demonstrations in the streets of Khartoum, women were allowed to vote in the parliamentary election of

29 See in this regard, Nafisa Ahmed al-Amin and Professor Ahmed M. Magied, 'A History of Sudanese Women Organizations and the Strive for Liberation and Empowerment (2001) *18 AhfJ* 17.

30 Art 5 of the Self-Government Statue of 1953.

31 Arts 6 and 7 ibid, and art 4(1–2) of the Interim Constitution 1956.

32 See in particular the Preamble and arts 1 and 2 of the UDHR.

33 Sudan has not ratified the convention as of May 2018.

34 Haja K Badri, *The Women's Movement in Sudan* (Khartoum University Press 2002) (Arabic) 114.

1953.[35] Their right to vote, however, was restricted to the graduates' constituencies and moreover confined to educated women who had completed high school or university, while men were allowed to vote without any such restrictions.[36] In 1958, a Revolutionary Command Council (RCC) seized power, ending the first democratic rule in Sudan. It immediately suspended the constitution and all rights guaranteed under it. Women were not represented in the Council and had no role in governing the country.[37]

The Interim Constitution of 1964, adopted following the end of military rule, reproduced its predecessors, with limited amendments passed in 1965, 1966 and 1967. The section on fundamental rights was maintained, with minor changes in article 4, which prohibits the deprivation of any Sudanese of his (or her) rights by reasons of birth, religion, race or gender in regard to public offices, employment in the private sector, occupation or profession. Women's rights underwent major developments in practice, as women were allowed to vote and run for election in the democratic election, with the first Sudanese woman entering the constituent assembly in 1965. Yet soon thereafter, women lost their presence in the third constituent assembly following the abolition of the graduates' colleges in 1968.[38]

3.1.2 The 2nd military government and the Permanent Constitution of 1973

The Permanent Constitution of Sudan 1973, enacted by the Nimeri regime, lacked the basic elements of democracy. It concentrated powers in the hands of the President and recognized no political parties other than the ruling one.[39] Yet, it significantly broadened the corpus of constitutional rights, including civil, political, economic, social and cultural rights.[40] According to its preamble, the constitution's ultimate goal was to create a society based on welfare, equality and justice; further, Sudanese society is founded on the principles of national unity, solidarity, freedom, equality and justice.[41] The Permanent Constitution recognized equality before the law, and equality rights and duties of citizens 'irrespective of origin, race, locality, sex, language or religion'.[42] It also guaranteed

35 Sara Abbas, 'The Sudanese Women's Movement and the Mobilisation for the 2008 Legislative Quota and its Aftermath' (2010) 41 *IDS Bulletin* 100, 101.

36 See art 33 of the Self-Government Statute of 1953.

37 See Mohammed Ahmed Salim, 'Towards a distinctive role for women in the next constitution', Paper presented in 'Constitution-making Forum: A Government Consultation' (Advisory Council of Human Rights, UNDP and UNMIS, Khartoum 24–25 May 2011).

38 Ibid.

39 Art 4 of the Permanent Constitution of the Democratic Republic of Sudan of 1973.

40 Part III ibid.

41 Art 14 ibid.

42 Art 38 ibid.

the rights to political participation, education, health, mother and childcare, and equality of opportunities for all Sudanese.[43]

Even though the 1973 Permanent Constitution was adopted by a military regime, it constituted the first attempt to incorporate international human rights standards. It also vested the State with a series of responsibilities to ensure the 'social fundamentals' of Sudanese society, such as education, rural development, and social security.[44] Controversially, it recognized religion as part of the constitutional framework. Its article 16 reads: 'Islam is the religion of the State; society adheres to its commands and the State promotes its values, whereas Christianity is the religion of a large number of citizens and State promotes its values.' Article 9, for the first time, made an explicit link between religion and the law, stipulating: 'Islamic Shari'a and custom are the main sources of legislation, and the personal matters of non-Muslims are to be governed by their own law.'

Initially, women assumed important roles in public life, and enjoyed more rights and better protection compared to past constitutions. This can be attributed to the broad scope of constitutional socio-economic rights, in addition to the general duties incumbent on the State to eradicate poverty and enhance living standards, especially for women and other groups. These rights flowed from the socialist orientation of the regime when seizing power, and its reliance on women to gain and/or legitimize power. Towards the end of the regime, a sharp decline in women's position and rights occurred as the result of the regime's sudden political shift, with the imposition of the Islamic laws in 1983 and the attendant curtailment of women's rights and freedoms.[45]

3.1.3 The democratic transition and Transitional Constitution of 1985

The Transitional Constitution of Sudan of 1985 was passed in the aftermath of the popular uprising that overthrew military rule. The constitution removed the article on State religion introduced in the 1973 Constitution. However, it retained the provision that acknowledged *Shari'a* and custom as the main sources of legislation, while permitting non-Muslims to regulate their personal matters by their own law.[46] It elaborated a range of civil and political rights, including equality of all persons before the law and equality of citizens in holding rights and duties without discrimination due to birth, race, colour, sex, religion or political opinion, and prohibited restriction of the rights and freedoms except by legislation from the legislative authority aimed at protecting public security, morality, public health or national economy.[47] Unlike its predecessor, it did not recognize any economic, social and cultural rights and the scope of civil and political rights was limited with no reference to the basic right to life and the prohibition of

43 Arts 45, 46, 53, 54, 55 and 56 ibid.
44 Chapter 1 ibid.
45 See Medani (n 7).
46 Art 4 of the Transitional Constitution of Sudan 1985.
47 Arts 17–32 ibid.

torture, inhuman, cruel treatment and punishment. The constitution was also deficient regarding the protection of the rights of women, children, persons with disabilities and the elderly. In fact, it adversely affected women by providing for the continuity of all laws in force until repealed or amended by the competent authority, which sanctioned the discriminatory September Laws.[48]

The most significant achievement of the democratic government that came to power in 1986 was the ratification of the International Covenant on Civil and Political Rights (ICCPR), the International Covenant on Economic, Social and Cultural Rights (ICESCR) and the African Charter on Human and Peoples' Rights (ACHPR). However, it did not ratify the UN Convention of the Elimination of All Forms of Discrimination against Women (CEDAW) and the UN Convention against Torture and Other Cruel, Inhuman or Degrading Treatment or Punishment (CAT). Lack of political will was also apparent concerning women's call for reforms to rectify the catastrophic impact of the measures taken under the September *Shari'a* laws (1983). The era was particularly challenging, with war, famine, displacement and poverty combining with, and resulting in, socio-economic instability. Women and children bore the brunt of these developments. Instead of the much needed recognition of women's concerns and contribution, however, they had minimal representation in the legislative assembly of 1986, with two seats out of 301 (0.7 per cent) in the graduates' constituencies.[49]

3.1.4 The 3rd coup d'état and the 1998 Constitution

The 1998 Constitution was passed as a step towards transforming the 3rd military *Inqaz* regime into a *de jure* government nine years after it had seized power, suspended the constitution, dissolved all political parties and declared its programme of Islamization of the state. A sharp decline in women's role and position had occurred in the first years of the regime with the imposition of various restrictions that violated their basic rights and freedoms, namely the rights to equality and non-discrimination, privacy, work, movement, protection against torture, safety and personal security.[50] The 1998 Constitution did not recognize economic and social rights. The scope of civil and political rights was limited compared to the ICCPR, and restricted, if not altogether undermined, by phrases such 'as regulated by law' and 'in accordance to the law'. Women's rights were further limited by article 65 that identified Islamic *Shari'a* and the 'consensus of the nation' as the only sources of legislation.

The 1998 Constitution incorporated directive principles that obliged the State to care for the family, facilitate marriage, develop population policies, provide child care, care for pregnant women, liberate women from prejudice in all aspects of life, encourage women's role in the family and public life, in a significant

48 Art 134 ibid.
49 Abbas (n 35) 102.
50 Ibid.

move to change women's feeble position caused by the regime itself in its first nine years in power.[51] Nonetheless, women's right to move freely was severely restricted in and outside the country by statutory provisions; male companionship, a father, son or husband, was required and guardian approval was mandatory for travel abroad.[52] The ban on women to assume certain positions continued despite the adoption of the constitution. The constitution's major deficiency was its failure to provide for equality between men and women and equality before the law; it also did not include any provision on non-discrimination. Yet, the 1998 Constitution made some significant contributions to women's rights. Its article 22 recognized for the first time women's right to pass their nationality to their children on an equal footing. Further, its article 67 included a positive discrimination clause as a measure to advance particular groups, including women, and allocated a 25 per cent proportional representation for women in special, indirect election at national and State constituencies. The government sought women's support by appointing a percentage of 8.8 per cent women parliamentarians in 1992, 5.1 per cent in 1996 and 9.7 per cent in 2001, chosen from female members of the ruling political party.[53] However, women's actual contribution was negligible, and women's issues did not feature on the agendas of the legislative or ministerial councils.

3.2 Women's rights and the Interim National Constitution (INC) 2005

3.2.1 Overview

A series of developments compelled the regime to agree to fundamental changes. Against the backdrop of mounting support for the Southern military opposition and the growing conflict in Darfur, the regime concluded the Comprehensive Peace Agreement (CPA) with the Sudan People's Liberation Movement/Army (SPLM/A) and adopted the 2005 INC. Notwithstanding the discontent concerning the process of its formulation and adoption, the INC remains the best constitution Sudan has had in terms of the principles, directives and rights it incorporates. Being a product of exhaustive negotiations between South–North and international–regional forces, the INC is greatly influenced by international and regional human rights standards. In its preamble, it affirms the pluralistic nature of the State and the ethnic, racial, religious and cultural diversity of the population and declares its commitment to a decentralized, multi-party democratic system of governance and peaceful transfer of power. It further pledges to promote economic development, social harmony and religious tolerance, build

51 Art 15 ibid.

52 See the Muslim Personal Status Act of 1991.

53 See further on Islamists and women's rights, 'Al-Turabi and the Women of Sudan: Commitment to Women's Rights or Political Ambition?' (compiled on the basis of an unpublished study by Abulkhalig El-Sir) (2017) 3 *Women in Islam* (SIHA Journal) 8.

trust among Sudanese people and uphold values of justice, human dignity and equality of men and women in rights and in duties.[54]

3.2.2 Preamble, guiding principles and directives

Alongside the symbolic statements regarding the nature of the State, sovereignty of the people, national economy, environment and natural resources, social justice, foreign policy and national reconciliation, part I of the INC includes a number of rights meant to guide the State in legislation and policy-making as denoted in article 22. However, they are not justiciable. While some of these rights are elaborated in the Bill of Rights, other rights of fundamental importance, such as the right to health and work, are not. According to article 1 and 4 of the INC, equality is one of the founding layers of the State and basic principles of the constitution. Prohibition of discrimination in employment or work for qualified persons by reason of disability, the right of elderly persons and people with special needs to participate in social, professional, creative and entertainment activities, promotion of education and the State's obligation to make primary education and eradication of illiteracy compulsory and free of charge, are among the rights stipulated herein. However, some entitlements provided for by article 13 of the ICESCR are left out, including parents' choice concerning their children's education, the State's obligation regarding availability of technical and professional education, and equal access to higher education for all based on merit.

Two provisions in this part are of exceptional significance to women. Article 5 of the INC provides that nationally enacted legislation shall have as its sources of legislation Islamic *Shari'a* and consensus of the people. Under the title of morals and public integrity, article 16 authorizes the State 'to enact laws to protect the society from corruption, delinquency and social evils and steer the society as a whole towards virtuous social values consistent with religions and cultures of the Sudan'. The two provisions generate considerable confusion and uncertainty, particularly for women. They endanger the supremacy of a number of constitutional provisions over statutory law in spite of article 3. Women's rights to equality and non-discrimination, and other rights will all be open to limitation when read and applied in light of *Shari'a* law as pursued in its historical and cultural context. In practice, this may lead to a conflict of norms and interpretations incompatible with international human rights law.[55]

3.2.3 Gender-specific provisions

The INC was originally drafted with minimal input from women; nonetheless, some gender-specific provisions found their way in. Its preamble makes clear reference to 'equality between men and women in rights and duties'. However, the

54 The Preamble and arts 1–4 of the INC 2005.

55 See further Halim (n 9) and Equal Rights Trust (n 3).

Bill of Rights does not provide such commitment to equality with equal clarity; the provision of equality and non-discrimination are weak and limited as discussed in the next section of this chapter. There are nine articles in the INC that make explicit statements regarding gender:

- Article 7 of the Guiding Principles and Directives affirms the inalienable right of every person born to a Sudanese mother or father to enjoy Sudanese nationality and citizenship. It further declares citizenship as the sole basis for equal rights and duties for all Sudanese.
- Article 15(1) recognizes the right of men and women to marry and to found a family, according to their respective family laws, and to enter into marriage with free and full consent. The significance of this provision stems from the fact that early marriage is a social practice in different parts of Sudan, sanctioned by culture and endorsed by legislation. The State is obliged to take measures to realize this constitutional provision, for instance, by amending the Muslim Personal Status Act 1991.
- Article 15(2) obligates the State to protect motherhood and women from injustice, promote gender equality and the role of women in family, and empower them in public life. This provision, although setting out potentially conflicting goals, can bring a paradigm shift in women's position in the private and public sphere, if used by the State to enact laws and develop polices and plans to rectify the gender disparity.
- Article 31 of the Bill of Rights recognizes the right of all persons to equality before the law without discrimination, as to race, colour, sex, language, religious creed, political opinion, or ethnic origin, and to the equal protection of the law.
- Article 32 requires the State to guarantee the equal right of men and women to enjoy all civil, political, social, cultural and economic rights, including the right to equal pay for equal work and other related benefits; promote women's rights through affirmative action; combat harmful customs and traditions which undermine the dignity and status of women; and provide maternity and child care and medical care for pregnant women.
- Article 44 provides for the right to education for every citizen; it obliges the State to give access to it without discrimination as to religion, race, ethnicity, gender or disability, and to make primary education compulsory and free of charge.
- Article 136 states that the national civil services, particularly at the senior and middle levels, shall be representative of the people of the Sudan. To ensure this, the imbalances and disadvantages in recruitment shall be redressed, no level of government shall discriminate against any qualified Sudanese citizen on the basis of religion, ethnicity, region or gender, and application of affirmative action and job training to achieve targets for equitable representation within a specified timeframe shall be observed.
- Article 185 provides for equitable sharing of resources and common wealth, stating that resources and common wealth shall be shared equitably to enable

each level of government to discharge its legal and constitutional responsibilities and duties and to ensure the promotion of quality of life, dignity and living conditions of all citizens without discrimination on grounds of gender, race, religion, political affiliation, ethnicity, language or region.

- Article 211 upholds, among other rights, the right to non-discrimination on the basis of race, sex, religious creed, the right in litigation or the right to fair trial during the state of emergency as part of the non-derogable rights. This provision is of great importance, especially for women living in areas where emergency situations become the norm and power is widely utilized.

These are the provisions that make clear reference to gender or women; some of them are justiciable (articles 31, 32 and 44 as part of the Bill of Rights), while others, despite their fundamentality, are non-justiciable guiding principles for State practice (articles 7 and 15). Furthermore, subjecting some of these rights to statutory law through drawback clauses makes them weak and vulnerable to limitation. On the other hand, article 136 is a good example of an affirmative action provision with specific means of implementation, likewise article 185, which lays the ground for women to claim the right to share resources and wealth in the future constitutional set up.

3.2.4 The Bill of Rights and human rights treaties: gains, gaps and limitations

The Bill of Rights (articles 27 to 48) constitutes a major achievement in Sudan's constitutional history. Its most important feature is the State's obligation under article 27 to promote, include and enforce it, and to incorporate all rights and freedoms recognized by international treaties that bind Sudan, as an integral part of it. This includes the ICCPR, the ICESCR, the International Convention on the Elimination of All Forms of Racial Discrimination (ICERD), the Convention on the Rights of the Child (CRC), the Convention on the Rights of Persons with Disabilities (CRPD) and the ACHPR. A further major characteristic is the explicit stipulation of the relationship between the Bill of Rights and other laws, which is one of regulation and not elimination or curtailment of prescribed rights and freedoms.[56] Another important provision is article 48 which authorizes the constitutional court and other competent courts to protect and enforce the Bill of Rights and the Human Rights Commission to monitor its execution by the State in a pioneering move towards promotion, implementation and protection, at least at the theoretical level. The Bill of Rights incorporates a series of civil, political and some socio-economic rights that women enjoy by virtue of being citizens, and, as highlighted above, incorporates specific provisions pertaining to women (articles 31 and 32).

56 Art 27(4) of the Bill of Rights.

Notwithstanding its strengths, the Bill of Rights has major gaps and limitations, especially when examined in light of international and regional human rights treaties ratified by Sudan, which are deemed to be part of the INC by virtue of article 27(3). These limitations have a considerable impact on women's enjoyment of the rights and freedoms protected by the constitution.

GAPS AND DEFINITIONAL LIMITATIONS

The prohibition of discrimination is not set out as a general right as stipulated in the ICCPR and ICESCR. Article 31 stipulates it in relation to equality before the law only, and fails to include important grounds of discrimination such as disability, wealth, gender or others. The equal right of men and women to enjoy all rights is mentioned in article 32, titled the 'Rights of Women and Children', and is linked to the right to equal pay for equal work and other related benefits, rather than being granted as an independent general right as in article 3 of the ICCPR and ICESCR.

The INC does not recognize the right of every person to a legal personality as set out in article 16 of the ICCPR and article 5 of the ACHPR, or the right to equality before the courts and tribunals guaranteed under article 14 of the ICCPR. Further, its article 33 does not mention cruel, inhuman or degrading 'punishment', in clear divergence from article 7 of the ICCPR and article 5 of the ACHPR. Such prohibition, if included, could be used to contest lashing women upon suspicion of committing crimes that fall within Sudan's public order regime.[57] The ACHPR, in article 13, enlarges the right to political participation, recognized in article 41 of the Bill of Rights, to include the right of every citizen to equal access to public property and services, as well as access to public service of her or his country, in strict equality of all persons before the law. In theory, these rights form an integral part of the Bill of Rights, but there is no implementing legislation to make these rights effective.

As for socio-economic rights, the Bill of Rights lacks the basic right to work; a single reference is made to it in the guiding principle on social justice: 'No qualified person shall be denied access to a profession or employment on the basis of disability.'[58] The INC does not recognize the right to work and the equitable conditions of work as specified in articles 6 and 7 of the ICESCR respectively, nor the right to social security and social insurance stipulated in article 9 of the ICESCR. An important missing right is the right to an adequate standard of living for oneself and the family, in particular, the right to food, to be free from hunger, clothing, housing, medical care and continuous improvement of living conditions, stipulated by article 11 of the ICESCR.

57 See REDRESS and Sudanese Human Rights Monitor, *No More Cracking of the Whip: Time to End Corporal Punishment in Sudan* (March 2012).
58 Art 12(2) of the INC 2005.

Last but not least, the right to health is incorporated as guiding principle and justiciable right. Article 46 of the Bill of Right, a replicate of article 19 of the guiding principles, reads: 'The State undertakes to develop public health, establishes, enhances and rehabilitates basic treatment and diagnostic institutions, and to provide primary healthcare and emergency services, free of charge, for all citizens.' This provision differs substantially from the right to health as stipulated in articles 12 of ICESCR and 16 of the ACHPR, where every individual has the right to enjoy the highest attainable standard of physical and mental health. To realize this right, the treaties place an obligation on the State to take the necessary measures to reduce the stillbirth-rate and infant mortality, ensure healthy development of the child, improve all aspects of environmental and industrial hygiene, and create conditions which would assure to all medical service and medical attention in the event of sickness.[59] The significant gap between the national obligation to promote public health and the international obligation to recognize the right to the highest physical and mental health needs to be addressed.

LEGISLATIVE LIMITATIONS BASED ON SOCIO-RELIGIOUS CONVICTION

Article 48 of the INC makes it inadmissible to curtail the rights and freedoms entrenched in the Bill of Rights, whereas article 27(4) confirms that legislation regulates the prescribed rights and freedoms and does not detract or derogate from them. In addition, article 3 declares the INC the supreme law of the land and that states' constitutions and all laws shall comply with it. Despite these guarantees, legislative provisions restrain most of the prescribed rights and freedoms of women, at times explicitly discriminating against them, in the name of religion and outdated believes. The drawback clauses, whether provided for as general directives or within the Bill of Rights, are often used to justify such curtailment.

Article 32 stipulates the equal right of men and women and article 7(2) provides that 'every person born to a Sudanese mother or father shall have an inalienable right to enjoy Sudanese nationality and citizenship'. The Sudanese Nationality Act 1994, as amended, however, makes the right of the person born of a Sudanese mother conditional on an application to the competent authorities, whereas a person born to a Sudanese father acquires it automatically.[60] Another distinction made by the Act concerns the acquisition of Sudanese nationality by residence, where nationality is granted if ancestors in the paternal line have been domiciled in Sudan since January 1956.[61] Further, the Act grants foreign women married to Sudanese men the right to apply for Sudanese nationality

59 UN Committee on Economic, Social and Cultural Rights (CESCR), *General Comment No 14: The Right to the Highest Attainable Standard of Health (Art. 12 of the Covenant)* UN doc E/C.12/2000/4 (11 August 2000). E/C.12/2000/4.

60 Art. 4(2) and (3) of the Sudanese Nationality Act 1994 (as amended, 2005, 2011).

61 Art 4(1)(b)(ii) ibid.

upon completion of a two-year residency in Sudan, while foreign men married to Sudanese women do not enjoy the same right.[62]

Article 15 enhances equality between the two sexes, ensures women's role in the family, empowers them in public life and declares the inadmissibility of any marriage unless entered into with full and free choice of the two parties. However, the Muslim Personal Status Act 1991, which is derived from *Shari'a* and deals with issues pertaining to marriage, divorce, maintenance, custody, inheritance and will, is discriminatory and incompatible with these constitutional guarantees. Under the Act, women cannot conclude marriage other than through a guardian, who has to be male, Muslim, adult and of sound mind.[63] If the guardian fails to complete the marriage without legitimate reasons, a woman shall request a judge to conclude the marriage contract. The Act permits the guardian to conclude a child marriage, wedding a girl at the age of ten (age of puberty) with judicial permission if the judge believes that it serves her best interest, conditional upon the man's status as a 'proper husband' and an appropriate dowry.[64]

In law, only a man has the right to dissolve marriage, and to withdraw from divorce without a woman's consent or even knowledge. Although women are entitled to seek divorce on the basis of a marriage contract, where concluded, or due to husband's impotence or incurable physical or mental sickness, they have to prove such a claim trough medical evidence by a Muslim doctor, and wait up to one year to acquire divorce.[65] Rights and duties within marriage are a source of discontent and debate, particularly the requirement to call the guardian or agent (*wakeel*) to conclude the marriage contract and to request a husbands' permission to leave the house, including to visit family or to work.[66] Males are given preference in inheritance rules, with women in most cases entitled to only half of the males' share.[67]

Another inconsistency concerns the provisions setting out the age of legal capacity/liability in the INC, the CRC, to which Sudan is a party, and the Sudan Child Act (2010) on the one hand and the Muslim Personal Status Act (1991) on the other. In several rape cases involving minor girls, the courts, in deciding the age of legal liability, relied on the *Shari'a*-based provision of the Personal Status Act where puberty is the only criterion. The court did not only dismiss the cases due to pregnancy, but accused the victims who claimed to be raped of perpetrating adultery.[68]

The public order regime discriminates against women and restricts their rights to privacy, freedom of movement and freedom from torture, inhuman or

62 Art 4(3) ibid.
63 Art 33 of the Muslim Personal Status Act 1991.
64 Arts 25, 33, 37 and 40 ibid.
65 Art 151 ibid.
66 Arts 132–9, 151–61, and 51–2 ibid.
67 Arts 44, 357–400 ibid.
68 Amin M Medani, 'A Reading into Women's Position in the Sudanese Criminal Act', in UNMIS, *A Collection of Essays on Violence against Women* (2006) 21.

degrading treatment or punishment. Article 152 of the Criminal Act 1991 criminalizes any inappropriate act or conduct as well as indecent dress in public places to the annoyance of the public. The accused is liable to a punishment of 40 lashes, a fine or both, and such punishment is frequently applied against women. Given the lack of clear criteria of what amounts to 'improper' conduct or 'indecent' dress, a large number of women and girls have experienced humiliation at the hands of the community order police, being whipped following a summary trial by public order courts.[69]

Eight out of twenty-five provisions of the Public Order Act of Khartoum State 1998 are exclusively directed at women and eight others shared between men and women.[70] A number of sections explicitly discriminate against women, such as the section prohibiting women from dancing in front of men[71] and the one allocating a small percentage of seats in public transport that does not reflect the actual number of women using public transportation.[72] The Act also limits the exercise of certain employment, such as hairdressing,[73] and vests the police with the power to enter the premises at any time to search and ensure compliance with the requirements of the Act.[74]

The State's obligation to promote women's rights through affirmative action under article 32(2) of the INC is strengthened by article 136, which provides general directives for recruitment in civil service, among which are addressing the imbalance and inequality in recruitment, discrimination at any level of government against qualified Sudanese based on religion, ethnicity, region or gender, and positive discrimination measures to achieve equitable employment within a specific timeframe. Section 19 of the National Civil Services Act of 2007 includes the constitutional directives as an integral part of the National Civil Services Committee mandate. However, recent statistics indicate a considerable gap of women's participation in different institutions,[75] and judicial and administrative decisions have failed to reflect the spirit and scope of the constitutional entitlement.[76]

69 See further REDRESS and SIHA (n 12).

70 See Nabil Adib, 'Public Order Act as Means for Using Violence against Women', *Al-Sudani* (May 2010) (Arabic).

71 S 7 of the Public Order Act of 1998.

72 S 9 ibid.

73 Ss 14–16 ibid.

74 Ss 17 ibid.

75 Women in the diplomatic corps (entered into as early as 1970) represent 12.4 per cent and 26 per cent in civil services with 4 per cent in high positions, 41 per cent of women get training in public services; 71 per cent of them in administrative work, 29 per cent in management and 26 per cent only in leadership. The percentage of women is even lesser in the private sector with 2.6 per cent in management, 9.9 per cent in professional and technical jobs and 97 per cent in the services sector. See Issa (n 14) 159ff.

76 See Equal Right Trust (n 3). The report discussed a number of decisions of administrative tribunals and the constitutional court involving cases of discrimination practiced against women and persons with disabilities in the employment area, pointing out the shortsighted interpretation of constitutional and legal provisions.

Further examples have been presented in other studies, workshops and forums in relation to women's right to movement, residence, privacy and personal freedom, property and ownership and inheritance, as well as to their rights in matrimonial and family matters.[77] These violations are in principle subject to review by the Constitutional Court. However, lack of effective access to courts and the jurisprudence of the Constitutional Court,[78] which has been reluctant to strike down laws, practices and interpretation, has allowed the discrepancy between constitutional rights and national legislation to persist. It is pertinent to reform national legislation to be in conformity with the constitution and strengthen the courts to assume and effectively exercise their supposed role in protecting and promoting human rights.

4 The role and rights of women in the forthcoming constitution

The debate on women's role and rights in any future constitutional set-up needs to be conscious of Sudan's constitutional history and the reality of women's lives in the country. It requires an acknowledgement of the violations experienced by women in the public and private sphere. A comprehensive approach is required to fully consider the socio-cultural, economic and political causes of inequality, discrimination and marginalization, and develop adequate provisions for constitutional protection against the same. Reviewing the gaps and limitations in past and current texts is a necessary exercise that allows women to build up knowledge, re-conceptualize their vision and develop a core agenda.

4.1 Women and the constitution: the contents and process

Three issues need to be addressed before discussing women's main constitutional concerns. Firstly, the women's question needs to be disentangled from that of other marginalized groups – namely, children, persons with disabilities, the elderly, internally displaced persons, refugees and religious or ethnic minorities. While inequality and discrimination is a shared factor between women and minority groups in general, women endure multiple (intersectional) discrimination by virtue of being members of marginalized groups. It is therefore time to document women's life stories, experiences and conditions in the context of the community and environment they live in and to identify the reasons for, and factors contributing to, their subordination and inferiority.[79] At the constitutional

77 Mohamed A Babiker, 'Gender and Migration in Sudan', CARIM-AS 2011(European University Institute 2011); Nasreldeen Abdulbari, 'Citizenship Rules in Sudan and Post Session Problems' (2010), www.cmi/no/sudan/doc/id=1284, accessed 23 March 2018; and Sudanese Organization for Research and Development (SORD), ***Towards Gender Equity in Sudan: Draft Legislation of Family Law for Muslim*** (2011).

78 Equal Rights Trust (n 3).

79 Hale (n 5).

level, recognition of women's experience of subordination, prejudices and stereotypes shall be reflected both in the constitution-making process and in the preamble with affirmation of their equal status, role and rights specified in the other parts.

Secondly, it is important that women's issues be mainstreamed in the text of the constitution. The broad symbolic political statements relating to the nature of the State, society, people and their national identity is of particular significance to women since it connotes how the nation views itself, where its values lie and what principles it adopts. Courts and other mechanisms play a fundamental role in interpreting, enforcing and defending the constitutional text and women's rights therein; their composition and role is therefore critical for the effective application of women's rights.

The constitution places three types of obligations on the State when providing for fundamental human rights; it prohibits, mandates or permits certain acts to ensure the full enjoyment of entrenched rights. Lifting discrimination and realizing women's constitutional rights depends largely on limiting State power and the mandatory measures the State is required to take. Few of these obligations appear in sections on particular institutions, as the majority relate to the human rights part. Limitations on the State power may extend beyond the text by inclusion of or reference to outside sources such as international human rights treaties. Article 27(3) of the INC is a good example of incorporation of outside sources into the national legal system; treaties to which Sudan is a party directly bind and automatically trump any constitutional or legislative provisions that contradict them. However, key treaties such as CEDAW, CAT and the Maputo Protocol (2003)[80] have not been ratified by Sudan despite repeated calls and campaigns for their ratification

An issue of fundamental significance is the role of women in the process of constitution-making. Efforts to raise women's awareness of their rights are not limited to the content of the constitution but extend to the process of negotiating and constructing the document. Human rights and women's rights advocates play a central role in mobilizing and educating women on outstanding issues, including but not limited to, identity, good governance, peace and security, power- and wealth-sharing, human rights and fundamental freedoms. Discussions of women's issues shall be conducted on the premise that women are a diverse group, members of which differ in terms of ethnicity, religion, social and political background, rural-urban status, economic conditions, abilities, capabilities and concerns. This recognition is crucial for adequate representation, that is which groups should participate and claim to speak on behalf of women's rights in the constitution-making process.

80 Protocol to the African Charter on Human and Peoples' Rights on the Rights of Women in Africa (2003).

4.2 Women' constitutional agenda: areas of concern

4.2.1 The external and internal sources of rights: socio-religious and legislative limitations

Addressing the challenge of religious and social constrains on women's rights is a key priority. The ongoing socio-religious controversy over women's status, role and rights poses a genuine obstacle to women's entitlement and enjoyment of human rights. The limited understanding and/or misinterpretation of *Shari'a* principles across the globe nourish the perspective of gender inequality and women's subordination in Muslim communities.[81] To date, Muslims have largely failed to develop a new understanding and interpretation of *Shari'a* law that is able to accommodate contemporary challenges and respond to current needs, including those of women. The conventional religious view continues to read and use most of the Islamic jurisprudence and rules, especially in relation to women, in their historical context with no or little consideration of the realities of today.[82]

Therefore, the need to revisit *Shari'a* rules in light of rapid transformations of Muslim communities and the gradual shift in individuals' roles occasioned by political, economic and social developments is critical. The religious decree that supports the preferential position for males (the *Giwama*) based on knowledge and provision for the family, for instance, is under increasing scrutiny as more women are seeking education and knowledge than men and a substantial number of them are, by choice or necessity, the sole breadwinners or major contributors in providing for the family, or at the very least for themselves.[83] The debate has already begun in different Muslim communities and has been reflected on by radical, conservative and liberal scholars alike.[84] Among women's groups in Sudan there is a general consensus to press for dialogue at all fronts, in civil society, across political parties, within government agencies and at grassroots level, to shake the outdated beliefs and instigate social change. There is an urgent need to exert efforts to commit all stakeholders to work jointly with a view to modifying the social and cultural patterns of conduct of women and men through public education, information and communication strategies, in order to eliminate harmful cultural and traditional practices that are based on the idea of inferiority of women or stereotyped roles for women and men.

At the constitutional level, the incorporation of two potentially conflicting provisions – namely article 5 that stipulates Islamic *Shari'a* and consensus as

81 Norani Othman, 'Muslim Women and the Challenge of Islamic Fundamentalism/Extremis: An Overview of Southeast Asian Muslim Women's Struggle for Human Rights and Gender Equity' (2006) 29 *Wom Stud Int For* 339.

82 See Abdullahi A. An-Na'im, 'Human Rights in Muslim World: Socio-Political Conditions and Scriptural Imperatives' (1990) 13 *HHRJ* 13.

83 According to the '*al-Giwama*' principle in *Shari'a*, men have authority to administer women affairs based on their merit and material support (Holy Qur'an, su'ra Al-Ni'saa (4:33).

84 See for example the multiple contributions, and special dossiers, in the annual SIHA Journal, *Women in Islam*.

main sources of legislation, and article 27(3) which refers to all rights and freedoms protected by international treaties ratified by Sudan – as part of the Bill of Rights-generates scope for uncertainty and interpretation that is incompatible with internationally recognized women's rights. Women's entitlement and enjoyment of certain basic rights have been curtailed when interpreted in the light of *Shari'a* rules.[85] Some scholars have held a discussion challenging the meaning of '*Shari'a*', concluding that it should be interpreted as general, directive principles, including spiritual values and social ideals of justice, freedom, *Shura* (deliberation) and public interest, as well as internationally affirmed rights and freedoms.[86]

To circumvent any possible curbing of constitutional human rights on a socio-religious basis, three viewpoints are presented by women. The first one suggests making reference to the 'overall principles and directives of the Islamic *Shari'a*, which include spiritual values and social ideals of justice, peace security, equity and equality' as the source of legislation, instead of 'Islamic *Shari'a*' as set out in article 5 of the INC. The second opinion proposes eliminating the article on the sources of legislation altogether by following the trend prior to the Permanent Constitution of 1973. If the constitution includes a provision on sources of legislation, then rules of Islamic *Shari'a* must continue to be the main source of legislation. The third, majority view, recommends keeping silent on the sources of legislation, but if reference is made, then it shall be to international and regional standards.[87]

Accordingly, the preferable approach is for the forthcoming constitution to altogether omit the article on sources of legislation. It is also fundamental to repeal or amend provisions that pose a threat to rights. A case in point is article 16, which provides that '[t]he State shall enact laws to protect the society from corruption delinquency and social evils and steer the society as a whole towards virtuous social values consistent with religions and cultures of the Sudan'. Such provision opens the door for limitations and dilutes the supremacy of the constitution (article 3), unless it includes the phrase 'provided that the enacted laws shall not contradict any of the provisions of the bill of rights'. Resolving the conflict between religious rules and international treaties on women's status and rights is fundamental for the forthcoming constitution to be legitimate and respected, not only by women's rights' advocates but also by those who believe human rights to be universal, indivisible and derived from the inherent dignity of the human person without distinction on any ground.

85 See above at 3.2.4.

86 See Mohamed I. Khalil, 'Religion and State in the Sudanese Constitutions', and Al-Tayeb Zain El-Abdeen, 'The Relationship of Religion and State in the Constitution', in Mahjoub M Saleh (ed.), *Studies on the Constitution* vol 1 (Alayam Center for Cultural Studies and Development 2012) (Arabic).

87 UN-Women in collaboration with IDSR - University of Khartoum, 'Women's Common Agenda for Forthcoming Constitution of the Sudan, Position Paper' (2015).

4.2.2 Equality and non-discrimination clause

Sudan's past constitutions have failed to incorporate comprehensive equality and non-discrimination clauses equivalent to those found in international human rights instruments; they lack both provisions, include the equality principle but not the non-discrimination clause, or integrate them inadequately. Relevant international treaties have, with no exception, integrated, alongside the preamble, two provisions; one guarantees the equal right of men and women to the enjoyment all prescribed rights, and another prohibits all forms of discrimination on the grounds of race, sex, colour, language, religion, political or other opinion, national or social origin, disability, gender, wealth, birth or any other status. Equality before the law, recognition as a person before the law, and equality before the courts and tribunals are important, interrelated rights.

As a State party, Sudan is obliged to guarantee the enjoyment of rights recognized by the relevant treaties in its constitution, legislations and policies. To guarantee equality and repress gender inequality at all levels, women shall ensure that the forthcoming constitution incorporates equality and non-discrimination provisions in line with articles 3 and 2 respectively of the ICCPR and ICESCR,[88] along with the interconnected articles on equality and recognition before the law and equality before the courts and tribunals enshrined by the ICCPR (articles 26, 16 and 14 respectively). Further, the constitution shall include a provision obliging the State to take necessary legislative, institutional and regulatory measures to combat all forms of discrimination against women. Inclusion of comprehensive non-discrimination and equality provisions will pave the way to end discriminatory practices related to inheritance, land ownership and family matters.

The proposed constitution would benefit from taking note of the elaborate definition of discrimination stipulated in the two standards on women rights not yet ratified by Sudan; that is CEDAW and the Maputo Protocol. The former has extended the meaning of discrimination in article 1 to include 'any exclusion or restriction based on sex that has the effect or purpose of impairing or nullifying recognition of women's human rights or fundamental freedoms in the political, economic, social, cultural, civil or any other fields, regardless of their marital status and in equality with men'. The latter expands, in its article 1(f), the definition further to include 'any distinction, exclusion or restriction or any differential treatment based on sex and whose objectives or effects compromise or destroy the recognition, enjoyment or the exercise by women, regardless of their marital status, of human rights and fundamental freedoms in all spheres of life'. The detailed definitions are effective in elaborating the scope of equality and non-discrimination and enhance their utility as a tool to guide State practice and process of implementation.

88 As well as the UDHR, CRC, CRPD, CERD and ACHPR.

4.2.3 Public and political participation: the affirmative action and quota system

The third key question concerns women's participation in public and political life. One of the INC's important articles is the one that introduces affirmative action as a tool to improve women participation in public life (article 32(2)). Despite its shortcomings, it is considered as a quantum leap in the way to bridge the gender gap in the State system. Thirteen years have passed since the INC has been adopted and the impact of the affirmative action clause on women's participation remains negligible. The same has been the fate of article 136 which provides general directives for recruitment in the civil service. Again, no effective measures have been taken to increase women's representation in public service or the private sector. Therefore, a quota requiring a minimum percentage of female employees is needed to specify outcomes and increase the number of women at the higher and medium level of public service.

As for the right to political participation, Sudanese women, after a strong, relentless campaign, succeeded in acquiring the quota of 25 per cent (amended to 30 per cent in 2014) in the National Election Act 2008. Section 29 reads: 'Twenty five percent of women members of the national assembly shall be elected on the basis of proportional representation at the State level from a separate and closed party list.' In practice, however, the impact of the quota system in redressing gender difference remains limited as (i) only women members of political parties can benefit from the quota measure, since independent and professional women candidates are not eligible to compete in the women's list, (ii) the quota is only applied at the national and state election, but not at local authorities and other public offices, (iii) more importantly, the quota system applies to one congress of the legislative body, i.e. the National Council, but not to States' Council members, and (iv) the women's list is a closed list.[89]

To guarantee equal and effective participation for women in public and political life, the upcoming constitution shall incorporate provisions that secure the right to participation as recognized under international law. It shall explicitly oblige the State to implement the affirmative action clause, with specific proportion in the light of the Sustainable Development Goals, at all government branches, legislative, executive, judicial and independent commissions and agencies at national, state and local ones, and at all levels, especially leading and decision-making positions. Based on article 40(3) of the INC and section 14 of the Political Parties Regulation Act 2007, where both have called for representation of women within political parties, a minimum percentage shall be specified and divided along the party hierarchy. It shall impose a direct obligation on the state to enact laws and policies to implement it.

89 See Elrayh (n 6).

4.2.4 Socio-economic rights

Economic and social rights provide that particular base-line levels of health, food, housing, work, social security and education are fundamental human rights which ought to be protected for everyone. They are particularly important for women, in Sudan as everywhere, who are the primary victims of poverty, hunger, sickness, displacement, illiteracy and unemployment, and as such, are the main beneficiaries of this category of rights.[90] Generally speaking, women earn less money than men. They are over-represented in the informal sector, part-time employment and unpaid informal care work. Their socio-economic position is less secure than that of men; and consequently they tend to have less economic independence. Sudanese women therefore have much to gain from socio-economic rights and such rights could be expected to go some way towards improving the substantive equality of men and women.

Under the current constitution, the economic and social rights are inadequately addressed. The Bill of Rights has made strong reference to international standards by considering treaties ratified by Sudan as an integral part of it, including the ICESCR. However, in contrast to civil and political rights, the list of socio-economic rights is limited to the right to free primary education, equal pay for work of equal value, acquisition and ownership, and a duty-like provision that obliges the State to promote primary care and provide free primacy and emergency care. The lack of adequate constitutional protection is combined with inadequate judicial recognition and interpretation, and general disrespect of this class of rights in governmental practice.[91]

Given the numerous pertinent challenges in Sudan, recognition, respect and promotion of social and economic rights must be one of the priorities in Sudan's future constitution. The proposed constitution shall hold the position that socio-economic rights are not subordinate to civil and political rights; they are interconnected, interdependent and mutually reinforcing, as affirmed by the Committee on Economic, Social and Cultural Rights in General Comment 3 (1991) and the preamble of the African Charter.[92] Catering for the basic needs of women, the constitution shall emphasize the importance of these rights by integrating them into the Bill of Rights. Article 13 and 24 of the African Protocol on Women's Rights (Maputo, 2003), to which Sudan is signatory, is a good model in this respect. It will certainly facilitate reference, implementation and adjudication if the proposed constitution follows in the footsteps of South Africa and Kenya in incorporating socio-economic rights in a justiciable manner and allowing courts

90 CESCR, *Concluding Observations on the Second State Party Report of the Sudan*, UN doc E/C.12/SDN/CO/2 (27 October 2015) paras 29, 31 and 43.

91 Equal Rights Trust (n 4).

92 CESCR, *General Comment No 3: The Nature of States Parties' Obligations (Art. 2, Para. 1, of the Covenant)* UN doc E/1991/23 (14 December 1990).

to question the government's adequate allocation of resources.[93] The challenge to enforce this class of rights will be enormous taking into account present economic and political volatility, yet it is a necessary approach to improve the life of the vast majority of Sudanese people and most women.

4.2.5 Violence against women

Violence against women is one of the most pressing questions that needs to be tackled in any forthcoming constitution. According to the UN Special Rapporteur on Violence against Women, 'the silences and denials about the existence of violence against women in Sudan, except in minimal and certain contexts, is a challenge that needs to be addressed as a matter of priority'.[94] Studies and reports indicate that women's situation in Sudan is constrained due to the high levels of gender-based violence and sexual violence against them, in both the public and private sphere.[95] Violence comes from different sources, takes different shapes and is practiced at different levels. Equally, violent acts are committed by individuals, family members, and State agents. It takes different forms, namely, rape, including marital rape, female circumcision (genital mutilation), domestic violence, early and forced marriage, sexual, physical and verbal harassment, human trafficking and forced prostitution. Several factors come into play when examining the causes of violence. Sudan is a low-income country and a male-dominated society, where husband violence is accepted as a cultural norm and viewed as normal behaviour within the family and in society. Poor socio-economic conditions contribute significantly to domestic violence against women.[96] Like other Muslim communities, the social set-up in Sudan strongly encourages women to accept the misconduct and violent behaviour of the husband as part of religious commands.[97] Further, the level of violence against women is particularly high in conflict zones, particularly in South Kordofan, Blue Nile and Darfur.[98]

93 See Sandra Liebenberg, 'Direct Constitutional Protection of Economic, Social and Cultural Rights in South Africa' in Danwood Mzikenge Chirwa and Lilian Chenwi (eds), *The Protection of Economic, Social and Cultural Rights in Africa: International, Regional and National Perspectives* (CUP 2016) and Godfrey O Odongo and Godfrey M Musila, 'Direct Constitutional Protection of Economic, Social and Cultural Rights under Kenya's 2010 Constitution' in ibid.

94 'Special Rapporteur on violence against women finalizes country mission to Sudan and calls for more open and constructive dialogues on violence against women, its causes and consequences' *UNOHCHR* (24 May 2016), www.ohchr.org/EN/NewsEvents/Pages/DisplayNews.aspx?NewsID=16009, accessed 23 March 2018.

95 See in particular *Report of the Special Rapporteur on Violence Against Women, its Causes and Consequences on her Mission to the Sudan*, UN doc A/HRC/32/42/Add.1 (18 April 2016).

96 Ibid para 17.

97 Lisa Hajjar, 'Religion, State Power, and Domestic Violence in Muslim Societies: A Framework for Comparative Analysis' (2004) 29 *Law & Soc Inq* 1.

98 Report of the Special Rapporteur (n 95) 12, 22–5.

When seeking to access justice, women victims of violence are confronted with a number of challenges and limitations. There is a *de jure* or *de facto* acceptance of violent conduct against women in different parts of Sudan, and a general categorization of crimes against women as minor offences. Lack of criminalization of some violent acts, stigma and fear of social exclusion, limited availability of segregated data, absence of effective procedures to protect victims and witnesses, and lack of remedies for victims are additional challenges.[99] Most of the time families resort to reconciliation instead of accountability for crimes against women and girls.[100] Deficiency of the definition of rape as a criminal offence and overly narrow evidentiary rules applicable in such cases are also a major limitation. Article 149 of the Criminal Act 1991 had failed, prior to its reform in 2015, the effectiveness of which remains to be seen, to provide adequate protection against rape and sexual harassment; to the contrary, it exposed women to potential prosecution for adultery, in divergence from the positive obligation of the State to protect women from harm and injustice under the constitution.[101] Abusive acts such as female genital mutilation and marital rape are not criminalized, while illegal early and forced marriage is widely tolerated, with the laws against them rarely enforced.[102]

Sudan's constitutional and legislative framework falls short of protecting women from all forms of violence. No reference is made to violence against women in the INC. Despite repeated calls from women's groups and members of the international community to tackle the issue, the legal gap in the area of violence against women persists, creating a sphere of fear that lessens protection and enhances cruelty of crimes committed in this context. The forthcoming constitution shall seek to rectify the status quo by incorporating provisions prohibiting all forms of physical, mental, sexual and psychological or other type of violence or exploitation against women, on the basis of religious, social, cultural tradition, custom or any other ground. It shall further obligate the State to enact legislation, regulations and policies, to combat violence, protect women against it, punish its perpetrators and provide reparation to the victims. The constitution shall direct the State to establish an independent body/authority to oversee government fulfilment of the constitutional decrees and implementation of related international instruments regarding violence against women.

4.2.6 Women's commission and other mechanisms

To secure implementation of women constitutional rights, it is important to consider all layers of government at the national, state and local levels. To begin with, the legislative institutions shall ensure the translation of human rights provisions into states' constitutions and local laws, regulations, and policies. Legislation

99 Ibid para 14.
100 Ibid para 95.
101 Ibid para 20.
102 Rogaia M Abusharaf, 'Rethinking Feminist Discourses on Female Genital Mutilation: The Case of the Sudan' (1995) *Can Wom Stud* 52.

that contradicts constitutional rules shall be amended or repealed within a specific timeframe. The judiciary is another key body whose task is to interpret and enforce constitutional rights. Judicial independence needs to be strengthened, and knowledge of the constitutional Bill of Rights and international human rights standards needs to be enhanced. Limitations on the mandate of the constitutional court shall be lifted to allow it to examine all matters relating to breach of the constitutional human rights.

A key mechanism to consider for the protection of women's rights is a women's commission. The proposed constitution shall establish an independent commission with a comprehensive mandate, proper authority and adequate resources to oversee the implementation of women's rights in practice. This includes ensuring State compliance with its obligations to take the appropriate actions to realize women rights; reviewing the enforcement of the affirmative action measures; advising stakeholders at official and civil society level on women's constitutional rights and concerns; carrying out and taking part in civic education programmes on human and women rights; and receiving individual and collective complaints on suspected violations of human rights involving women. It shall work closely and coordinate with other national institutions and commissions on issues related to women that fall under their jurisdiction, namely, the Human Rights Commission, National Civil Services Commission, National Employment Justice Chamber and the Public Grievances Chamber. It shall participate in civic education on human rights in general and women rights directed towards people at the grassroots level.

5 Conclusion

The State has failed to secure women rights, notwithstanding the INC of 2005. The question of women's status, role and rights is complex and challenging as it is influenced by different socio-cultural, economic and political factors. To redress women's grievances and rectify injustices, there is a need for a paradigm shift to overcome outdated religious and social beliefs about women's value and roles, eliminate stereotypes and gender bias, and remove multifaceted economic, political and legal barriers. The legitimacy of the constitution-making process will depend on its ability to include women's views and visions, not only on women's issues, but on all outstanding questions of governance, law-making, power- and wealth-sharing, development, peace- and state-building. Women's initiatives face the challenge of making a concerted effort to bring women together and facilitate their internal dialogue on outstanding issues and women concerns. This includes campaigning for the ratification of CEDAW and the Maputo Protocol, and working on comprehensive law reform to ensure compliance with international and regional human rights standards. Women in Sudan are looking ahead more than ever to end the state of uncertainty concerning their role and rights in society and the State, to remove physical and psychological barriers, to resolve the Islamism–secularism dilemma, and to assume their equal place in the private and public domain.

Appendix

Human rights provisions in the constitutions of Sudan and South Sudan and selected constitutional court cases

1 The Self-Government Statute (1953)[1]

Chapter II: Fundamental Rights

Article 5: Right to freedom and equality

(1) All persons in the Sudan are free and are equal before the law.
(2) No disability shall attach to any Sudanese by reason of birth, religion, race or sex in regard to public or private employment or in the admission to or in the exercise of any occupation, trade, business or profession.

Article 6: Freedom from arrests and confiscations

No person may be arrested, detained, imprisoned or deprived of the use or ownership of his property except by due process of law.

Article 7: Freedom of religion and association

(1) All persons shall enjoy freedom of conscience, and the right freely to profess their religion, subject only to such conditions relating to morality, public order, or health as may be imposed by law.
(2) All persons shall have the right of free expression of opinion, and the right of free association and combination, subject to the law.

Article 8: The rule of law

All persons and associations of persons, official or otherwise, are subject to the law as administered by the Courts of Justice, saying only the established privileges of Parliament.

1 The Self-Government Statute, Special Legislative Supplement to Sudan Government Gazette No. 854 (21st March 1953). See also Agreement between the Government of the United Kingdom of Great Britain and Northern Ireland and the Egyptian Government concerning Self-Government and Self-Determination for the Sudan, Cairo, February 12, 1953, Treaty Series No. 47 (1953) 13ff.

Article 9: Independence of judiciary

The Judiciary shall have be independent and free from interference or control by any organ of the Government, executive or legislative.

Article 10: Right to constitutional remedy

Any person may apply to the High Court for protection or enforcement of any of the rights conferred by this Chapter, and the High Court shall have power to make all such orders as may be necessary and appropriate to secure to the applicant the enjoyment of any of the said rights.

Note: the provisions contained in Chapter II were copied verbatim in the 1956 and 1964 constitutions.

2 The Permanent Constitution of the Sudan (1973)[2]

Part III: Freedoms, Rights and Duties

Article 38

All persons in the Democratic Republic of the Sudan are equal before Courts of law. The Sudanese have equal rights and duties, irrespective of origin, race, locality, sex, language or religion.

Article 39

Punishment is personal provided that blood-money (Diya), compensation or collective fine may be imposed in accordance with custom or local social order.

Article 40

No Sudanese shall be deported from Sudanese lands or be prevented from entering them.

Article 41

Freedom of movement and residence shall be guaranteed for all citizens, except for reasons of security and public health as prescribed by law, provided that the period and extent of any restriction thereon shall be fixed.

2 The Permanent Constitution of the Sudan (issued on 8th of May 1973) Democratic Republic of the Sudan Gazette (1973).

Article 42

The private life of citizens is inviolable. The State shall guarantee the freedom and secrecy of postal, telegraphic and telephonic communications in accordance with the law.

Article 43

Dwellings are inviolable and they shall not be entered or searched without the permission of their occupants, except in the cases, and in the manner, prescribed by law.

Article 44

Political refugees in the Democratic Republic of the Sudan shall not be extradited to another State, except within the limits permitted by the principles of International law and laws of the Sudan.

Article 45

Every citizen shall have the right to participate in elections and referendums when he attains eighteen years of age and fulfills conditions of eligibility as prescribed by law.

Article 46

The right of citizens to participate in public life and in nomination of themselves for public posts and office, in accordance with the provisions of the Constitution and the law, is guaranteed.

Article 47

Freedom of belief, prayer and performance of religious practices, without infringement of public order or morals, is guaranteed.

Article 48

Freedom of opinion is guaranteed. Every Sudanese shall have the right to express his opinion in writing or verbally or by other means of expression in accordance with the law.

Article 49

The press shall be free within the limits of the law, as a means to educate and enlighten the people, and it shall be directed to serve the objectives of the people.

Article 50

The Sudanese shall have the right to hold peaceful meetings and to take part in quiet and peaceful processions in accordance with the provisions of the law.

Article 51

The right to form trade unions, associations and societies is guaranteed for Sudanese, in accordance with the provisions of the law.

Article 52

The State shall prohibit conscript labour. Forced labour shall only be allowed for a military or civil necessity, or in execution of a criminal penalty in accordance with the provisions of the law.

Article 53

Education is a right of every citizen and the State shall endeavour to spread and provide it free in all stages.

Article 54

Health care and medical treatment are a right of every citizen and the State shall endeavour to spread and provide it free.

Article 55

Mothers and children shall be accorded care and attention and the State shall ensure adequate guarantees for mothers and the working women.

Article 56

The State shall ensure equality of opportunities for all Sudanese and prohibit any discrimination in work opportunities or conditions or pay on the grounds of origin, sex, or geographical affiliations.

Article 57

The defence of the country, upholding of the Constitution and protection of the revolutionary achievements shall be a sacred duty of every citizen.

Article 58

Subject to Article 111 hereof, any person aggrieved by any law passed by any legislative authority may institute a civil suit before the Supreme Court to declare such law void on the ground of its violation of the freedoms and rights guaranteed by this Constitution.

3 Constitution of the Republic of Sudan (1998)[3]

Chapter I: Freedoms, Sanctities and Rights

Article 20: Freedom and sanctity of life

Every human being shall have the right to life, freedom, safety of person and dignity of honour save by right in accordance with the law; and he is free of subjection to slavery, forced labour, humiliation or torture.

Article 21: Right to equality

All people are equal before the courts of law. Sudanese are equal in rights and duties as regards to functions of public life; and there shall be no discrimination only by reason of race, sex or religious creed. They are equal in eligibility for public posts and offices not being discriminated on the basis of wealth.

Article 22: Sanctity of nationality

Every person born to a Sudanese mother or father shall have a non-alienable right to enjoy the country's nationality and its rights and bear its obligations. Whoever is brought up or is resident in the Sudan for several years shall have the right to nationality as regulated by law.

Article 23: Freedom and right of movement

Every citizen shall have the right of freedom of movement, residence in, exit from and entry into the country; and his freedom shall not be restricted save under safeguards of the law.

Article 24: Freedom of creed and worship

Every human being shall have the right of freedom of conscience and religious creed, and he shall have the right to declare his religion or creed, and manifest the same by way of worship, education, practice or performance of rites or ceremonies; and no one shall be coerced to adopt such faith, as he does not believe in, nor to practice rites or services he does not voluntarily consent to; and that is without prejudice to the right of choice of religion, injury to the feelings of others, or to public order, all as may be regulated by law.

3 Constitution of the Republic of Sudan (passed by the National Assembly on 28 March 1998), English version, www.ilo.org/dyn/natlex/docs/ELECTRONIC/52652/90486/F1708365755/SDN52652%20English.pdf, accessed 12 June 2018.

Article 25: Freedom of thought and expression

There shall be guaranteed for citizens the freedom of pursuing any science or adopting any doctrine of opinion or thought without coercion by authority; and there shall be guaranteed the freedom of expression, reception of information, publication and the press without prejudice security, order, safety and public morals, all as regulated by law.

Article 26: Freedom of association and organization

(1) Citizens shall have the right of association and organization for cultural social, economic, professional or trade union purposes without restriction save in accordance with the law.
(2) There shall be guaranteed for citizens the right to organize political association; and shall not be restricted save by the condition of consultative decision making and democracy in the leadership of the organization, and use of propagation not material force in competition and abiding by the fundamentals of the Constitution, that as regulated by law.

Article 27: Sanctity of cultural communities

There shall be guaranteed for every community or group of citizens the right to preserve their particular culture, language or religion, and rear children freely within the framework of their particularity, and the same shall not by coercion be effaced.

Article 28: Sanctity of earning and property

(1) Every person shall have his right to acquire property and knowledge, and shall enjoy the privacy of his earning; and there shall be no expropriation of whatever he has gained of livelihood, property, land, invention, or manual, scientific, literary or artistic production, save by such law as may charge him with the tax of contribution for public need or public interest in consideration of just compensation.
(2) No taxes, fees, or other fiscal dues shall be levied save by law.

Article 29: Inviolability of communication and privacy

(1) There shall be guaranteed for citizens the freedom and secrecy of communication and correspondence; and the same shall neither be tapped nor perused save upon controls provided by law.
(2) All privacies of a human being in residence, livings, effects and family shall be inviolabilities not to be infringed save upon permission or by law.

Article 30: Immunity against detention

A human being is free. He shall neither be arrested, detained, nor confined, save by such law that shall require stating the charge, the duration of detention, facilitation of release and respect for dignity in treatment.

Article 31: Right and sanctity in litigation

The right to litigate shall be guaranteed for all persons and no one shall be denied the right to sue or shall be involved in a criminal or civil litigation save in accordance to the procedures and rules of law.

Article 32: Right of innocence and defense

No person shall be incriminated or punished for an act save in accordance with a prior law incriminating the act and punishing therefor. A person accused of an offence shall be innocent until his conviction is judicially proved; and he shall have the right to a prompt and fair trial and to defend himself and choose whoever may represent him in defence.

Article 33: Sanctity from death save in justice

(1) No death penalty shall be inflicted, save as retribution or punishment for extremely serious offences by law.
(2) No death penalty shall be inflicted for offences committed by a person under eighteen years of age; and such penalty shall be executed upon neither pregnant nor suckling women, save after two years of lactation; nor shall the same be inflicted upon a person who passed seventy years of age other than in retribution and prescribed penalties (*hudud*).

Article 34: Protection of freedoms, sanctities and rights

Every aggrieved person who has exhausted means of grievance and complaint to the executive and administrative organs, shall have the right of access to the Constitutional Court to protect the freedoms, sanctities and rights set out in this Chapter; and the Constitutional Court may according to due process exercise the power to annul any law or order that contravenes the Constitution and restore the right to the aggrieved or compensate him for damage sustained.

4 The Interim National Constitution of the Republic of the Sudan (2005: (as amended))[4]

Part Two: BILL OF RIGHTS

Article 27: Nature of the Bill of Rights

(1) The Bill of Rights is a covenant among the Sudanese people and between them and their governments at every level and a commitment to respect

4 The Interim National Constitution of the Republic of the Sudan, Official Gazette (in Arabic) (17 July 2005) No. 1722. English version, www.ilo.org/dyn/natlex/docs/ELECTRONIC/72048/92191/F961646467/SDN72048.pdf, accessed 12 June 2018. On the 2017

and promote human rights and fundamental freedoms enshrined in this Constitution; it is the cornerstone of social justice, equality and democracy in the Sudan.

(2) The State shall protect, promote, guarantee and implement this Bill.

(3) All rights and freedoms enshrined in international human rights treaties, covenants and instruments ratified by the Republic of the Sudan shall be an integral part of this Bill.

(4) Legislation shall regulate the rights and freedoms enshrined in this Bill and shall not detract from or derogate any of these rights.

Article 28: Life and Human Dignity

Every human being has the inherent right to life, dignity and the integrity of his/her person, which shall be protected by law; no one shall arbitrarily be deprived of his/her life.[5]

Article 29: Personal Liberty[6]

Every person has the right to liberty and security of person; no person shall be subjected to arrest, detention, deprivation or restriction of his/her liberty except for reasons and in accordance with procedures prescribed by law.

Article 30: Sanctity from Slavery and Forced Labor:

(1) Slavery and slave trade in every form is prohibited. No person shall be held in slavery or servitude.

(2) No person shall be required to perform forced or compulsory labour except as a penalty upon conviction by a competent court of law.[7]

amendments, see Arabic text of INC 2005 (as amended in 2017), approved in two separate sessions by the National Legislature on 25 April 2017, and the Council of States, on 24 April 2017. It was signed by the President of the National Legislature, Ibrahim Ahmed Omer, and approved by the President of the Republic, Omer Hassan Ahmed Al-Basheer, on 3rd May 2017. Translation of the 2017 amendments is the editor's unofficial translation from Arabic into English.

5 Art 28 was amended by constitutional amendments 2017. It now reads: 'Every person has the right to personal security and safety and freedom in life and shall not be deprived of his inherent right to life except in accordance with a final judicial decision.'

6 Article 29 was repealed and replaced by constitutional amendments of 2017. Article 29(1) now reads: 'Everyone has the right to freedom and the security of his endeavours'. Article 29(2) reads: 'No person should be arrested and kept in custody without having the right to liberty except under restrictions and regulations detailed under the law'. (editor's translation from Arabic)

See Arabic text of INC 2005 (amendments 2017), approved in two separate sessions by the National Legislature on 25 April 2017, and the Council of States, on 24 April 2017. It was signed by the President of the National Legislature, Ibrahim Ahmed Omer, and approved by the President of the Republic, Omer Hassan Ahmed Al-Basheer, on 3rd May 2017.

7 Art 30 was amended in 2017. It now reads: 'Slavery and human trafficking are absolutely prohibited in every form and no one shall be subjected to detention except in accordance with the law; no one shall be forced to perform compulsory work or held in servitude.'

Article 31: Equality before the Law:[8]

All persons are equal before the law and are entitled without discrimination, as to race, colour, sex, language, religious creed, political opinion, or ethnic origin, to the equal protection of the law.

Article 32: Rights of Women and Children:

(1) The State shall guarantee equal right of men and women to the enjoyment of all civil, political, social, cultural and economic rights, including the right to equal pay for equal work and other related benefits.
(2) The State shall promote woman rights through affirmative action.
(3) The State shall combat harmful customs and traditions which undermine the dignity and the status of women.
(4) The State shall provide maternity and child care and medical care for pregnant women.
(5) The State shall protect the rights of the child as provided in the international and regional conventions ratified by the Sudan.

Article 33: Sanctity from Torture

No person shall be subjected to torture or to cruel, inhuman or degrading treatment.

Article 34: Fair Trial

(1) An accused is presumed to be innocent until his/her guilt is proved according to the law.
(2) Every person who is arrested shall be informed, at the time of arrest, of the reasons for his/her arrest and shall be promptly informed of any charges against him/her.
(3) In all civil and criminal proceedings, every person shall be entitled to a fair and public hearing by an ordinary competent court of law in accordance with procedures prescribed by law.
(4) No person shall be charged of any act or omission which did not constitute an offence at the time of its commission.
(5) Any person shall be entitled to be tried in his/her presence in any criminal charge without undue delay; the law shall regulate trial in absentia.

8 Article 31 was amended by the 2017 constitutional amendments. Its new article 31(1) replaces the words 'political opinion' with 'political allegiance' .

A new article 31(2) was added: 'All people are equal with regards to holding election posts, or holding public posts, or disputes, or judicial transactions or humanitarian public affairs or legal or national transactions without discrimination among them unless based on qualification and competence.'

(6) Any accused person has the right to defend himself/herself in person or through a lawyer of his/her own choice and to have legal aid assigned to him/her by the State where he/she is unable to defend himself/herself in serious offences.

Article 35: Right to Litigation

The right to litigation shall be guaranteed for all persons; no person shall be denied the right to resort to justice.

Article 36: Restriction on Death Penalty

(1) No death penalty shall be imposed, save as retribution, hudud or punishment for extremely serious offences in accordance with the law.
(2) The death penalty shall not be imposed on a person under the age of eighteen or a person who has attained the age of seventy except in cases of retribution or hudud.
(3) No death penalty shall be executed upon pregnant or lactating women, save after two years of lactation.

Article 37: Privacy

The privacy of all persons shall be inviolable; no person shall be subjected to interference with his/her private life, family, home or correspondence, save in accordance with the law.[9]

Article 38: Freedom of Creed and Worship

Every person shall have the right to the freedom of religious creed and worship, and to declare his/her religion or creed and manifest the same, by way of worship, education, practice or performance of rites or ceremonies, subject to requirements of law and public order; no person shall be coerced to adopt such faith, that he/she does not believe in, nor to practice rites or services to which he/she does not voluntarily consent.[10]

9 Art 37 was amended in 2017, with the title Sanctity of Privacy. It now reads: 'The privacy of all persons shall be inviolable in all aspects of life in residency, private speeches (nagwa), and in correspondences with others through voice or images, or a written form save in accordance with a judicial decision or a decision from the public prosecution office, or a decision from a security authority affecting national security.'

10 Art 38 was amended in 2017, with the title: Freedom of Creed, Worship and Mazhab (in Arabic denotes religious school of thought). It now reads: 'Every person shall have the right to freedom of creed and religious practices. No person shall be coerced to adopt a faith that he does not believe in, and has the right to express his religion and creed in accordance with, and as regulated by the law.'

Article 39: Freedom of Expression and Media

(1) Every citizen shall have an unrestricted right to the freedom of expression, reception and dissemination of information, publication, and access to the press without prejudice to order, safety or public morals as determined by law.[11]
(2) The State shall guarantee the freedom of the press and other media as shall be regulated by law in a democratic society.[12]
(3) All media shall abide by professional ethics, shall refrain from inciting religious, ethnic, racial or cultural hatred and shall not agitate for violence or war.

Article 40: Freedom of Assembly and Association

(1) The right to peaceful assembly shall be guaranteed; every person shall have the right to freedom of association with others, including the right to form or join political parties, associations and trade or professional unions for the protection of his/her interests.
(2) Formation and registration of political parties, associations and trade unions shall be regulated by law as is necessary in a democratic society.
(3) No association shall function as a political party at national, Southern Sudan or state level unless it has:

    (a) its membership open to any Sudanese irrespective of religion, ethnic origin or place of birth,
    (b) a programme that does not contradict the provisions of this Constitution,
    (c) democratically elected leadership and institutions,
    (d) disclosed and transparent sources of funding.[13]

11 Article 39 (1) was amended in 2017. It now reads:
'Every citizen has the free right to express and reflect his opinion to the public through media outlets and through public discourse, written and visual publications and through public demonstrations and in processions to advocate for his causes and in accordance with the law regulating and balancing the right of freedom of expression and the right of persons not to be defamed and the reassurance of the society of its morals and its activities of public demonstration.'

12 Art 39(2) was slightly amended in 2017. The words 'democratic society' were removed from the text.

13 Art 40 was amended in 2017, with the title: Freedom of Succession (Mowala in Arabic), Assembly and Association. Art 40(1) reads: 'Members of the communities shall be allowed to engage in Mowala relationship, organize and assemble in associations, religious sects, political parties, commercial partnerships, charitable cooperatives, trade or professional unions in accordance with the regulations of the law.' Art 40(2): 'The entities in sub-section 1 above shall abide by the laws in administering their affairs and shall not be exploited to embezzle money (haram). They shall be registered with honest, independent and renewable will and be chosen through consultation (shura).' Art 40(3) was amended by removing the words 'Southern Sudan, or state' from the text.

Article 41: Right to Vote

(1) Every citizen shall have the right to take part in the conduct of public affairs, through voting as shall be regulated by law.
(2) Every citizen who has attained the age specified by this Constitution or the law, shall have the right to elect and be elected in periodic elections, through universal adult suffrage in secret ballot, which shall guarantee the free expression of the will of the electorate.

Article 42: Freedom of Movement and Residence

(1) Every citizen shall have the right to freedom of movement and the liberty to choose his/her residence except for reasons of public health and safety as shall be regulated by law.
(2) Every citizen shall have the right to leave the country as shall be regulated by law and shall have the right of return.

Article 43: Right to Own Property

(1) Every citizen shall have the right to acquire or own property as regulated by law.
(2) No private property may be expropriated save by law in the public interest and in consideration for prompt and fair compensation. No private property shall be confiscated save by an order of a court of law.

Article 44: Right to Education

(1) Education is a right for every citizen and the State shall provide access to education without discrimination as to religion, race, ethnicity, gender or disability.
(2) Primary education is compulsory and the State shall provide it free.

Article 45: Rights of Persons with Special Needs and the Elderly

(1) The State shall guarantee to persons with special needs the enjoyment of all the rights and freedoms set out in this Constitution; especially respect for their human dignity, access to suitable education, employment and full participation in society.
(2) The elderly shall have the right to the respect of their dignity. The State shall provide them with the necessary care and medical services as shall be regulated by law.

Article 46: Public Health Care

The State shall promote public health, establish, rehabilitate, develop basic medical and diagnostic institutions, provide free primary health care and emergency services for all citizens.

Article 47: Ethnic and Cultural Communities

Ethnic and cultural communities shall have the right to freely enjoy and develop their particular cultures; members of such communities shall have the right to practice their beliefs, use their languages, observe their religions and raise their children within the framework of their respective cultures and customs.

Article 48: Sanctity of Rights and Freedoms

Subject to Article 211 herein, no derogation from the rights and freedoms enshrined in this Bill shall be made. The Bill of Rights shall be upheld, protected and applied by the Constitutional Court and other competent courts; the Human Rights Commission shall monitor its application in the State pursuant to Article 142 herein.

5 The Transitional Constitution of the Republic of South Sudan, 2011[14]

Part Two: BILL OF RIGHTS

Nature of the Bill of Rights

9. (1) The Bill of Rights is a covenant among the people of South Sudan and between them and their government at every level and a commitment to respect and promote human rights and fundamental freedoms enshrined in this Constitution; it is the cornerstone of social justice, equality and democracy.
(2) The rights and freedoms of individuals and groups enshrined in this Bill shall be respected, upheld and promoted by all organs and agencies of Government and by all persons.
(3) All rights and freedoms enshrined in international human rights treaties, covenants and instruments ratified or acceded to by the Republic of South Sudan shall be an integral part of this Bill.
(4) This Bill of Rights shall be upheld by the Supreme Court and other competent courts and monitored by the Human Rights Commission.

Sanctity of Rights and Freedoms

10. Subject to Article 189 herein, no derogation from the rights and freedoms enshrined in this Bill shall be made. The Bill of Rights shall be upheld, protected and applied by the Supreme Court and other competent courts; the Human Rights Commission shall monitor its application in accordance with this Constitution and the law.

14 The Transitional Constitution of the Republic of South Sudan (signed into law by the President of the Republic on Independence Day 7 July 2011), www.gurtong.net/LinkClick.aspx?fileticket=SHBZGArJ8Ks%3d&tabid=106, accessed 12 June 2018.

Life and Human Dignity

11. Every person has the inherent right to life, dignity and the integrity of his or her person which shall be protected by law; no one shall be arbitrarily deprived of his or her life.

Personal Liberty

12. Every person has the right to liberty and security of person; no person shall be subjected to arrest, detention, deprivation or restriction of his or her liberty except for specified reasons and in accordance with procedures prescribed by law.

Freedom from Slavery, Servitude and Forced Labour

13. (1) Slavery and slave trade in all form are prohibited. No person shall be held in slavery or servitude.
(2) No person shall be required to perform forced or compulsory labour except as a penalty upon conviction by a competent court of law.

Equality before the Law

14. All persons are equal before the law and are entitled to the equal protection of the law without discrimination as to race, ethnic origin, colour, sex, language, religious creed, political opinion, birth, locality or social status.

Right to found a family

15. Every person of marriageable age shall have the right to marry a person of the opposite sex and to found a family according to their respective family laws, and no marriage shall be entered into without the free and full consent of the man and woman intending to marry.

Rights of Women

16. (1) Women shall be accorded full and equal dignity of the person with men.
(2) Women shall have the right to equal pay for equal work and other related benefits with men.
(3) Women shall have the right to participate equally with men in public life.
(4) All levels of government shall:

(a) promote women participation in public life and their representation in the legislative and executive organs by at least twenty-five per cent as an affirmative action to redress imbalances created by history, customs, and traditions;
(b) enact laws to combat harmful customs and traditions which undermine the dignity and status of women; and

(c) provide maternity and child care and medical care for pregnant and lactating women.

(3) Women shall have the right to own property and share in the estates of their deceased husbands together with any surviving legal heir of the deceased.

Rights of the Child

17. (1) Every child has the right:

(a) to life, survival and development;
(b) to a name and nationality;
(c) to know and be cared for by his or her parents or legal guardian;
(d) not to be subjected to exploitative practices or abuse, nor to be required to serve in the army nor permitted to perform work which may be hazardous or harmful to his or her education, health or well-being;
(e) to be free from any form of discrimination;
(f) to be free from corporal punishment and cruel and inhuman treatment by any person including parents, school administrations and other institutions;
(g) not to be subjected to negative and harmful cultural practices which affect his or her health, welfare or dignity; and
(h) to be protected from abduction and trafficking.

(2) In all actions concerning children undertaken by public and private welfare institutions, courts of law, administrative authorities or legislative bodies, the paramount consideration shall be the best interest of the child.
(3) All levels of government shall accord special protection to orphans and other vulnerable children; child adoption shall be regulated by law.
(4) For the purposes of this Constitution, a child is any person under the age of eighteen years.

Freedom from Torture

18. No person shall be subjected to torture or to cruel, inhuman or degrading treatment or punishment.

Fair Trial

19. (1) An accused person is presumed to be innocent until his or her guilt is proved according to the law.
(2) Any person who is arrested shall be informed, at the time of arrest, of the reasons for his or her arrest and shall be promptly informed of any charges against him or her.
(3) In all civil and criminal proceedings, every person shall be entitled to a fair and public hearing by a competent court of law in accordance with procedures prescribed by law.

(4) No person shall be charged with any act or omission which did not constitute an offence at the time of its commission.
(5) Every accused person shall be entitled to be tried in his or her presence in any criminal trial without undue delay; the law shall regulate trial in absentia.
(6) Any accused person has the right to defend himself or herself in person or through a lawyer of his or her own choice or to have legal aid assigned to him or her by the government where he or she cannot afford a lawyer to defend him or her in any serious offence.

Right to Litigation

20. The right to litigation shall be guaranteed for all persons; no person shall be denied the right to resort to courts of law to redress grievances whether against government or any individual or organization.

Restriction on Death Penalty

21. (1) No death penalty shall be imposed, save as punishment for extremely serious offences in accordance with the law.
(2) No death penalty shall be imposed on a person under the age of eighteen or a person who has attained the age of seventy.
(3) No death penalty shall be executed upon a pregnant or lactating woman, save after two years of lactation.

Privacy

22. The privacy of all persons shall be inviolable; no person shall be subjected to interference with his or her private life, family, home or correspondence, save in accordance with the law.

Religious Rights

23. The following religious rights are guaranteed by this Constitution:

(a) the right to worship or assemble in connection with any religion or belief and to establish and maintain places for these purposes;
(b) the right to establish and maintain appropriate faith-based, charitable or humanitarian institutions;
(c) the right to acquire, possess and own movable and/or immovable property and make, acquire and use the necessary articles and materials related to the rites or customs of religion or belief;
(d) the right to write, issue and disseminate religious publications;
(e) the right to teach religion or beliefs in places suitable for these purposes;

(f) the right to solicit and receive voluntary financial and other contributions from individuals, private and public institutions;
(g) the right to train, appoint, elect or designate by succession appropriate religious leaders called for by the requirements and standards of any religion or belief;
(h) the right to observe days of rest, celebrate holidays and ceremonies in accordance with the precepts of religious beliefs; and
(i) the right to communicate with individuals and communities in matters of religion and beliefs at national and international levels.

Freedom of Expression and Media

24. (1) Every citizen shall have the right to the freedom of expression, reception and dissemination of information, publication, and access to the press without prejudice to public order, safety or morals as prescribed by law.
(2) All levels of government shall guarantee the freedom of the press and other media as shall be regulated by law in a democratic society.
(3) All media shall abide by professional ethics.

Freedom of Assembly and Association

25. (1) The right to peaceful assembly is recognized and guaranteed; every person shall have the right to freedom of association with others, including the right to form or join political parties, associations and trade or professional unions for the protection of his or her interests.
(2) Formation and registration of political parties, associations and trade unions shall be regulated by law as is necessary in a democratic society.
(3) No association shall function as a political party at the National or state level unless it has:

(a) its membership open to any South Sudanese irrespective of religion, gender, ethnic origin or place of birth;
(b) a programme that does not contradict the provisions of this Constitution;
(c) a democratically elected leadership and institutions; and
(d) disclosed and transparent sources of funding.

Right to Participation and Voting

26. (1) Every citizen shall have the right to take part in any level of government directly or through freely chosen representative, and shall have the right to nominate himself or herself or be nominated for a public post or office in accordance with this Constitution and the law.
(2) Every citizen shall have the right to vote or be elected in accordance with this Constitution and the law.

Freedom of Movement and Residence

27. (1) Every citizen shall have the right to freedom of movement and the liberty to choose his or her residence except for reasons of public health and safety as shall be regulated by law.
(2) Every citizen shall have the right to leave and or return to South Sudan.

Right to Own Property

28. (1) Every person shall have the right to acquire or own property as regulated by law.
(2) No private property may be expropriated save by law in the public interest and in consideration for prompt and fair compensation. No private property shall be confiscated save by an order of a court of law.

Right to Education

29. (1) Education is a right for every citizen and all levels of government shall provide access to education without discrimination as to religion, race, ethnicity, health status including HIV/AIDS, gender or disability.
(2) All levels of government shall promote education at all levels and shall ensure free and compulsory education at the primary level; they shall also provide free illiteracy eradication programmes.

Rights of Persons with Special Needs and the Elderly

30. (1) All levels of government shall guarantee to persons with special needs participation in society and the enjoyment of rights and freedoms set out in this Constitution, especially access to public utilities, suitable education and employment.
(2) The elderly and persons with special needs shall have the right to the respect of their dignity. They shall be provided with the necessary care and medical services as shall be regulated by law.

Public Health Care

31. All levels of government shall promote public health, establish, rehabilitate and develop basic medical and diagnostic institutions and provide free primary health care and emergency services for all citizens.

Right of Access to Information

32. Every citizen has the right of access to official information and records, including electronic records in the possession of any level of government or any

organ or agency thereof, except where the release of such information is likely to prejudice public security or the right to privacy of any other person.

Rights of Ethnic and Cultural Communities

33. Ethnic and cultural communities shall have the right to freely enjoy and develop their particular cultures. Members of such communities shall have the right to practice their beliefs, use their languages, observe their religions and raise their children within the context of their respective cultures and customs in accordance with this Constitution and the law.

Right to Housing

34. (1) Every citizen has the right to have access to decent housing.
(2) The State shall formulate policies and take reasonable legislative measures within its available resources to achieve the progressive realization of these rights.
(3) No one shall be evicted from his or her lawfully acquired home or have his or her home demolished save in accordance with the law.

Selected Constitutional Court Cases

Death Penalty

Abd-Almoeiz Hamdoon Said v Sudan Government, (2003) 1 *Constitutional Court Journal* 93.

The Court laid down the principle that the death penalty shall not be imposed for offences committed by a person under 18 years old.

Abu-Abada Ali Al-Awad v Sudan Government, (2003) 1 *Constitutional Court Journal* 279.

The Court stipulated the principle that it would be a violation of the constitutional and natural right of the accused to be sentenced to death during his imprisonment without his knowledge or without him being asked or informed or given a chance to know what happened in his absence. It is a very basic rule of natural law that a person shall not be convicted without being heard even in civil cases.

Nagim Eldeen Gasm Elseed v (1) Government of Sudan and (2) blood heirs of Abdel Rahman Mohamed Ali, Case no, MDG/GD/18/2005, (2008) 2 *Constitutional Court Journal* 399.

The death penalty cannot be executed against an accused who at the time of the offence was under the age of 18 years.

Al-Omda Hussien Esaq Yhaya Sajo et al v Sudan Government, the Governor of Northern Darfur State, (2001) 2 *Constitutional Court Journal* 459.

For a suit to be accepted before the Constitutional Court there shall be direct interest. This interest requires a connection between the constitutional issue and the applicant's interest.

Fair trial and Administration of Justice

Twafuq Mohamed Abdalla v Bit Al-Mina Ibrahim, (2003) 1 *Constitutional Court Journal* 473.

The Constitution protects the right to litigation.

Sabah Al-Kier Haj Taha v Osman Yagoub Salih and Sudan Government, (2003) 1 *Constitutional Court Journal* 157.

An accused will be deprived of his or her constitutional right if he or she was denied a fair and prompt trial in which he or she was not able to defend him- or herself.

Rahmetalla Adam Medani v The deceased Guardians: Yagoub Musa Ibrahim and Sudan Government, (2003) 1 *Constitutional Court Journal* 290.

The right of the accused to be defended by a lawyer and his right to request the Attorney General to have a lawyer appointed in case of indigence does not impose a mandatory obligation on the State but it is a right of the accused to demand legal aid.

Hafiz Essa Mohamed Essa v Sudan Government, The deceased Guardians of Al-Hadi Abdalla, (2003) 1 *Constitutional Court Journal* 343.

The right of the accused to be defended by a lawyer in a case relating to serious offences does not make the appointment of a lawyer obligatory on the State, but it is a right of the accused to demand it if he wishes. In such case, the State is obliged, upon the request of the accused, to appoint an advocate and to bear all or part of the expenses.

Mohamed Awad Hamza v Abdalsalam Al-Awad Sudan Government, (2003) 1 *Constitutional Court Journal* 519.

The right to a fair trial guarantees procedural and substantive protection which shall be applied properly.

Saifeldeen Abdalraheem Ahamed v Khalifalla Ahmed, Al Zanieb Hassan Abass, Sudan Government, (2003) 1 *Constitutional Court Journal* 529.

A fair trial entails that the court shall be competent, and that the procedures be applied properly.

Mohamed Yahya Adam v the deceased Guardians, Sabir Ahmed Dwari, Sudan Government, (2003) 1 *Constitutional Court Journal* 675.

In this case, the Court defined the meaning of the right to a fair trial.

Elsheikh Taha Almahal Complex v Governor of Khartoum state, (2011) 2 *Constitutional Court Journal* 65.

The appellant was deprived of the right to a fair hearing since he was not provided with an opportunity to respond to the application for appeal by the appellate revision Court. The trial of the accused before the National Security court does not deprive him of the right to equality before the courts.

Awad Alla Al-Abass v Sudan Government, Deceased Guardians: Abdalmajed Al-Khadir, (2011) 2 *Constitutional Court Journal* 186.

The right of an accused to be defended by a lawyer (legal aid) is contingent upon the accused being indigent, and even then it depends upon his or her request.

Doctor Mahamoud Sharaniy et al v Sudan Government, Minister of Justice, Minister of Finance, (2011) 2 *Constitutional Court Journal* 338.

The requirement to pay court fees does not constitute a denial or diminish the right to litigation. If a litigant lacks financial means, he or she can submit a request to be exempted from court fees.

Makki Hamidan Hamodi Farah v The deceased guardians/ Ali Aboda Momein, (2012) 1 *Constitutional Court Journal* 111.

It is the right of an accused person to have or be defended by a lawyer or a litigator. As laid down in other precedents, the accused personally has to submit an application or request to the court to seek legal assistance if he is indigent or cannot afford to have a lawyer. In this case the court shall refer the accused to the Attorney General to appoint a lawyer. In his dissenting opinion Judge Eltayeb Abass Al-Jili stated: 'The right of the accused to be defended by a lawyer or a litigator should not be conditional on indigence but the accused's inability to defend himself, in particular in cases involving the death penalty.'

Trial of Civilians before Military Courts

Sol Nasr case. This case, though unpublished in the SJLR, was included in the book of the Sudanese Judge Henry Riyad, *The Most Famous Political Trials in Sudan: Exploitation of Power, Smuggling of the Flasha, Political Assassinations and Preventive Detention* (Beirut Dar al-Jil 1987) (Arabic).

It was the first constitutional case decided under the 1973 constitution. The Supreme Court ruled that the trial of civilians before military tribunals, using a penal law that had retroactive effect, offended the 'the letter and spirit' of the constitution. However, just as that court was about to deliver another decision, this time on the unconstitutionality of preventive detention, an attempted coup d'état against the Nimeri regime took place on 5 September 1975. The regime then used the incident as a pretext for far-reaching amendments to the constitution, which sought, *inter alia*, to greatly enhance the powers of the President, and ensure the constitutionality of preventive detention and special criminal courts. The constitutional amendments were made with retrospective effect.

Henry Poma Arol v Sudan Government, (2003) 1 *Constitutional Court Journal* 82.

Trying civilians before military courts is not prohibited provided that the offences against state concern charges that are related to disciplined forces and sedition; this shall be decided by Attorney upon Minister of Justice approval according to section (4) sub-section (e) of the People's Armed Forces Act, 1406 Higreia (1983).

Emergency Powers

Ibrahim Yussef Habani et al v President of the Republic of Sudan, (2003) 1 *Constitutional Court Journal* 174.

The President has absolute discretionary powers to assess the circumstances to proclaim the state of emergency. The drafters of the Sudan Constitution, 1998, did not intend, when they articulated the President's powers, to deprive the President of the power to dissolve Parliament, but they intended him to act according to the constitutional customs, circumstances and necessity. In particular, he represents the supremacy of the State and is responsible for its security, stability and integrity.

Freedom of Association

Amal Abass Al-Ajab v National Press Council Sudan Government, (2003) 1 *Constitutional Court Journal* 108.

The right to form an association is a constitutional right. Under article (26) sub-section (1) of the Constitution of the Republic of Sudan, 1998, individuals are free to form such associations and its activities shall not be restricted unless provided for by law.

Freedom of Expression and Opinion

Alyom for printing, press and distribution v The Press National Council, Sudan Government, (2003) 1 *Constitutional Court Journal* 204.

The Principle of press freedom is a well-established principle in Sudan since its independence, in addition to Sudan's recognition of article 19 of the Universal Declaration of Human Rights (UDHR) which relates to the freedom of the press and opinion.

Joseph Garang and Others v Supreme Commission and Others, (1986) *Sudan Law Journal and Reports (SLJR)* 1.

In this case, on the pretext that communist students had uttered some blasphemous remarks about the prophet, the government secured from the Assembly a constitutional amendment that allowed it to outlaw any communist activity. The amendment was challenged before the High Court which declared, in this case, that the amendment was unconstitutional. Even though the decision was subject to an appeal, the government reacted by dismissing the decision as being merely declaratory and insisting that it would not abide by it. It subsequently obtained reaffirmation from the Constituent Assembly of its initial decision, and sought to preempt any future challenges by outlawing communist activities.

Economic, Social and Cultural rights

Alrakowa for Transportation and Investment et al v Sudan Government, The National Chamber of Travelling Bus, (2003) 1 *Constitutional Court Journal* 642.

The right to employment has been stipulated in articles 21 and 28 of the Constitution of the Republic of Sudan, 1998. It entails that every person in society has a right to be employed for work that is suitable and fits his or her abilities to enable him or her to live in dignity without discrimination based on race, sex or religion.

Index

Abuja Agreement (ESPA) 2006 5
accountability 3, 5, 10, 16, 23, 27–8, 30, 33–4, 37–8, 48, 57–8, 76–7, 107, 114, 117, 188
Addis Ababa Agreement (1972) 52, 54, 83
administration 39, 44–5, 69, 84, 109, 132, 151, 156, 164, 190, 196, 203; boundaries 85; British 44–5; colonial 44; decisions 179; military 55; native 20, 27; of justice 92, 95, 113; public 24; State 29; Turkish 43
African Charter on Human and People's Rights (ACHPR) 100, 108–9, 111, 142, 144, 171, 175–7
African Charter on the Rights and Welfare of the Child 120, 144
African Union (AU) 4, 17, 76, 123
African Union Commission of Inquiry on South Sudan (AUCISS) 155
African Union High Level Panel on Darfur 19, 57
age of legal capacity/liability 178
agreement 34, 47, 66, 72–3, 80–1, 85, 135, 154–5; dis- 72; framework 72, 135; lack of 6; peace 7, 11, 34–5, 37, 39–40, 43, 57, 60, 63–4, 67, 84, 139, 143, 146, 155–6, 158; self-determination 46; unilateral 60
Agreement on the Resolution of the Conflict in South Sudan (ARCISS) (2015) 64–5, 73–6, 84–5, 155
Akol, Lam 80, 86
Al-Azhari, Ismail 47
Al-Bashir, Omer 2, 36, 119, 134, 141–2, 145
Al-Turabi, Hassan 2
Anglo-Egyptian Agreement (1953) 46
Anglo-Egyptian Condominium 7, 19, 44
An Na'im, Abdullahi Ahmed 8, 18
apostasy 8, 31, 102–3, 105, 150
Assembly: Constituent 42, 47–50, 55, 74, 169, 211; Legislative 45, 69, 73–4, 76, 79, 81, 171; National 48, 55–6, 107, 128, 185; The People's 51–4
authority 56, 74, 88, 101, 123, 126, 188–9, 195; colonial 160; competent 171; flailing 32; higher 63; judicial 117; legislative 170, 193; symbolic 79
autonomy 2, 9, 26, 51, 54, 82–3, 107, 140, 142–3, 145; regional 67

Basic Rules Act (1983) 32
Bayart, Jean-François 123
Bill of Rights (BoR) 4–5, 7, 10, 15, 33–5, 56, 75, 85, 91–2, 120–1, 128, 139–40, 142, 147–50, 158, 161, 165–6, 173–7, 183, 186, 189, 197, 201–2
British-Egyptian condominium 124

citizenship: acquired 120; certificates 131; denial of 132; dual 120, 130; framework 123; granting of 132; inclusive 10, 158; inequality in 118; law 130–1; legal 133, 137; non-discriminatory 35; problem of 119, 137–8; rights 10, 119–23, 127, 130, 133, 136, 146, 153; space 119, 122, 130; struggle of 122, 130–1; unequal 118–19
class 9, 18, 25, 131, 136; lower 131; middle 28; of rights 186–7; political 37
Closed District Regulations 44
coercion 18, 26, 32, 35, 50, 195

commission: constitution amendment 45–6; independent 185, 189; international 46; national 47–8, 55; women's 189
Commission for the Protection of Non-Muslims in the Capital 153–4
Commission of Refugees (COR) 134
Commission on Human Rights in South Sudan 77
Commission on Truth, Reconciliation and Healing (CTRH) 37, 39, 76
Committee on the Elimination of Racial Discrimination 23, 148
Compensation and Reparations Authority (CRA) 76
Compensation Commission 57
Comprehensive Peace Agreement (CPA) (2005) 1–2, 7–8, 11, 15, 26, 30, 33–5, 38, 43, 55–8, 60–1, 64, 84, 87, 91, 111, 113–17, 121, 126, 143, 146–7, 149, 152–8, 172
condominium 20–1, 30, 32, 44–5, 124; colonial 9, 41; government 27
conflict 2, 6, 9–10, 16, 18, 20, 23, 35, 38, 49–50, 57, 63, 65, 69, 72–3, 75, 78, 81, 87, 101, 103, 110–11, 118, 127, 132, 134, 139–40, 142, 150, 158–9, 165, 172–3, 173, 187; armed 1–2, 15, 21–2, 29–31, 57–8, 69, 71, 79, 96, 102, 111–12, 118–19, 155–6; ethnic dimension of 23; large-scale 70; legacy of 38, 40, 75; mitigation 74, 88; North–South 31, 37, 146, 150; open 39, 66; post- 7, 56, 60, 75, 77, 87; postcolonial 126, 141; recurring 24, 34; resolution 24, 39; violent 78, 84
constituencies 68, 169, 171–2; geographical 185; Graduate College 162; Islamist 2; local 58
constitution: debates 1–3, 6; developments 2, 7, 41, 59–60, 113; framework 2, 7, 43, 57, 60, 63, 70, 87, 112, 138–9, 147, 158, 170; human rights protection 1, 9, 92; -making 1–10, 16–18, 36, 39–43, 52, 55, 61–2, 65–7, 70–6, 87–8, 121, 138, 152, 159, 161, 163, 166–7, 181, 189; standoffs, 66, 77–8
constitutionalism 1, 3–5, 8–10, 34, 39, 41, 54, 58–64, 66, 78, 84, 86, 88, 91–3, 117
Convention of the Elimination of All Forms of Discrimination against Women (CEDAW) 11, 137, 171, 181, 184, 189
Convention on the Rights of Persons with Disabilities (CRPD) 175
Convention on the Rights of the Child (CRC) 103, 144, 175, 178
coup 28, 31–3, 46, 51, 145, 163; attempted 54, 210; military 2, 4, 7, 22, 48, 60, 94
crimes 23, 57, 102–3, 165, 176, 188; against the state 102; against women 188; atrocity 76–7; *hudud* 102–3; international 21, 26, 31, 111; transnational 114; war 21, 38
Criminal Procedure Act (1991) 33, 99
crisis 63, 72, 79, 118, 141, 155; December (2013) 83, 86; humanitarian 3; human rights 16; of national identity 75, 118; political 34
culture 74–5, 95, 118, 122, 124, 138, 143–4, 146–7, 152–3, 173–4, 183, 195, 201, 207; destruction of 24; diversity of 134; dominant 134; governance 64; of impunity 38; political 10, 64; regional 134

Darfur Peace Agreement (DPA) 11, 43, 156
death penalty 102–3, 150, 196, 199, 204, 207–9
decentralization 31, 69, 83, 85
decree: constitutional 163, 188; emergency 4; executive 85; -making power 58; presidential 55, 63, 68, 82; religious 182
democracy 9, 35–6, 121, 158, 169, 195, 197, 201; lack of 38; liberal 59, 93; multiparty 34; parliamentary 46
democratization 4, 159
Deng, Francis 8, 141
detention 98–9, 101, 107, 114–15, 135, 163, 168, 197, 202; arbitrary 23, 95, 98–100, 114; duration of 196; incommunicado 100; legality of 100; pre-trial 98–9; preventive 44–5, 54, 210; prolonged 102, 104
dictatorship 6, 36, 48, 60
disability 92, 108–9, 144, 162, 168, 173–4, 176, 184, 190, 200, 206
discrimination: against women 25, 27; ethnic 21, 25, 38, 133, 141, 148, 162; incitement to 96; institutionalized 25–6; non- 25, 95–7, 120, 139, 144, 146–7, 157–8, 161,

163, 166–8, 171–5, 184; positive, 164, 167, 172, 179; prohibition of 92, 96, 147–8, 173, 176; racial 9, 141, 148; religious 21, 141, 148, 152, 162; social 132; systemic 19, 26
displacement 23–4, 29, 127, 161–2, 171, 186
diversity 1, 3, 24, 35, 37, 40, 72, 87, 119, 134, 138–9, 141, 146, 155, 158, 160; cultural 74, 87, 134, 146, 150, 153, 172; linguistic 146, 150; regional 39; religious 41, 146, 149–50, 153, 172; social 153
Doha Document for Peace in Darfur (DDPD) (2010) 5, 43, 57, 146, 156

East Sudan Peace Agreement (ESPA) 5, 43
education 22–3, 28, 108, 133, 160, 164–5, 170, 173–4, 182, 186, 189, 193–4, 199–200, 203, 206; access to 26, 108; children's 173; compulsory 108, 206; free 94, 108; institutions 49; militarization of 31; primary 173–4, 186, 200
election 34–5, 47, 51–3, 58, 64, 73–4, 79–81, 93, 97, 162, 168–9, 172, 192, 200; democratic 84, 169; general 47, 81, 85; national 79, 185; parliamentary 168; state 185
Engendering the Constitution Forum 167
equality 92–7, 121, 139, 144, 147, 158, 161, 163, 165–74, 176, 178, 183–4, 193, 197, 201, 209; absolute 167; in diversity 37; formal 26, 35; gender 25, 161, 168, 174; principles of 97, 168, 184, 186
ethnicity 21, 25, 38, 74, 108, 118, 122, 126–8, 130–1, 134, 136, 141, 144, 146, 162, 174–5, 179, 181, 200, 206
Evidence Act (1993) 101, 165

fair trial 100–2, 104, 175, 196, 198, 204, 208–9; un- 22
Falola, Toyin 122
federalism 2, 5, 9, 40, 47, 72, 75, 82–3, 85, 142, 155
forced labour 193–4, 202; prohibition of 94–5
Four Freedoms Agreement 135
freedom: collective 142; fighters 60; from arrest 92; from slavery 95, 202; from torture 178, 203; fundamental 50, 54, 113, 121, 160, 168, 181, 184, 197, 201; of action 50; of assembly 106, 205; of association 55, 92, 95, 195, 199, 205, 210; of belief 93, 105, 145, 192; of conscience, 190, 194; of creed 95, 104, 194, 199; of expression 29, 44, 50, 92, 95, 105–7, 113, 133, 168, 195, 199, 205, 210; of information laws 106; of movement 44, 93, 95, 178, 191, 194, 200, 206; of opinion 93, 192; of religion 8, 47, 49, 92–3, 104–5, 141, 144, 149–51, 163, 168; of residence 93, 135, 206; of the press 93, 106–7, 199, 205, 211; of property 135; of thought 95, 144–5, 195; personal 153, 180; political 36, 55; preservation of 52; right to 92, 99; to worship 105, 151
Freedom of Information Act (2015) 106, 130
Fukuyama, Francis 123

Garang, John 17, 20, 50, 154, 211
Gellner, Ernest 122
Ghai, Yash 61
Giwama 182
governance 4, 24, 32, 39–40, 43, 58, 62, 64–5, 67, 69, 87, 93, 141, 160–1, 172, 181, 189; democratic 39; lopsided 16, 29; military 38; modes of 9, 27, 31, 38, 117, 150; problems 16, 29, 37; self- 83–4; transitional 72
Guibernau, Montserrat 123

habeas corpus 44, 98–100
hegemony 18, 22, 56, 91; executive 62; national 29; regional 21; riverine 20
High Judicial Council (HJC) 116–17
Hobsbawm, Eric 122
humanitarian: aid 29, 38; assistance 23, 39; crisis 3; institutions 149, 205; law 111, 116; matters 97
human rights: international 8, 10, 91–2, 97, 100, 104, 106, 110, 117, 142, 157–8, 166, 170, 173, 181, 184, 189, 197, 202; law 110–13, 117, 142, 152, 157, 173; perspective 17, 103; protection 1–6, 8–10, 15, 33, 35–6, 58, 62, 87–8, 91–2, 110–13, 115, 117; standards 15, 34, 57, 92, 106, 117, 170, 172, 189; treaties 7, 97, 99, 101, 106, 110–11, 158, 176, 181, 197, 202; universal 8, 103;

violations 1, 10, 16–18, 23, 33–4, 38, 54, 57, 91, 112, 116–17, 143, 147, 155
Hybrid Court for South Sudan (HCSS) 76

Ibrahim, Maryam Yaḥya 150
Ibrahim, Safia Ishag 26
ideology 18, 30, 42, 59, 92; dominant 118; leftist 162; Islamist 22, 59, 94; religious 15; socialist 59, 94; tribalist 18
Igga, James Wani 81
inequality 18, 21, 118, 132–3, 179–80; gender 8, 164, 182; legitimate 26; societal 20
Inqaz Regime 163, 171
Intergovernmental Authority for Development (IGAD) 64, 72–3, 83–4
Interim Constitution of Southern Sudan (ICSS) 64, 67–70, 74, 87
Interim National Constitution (INC) 5, 7–8, 11, 15, 26, 30, 33–4, 41–2, 55–7, 60, 62, 91–2, 95–6, 104–6, 108–9, 112–17, 120–1, 125–6, 140, 142, 146–54, 158, 165, 172–4, 176–9, 181, 183, 185, 188–9
internally displaced persons (IDPs) 22, 158, 180
International Convention on the Elimination of All Forms of Racial Discrimination (ICERD) 96, 148, 157, 175
International Covenant on Civil and Political Rights (ICCPR) 7, 95–101, 105, 107, 111, 142–4, 147, 152, 157, 171, 175–6, 184
International Covenant on Economic, Social and Cultural Rights (ICESCR) 7, 108–9, 142, 171, 173, 175–7, 184, 186
International Criminal Court (ICC) 26, 33, 35, 37, 57
International Refugee Rights Initiative 137
Islam 2, 6, 8, 10, 20, 22, 31, 42–3, 47, 49, 94, 105, 118, 122, 134, 140–1, 151, 167, 170
Islamic: approach 163; character 55; civilization mission; constituencies 2; Constitution Front 167; faith 141; identity 2, 119; ideology 59, 94, 145; jurisprudence 182; law 32–3, 43, 91, 104, 110, 140, 144, 162, 170; model 162; orientation 92; penalties 103; perspectives 103; principles 166; reformation 8; scholars 150; –secularism dilemma 189; State 2–3, 8, 28, 119, 139, 145, 152; vision 158; world 119
Islamist 32, 60, 150; government 134; ideology 22; military coup 60; movement 2, 7, 55; project 134;
Islamization 2, 7, 59–60, 74, 134, 140–2, 145, 150, 171
Issa, Farouk Abu 36

Janjaweed 31
jihad 134, 150
Johnson, Douglas 82, 85
Juba Conference (1947) 45
judiciary 6, 11, 27–8, 33–5, 47, 56, 62–3, 69, 81, 86, 91, 93, 111, 113, 116–17, 163, 166, 168, 189; independent 5, 30, 32, 47, 56, 58, 113, 191; sophisticated 32
justice 10, 52, 57, 77, 153, 167, 169, 173, 198; access to 5, 22, 57, 138, 188; administration of 39, 92, 95, 113; criminal 58, 98; social 50, 121, 146, 164, 173, 176, 183, 197, 201; transitional 36–7, 39, 57, 75–7

Kiir, Salva 68, 72, 78, 81, 84

Land Commission 56
Law Reform Commission 115
League of Nations 143
legislation 11, 44, 73, 75–6, 85, 105, 111, 113, 115, 121, 148–50, 153, 165, 170–1, 173–4, 176–7, 183–4, 188, 197; anti-terrorism 99, 102; criminal 96, 148, lack of 25; national 5, 50, 111, 180; penal 85
legitimacy 6–7, 37, 40, 46, 61, 74, 79, 81, 87, 137, 160, 189; democratic 27, 64, 71; genuine 42; ideological 22; state 77, 87
liberty 98–9, 197, 200, 202, 206; deprivation of 98, 100; individual 44, 58; personal 100
Lwoki, Benjamin 82

Machakos Protocol (2002) 154
MacMichael, Harold 125
Madhol, Reuben 86
Madut,Chan Reec 86
Mahdiyya 16, 19, 32, 43, 43, 45

Mamdani, Mahmood 122
Manby, Bronwen 133, 135
Maputo Protocol (2003) *see* Protocol on the Rights of Women in Africa
marginalization 2, 19, 21, 25, 28, 32, 35, 40, 64, 79, 97, 133, 137–8, 141, 147, 151, 158, 161–2, 165, 167, 180
May Regime (1969-85) 162
Medani, Amin Mekki 36, 208
Miamingi, Remember 74
minority: cultural 145; ethnic 24, 141, 145, 148, 153, 157, 160, 180; groups 24, 49, 105, 140, 180; linguistic 96, 122, 140, 148, 157; national 153, 157–8; racial 141; religious 8, 11, 21, 25, 49, 104–5, 122, 139–41, 145–6, 148, 150–3, 158, 160, 180; representation 23; rights 2, 4, 9, 11, 23, 34–5, 139–40, 142–3, 146, 152–3, 155, 157–9; views of the 49
Muslim Personal Status Act (1991) 165, 174, 178

National Alliance 80
National Civil Services Commission 189
National Commission for the Allocation of Resources 30
National Commission for the Review of the Constitution 30
National Congress Party (NCP) 24, 35–6, 56, 58, 67, 94, 119, 153–4, 156
National Constitutional Review Commission (NCRC) 56, 65, 70–1, 73, 115
National Dialogue (2014) 5, 36, 58, 61
National Elections Commission (NEC) 80
National Employment Justice Chamber 189
National Human Rights Commission (NHRC) 8, 30, 56–7, 115–16, 175, 189, 201–2
National Intelligence and Security (NISS) Act (2010) 99, 101, 114
National Intelligence and Security Service (NISS) 26, 30–1, 34–5, 114–15
National Islamic Front (NIF) 2, 94
National Judicial Service Commission (NJSC) 30, 56, 115–17
National Legislative Assembly 69, 73–4, 81
National Press Council 107–8
National Security and Intelligence Act (2010) 33
National Unionist Party 47
Nimeri, Jaafar 32, 51, 54, 145; departure 55; dictatorship 6; regime 6–7, 31–2, 51, 55, 83, 94, 111, 149, 169, 210; years 2
No to Women Oppression 26

October Revolution 51
Ohmae, Kenichi 123

Penal Code (1983) 149
Police Act 2008 33, 102
police 24, 26, 114, 131, 164, 174, 179; checks 131; courts 102; harassment 163; intimidation 163; investigations 101; power 123
political instability 2, 9, 118, 133
Political Parties Regulation Act (2007) 185
poverty 22, 170–1, 186; extreme 23; line 164
Press Ordinance 44
Property Claims Commission 57
Protocol on Agreed Principles on Transitional Arrangements Towards Resolution of the Crisis in South Sudan 72
Protocol on the Rights of Women in Africa (Maputo Protocol) 11, 181–4, 186, 189
Public Grievances Chamber 189
Public Order Act of Khartoum State (1998) 165, 179
punishment 8, 32–3, 58, 95, 163, 171, 176, 179, 191, 196, 199, 203–4, 207; capital 102; corporal 103, 203; degrading 103, 179

Rapid Support Forces (RSF) 31
referendum 34, 42, 65, 67–8, 71, 74, 77, 93, 121, 124, 128, 134, 140, 143, 154–8, 192
religion 1, 4, 21, 25, 47, 49, 75, 92–5, 104–5, 108, 118, 120, 122–3, 134, 140–1, 143–7, 149–3, 162–3, 166–70, 173–5, 177, 179, 181, 183–4, 190–1, 194–5, 199–201, 204–7, 211
revolution 4, 43, 47, 51, 55, 79, 82, 94, 193
Revolutionary Command Council (RCC) 51, 165

sanctity: from death 196; from slavery and forced labour 197; from torture 98; in litigation 95, 196; of cultural communities 95, 195; of earning and property 95, 195; of life, 95, 194; of nationality 95, 194; of rights and freedoms 201–2
Sanderson, Mike 135–6
secession 2, 5, 10, 41, 64, 67–8, 105, 118–19, 121, 125, 128, 130, 134, 136, 139–41, 143, 151, 154–5, 157, 160
secularism 2, 5–6, 47, 49, 95, 152, 189
Self-Governing Statute (1953) 2, 6
September Laws 163, 171
Shari'a 7–8, 25–6, 32, 102, 105, 151, 153, 166–7, 170, 178, 183; -based constitution 5; Islamic 171, 173, 182–3; law 3, 5, 7–8, 11, 22, 31–2, 35, 59, 96, 110–11, 145–6, 148–51, 153, 166, 171, 173, 182; offences 103; principles 182; rules 182–3
social justice, 50, 109, 121, 146, 164, 173, 176, 197, 201
Stanley-Baker, Mr. Justice 45
statute 56, 76; book 44; Self-Governing (1953) 2, 6, 42, 46–7, 59, 92–3, 168; Self-Rule (1953) 41
Sudan: independence (1956) 2, 6, 16, 28, 32, 41, 47–8, 67, 82, 104, 122, 124–5, 140–1, 144–5, 149, 162, 168; independence of South (2011) 1–2, 5, 9–10, 16, 38, 41, 58, 64, 69, 78, 118–19, 130, 154, 157–8
Sudan Call 36
Sudan Child Act (2010) 178
Sudan People's Liberation Movement/Army (SPLM/A) 1, 5, 15, 17, 20, 38, 55–6, 60, 63–72, 78–82, 87, 154, 156, 172
Sudan People's Liberation Movement – Democratic Change (SPLM-DC) 80
Sudan People's Liberation Movement-in-Opposition (SPLM-IO) 72, 83–4
Sudan Socialist Union (SSU) 51–2
Sudanese Nationality Act (1994) 25, 125, 129, 177
Supreme Transitional Military Council 111
Sustainable Development Goals 185
Teny, Riek Mahar 70
Tier, Akolda 71
torture 22–3, 31, 39, 95, 99, 101, 104, 114, 163, 194, 198; freedom from 104, 178, 203; prohibition of 101, 103–4, 165, 170–1; protection against 171; reparation for 104
Transitional Cabinet of Ministers 111
Transitional Constitution of the Republic of South Sudan (2011) 5, 64–5, 68, 70–1, 73–5, 78–9, 81, 85, 87, 91, 155
Transitional National Legislative Assembly 73
Tripartite Memorandum of Understanding 134
Truth, Justice and Reconciliation Commission 57

United Nations (UN) 76; agencies 17; Charter 142
United Nations Convention against Torture and Other Cruel, Inhuman or Degrading Treatment or Punishment (CAT) 171, 181
United Nations High Commissioner for Refugees (UNHCR) 134–6
United Nations Human Rights Committee 23, 25, 100, 102
United Nations International Commission of Inquiry 35
United Nations Special Rapporteur on Violence against Women 187
Universal Declaration of Human Rights 1948 (UDHR) 168, 210–11
Universal Periodic Review 36

violence 9, 16, 24, 30–2, 35–6, 38, 64, 74, 77–8, 96, 148, 155, 165, 187–8, 199; against women 27, 187–8; conflict 78, 84; domestic 187; gender-based 26, 187; incitement of 105, 150; non- 87–8; sexual 26, 187; State 31; tribal 31; vulnerability to 26

The Westminster Model 46–7, 93

For Product Safety Concerns and Information please contact our EU representative GPSR@taylorandfrancis.com Taylor & Francis Verlag GmbH, Kaufingerstraße 24, 80331 München, Germany